A Kiss across the Ocean

Transatlantic Intimacies of

BRITISH POST-PUNK & US LATINIDAD

Richard T. Rodríguez

DUKE UNIVERSITY PRESS · DURHAM AND LONDON · 2022

Printed in the United States of America on acid-free paper ∞
Designed by Matthew Tauch
Project editor: Annie Lubinsky
Typeset in Arno Pro, Cronos Pro and Clairvaux LT Std
by Westchester Publishing Services

Library of Congress Cataloging-in-Publication Data
Names: Rodríguez, Richard T., [date] author.
Title: A kiss across the ocean : transatlantic intimacies of British post-punk and US Latinidad / Richard T. Rodríguez.
Description: Durham : Duke University Press, 2022. | Includes bibliographical references and index.
Identifiers: LCCN 2021052377 (print) | LCCN 2021052378 (ebook)
ISBN 9781478015949 (hardcover)
ISBN 9781478018582 (paperback)
ISBN 9781478023180 (ebook)
Subjects: LCSH: Rodríguez, Richard T., 1971– | Hispanic American gays—Social life and customs—20th century. | Hispanic American youth—Social life and customs—20th century. | Popular music—Social aspects—United States. | Popular music—Great Britain—Latin American influences. | Post-punk music—Cross-cultural studies. | Youth—Great Britain—Social life and customs—20th century. | BISAC: SOCIAL SCIENCE / Ethnic Studies / American / Hispanic American Studies | SOCIAL SCIENCE / LGBTQ Studies / General Classification: LCC E184.S75 R6736 2022 (print) | LCC E184.S75 (ebook) | DDC 305.868/073—dc23/eng/20220126
LC record available at https://lccn.loc.gov/2021052377
LC ebook record available at https://lccn.loc.gov/2021052378

Cover art: Siouxsie Sioux, London, 1979.
Photo by Sheila Rock.

No one seems to touch me in the way you do.

Eurythmics, "Right by Your Side" (1983)

So what translates in touch? I ask this not merely of the translation of different social forms of touch, in the manner of styles, but also of the physical link established by the touch.

Alfred Arteaga, *The House with the Blue Bed* (1997)

We would do well to listen more carefully to these sonic solicitations, just beyond the threshold of our acculturated sonic filters.

Dominic Pettman, *Sonic Intimacies: Voice, Species, Technics (Or, How to Listen to the World)* (2017)

The way you look at me, it speaks of intimacy.

Pet Shop Boys, "Thursday" (2013)

Contents

Acknowledgments

This book would not exist without the support of the many people who provided the encouragement to reflect on the music that saved me as a teen and, as evident in the following pages, motivates my intellectual pursuits as a middle-aged adult.

Glyn Davis and Jonny Murray's invitation to present at the "Pet Shop Boys Symposium" they organized in 2016 at the Edinburgh College of Art at the University of Edinburgh came attached with the license necessary for pursuing this project. I thank them for their continued collegiality and support. A group of stellar graduate students—Monica Mohseni, Tia Butler, and Xianyao Xiao—invited me to the University of Texas at Austin to keynote their perfectly titled conference, "Reclaiming the Swamp (Thing): Popular Culture and the Public Academy," which granted me hospitable space to test out many of the ideas in this book. As a result of this conference, I met two invaluable interlocutors—Elizabeth Richmond-Garza and Tom Garza—who offered keen feedback and cherished encouragement. Joshua Chambers-Letson, discovering my long-standing love of Siouxsie and the Banshees by spying a copy of *Downside Up* on my Chicago kitchen table, recruited me for the panel "The Racial Publics of Siouxsie Sioux" at the annual MoPop Pop Conference in Seattle. My mentor and friend Jorge Mariscal brought me to UC San Diego to lecture on many of the ideas appearing on the following pages. Claudia Milian's invitation to Duke University's Tenth Anniversary of the Program of Latina/o Studies in the Global South afforded the opportunity to present on this work in a supportive yet importantly critical environment. And the support of Ariana Ruiz, Rene Rocha, and Darrel Wanzer-Serrano to deliver a talk at the symposium "Imagining Latinidades: Articulations of National Belonging" at the University of Iowa supplied me with the confidence to finalize the manuscript and release it into the world.

I am deeply thankful to Ken Wissoker, who was an advocate of this book from its molten origins. He listened to my initial ideas and encouraged their development while patiently awaiting their realization. Courtney Berger did the same and has never given up hope in me. Joshua Gutterman Tranen,

Chad Royal, Matt Tauch, and Annie Lubinsky, also at Duke University Press, helped in many ways to shepherd the manuscript toward publication.

Many thanks to the staff members of the British Library in London and the Tomás Rivera Library at the University of California, Riverside—especially in the Interlibrary Loan office—who helped me locate numerous materials referenced in this book. Philip Chiu at Rivera Library has come to my rescue one too many times to recall.

Much appreciation to the visual artists whose work is featured in this book, including the late Peter Andreas, Janette Beckman, Che Bracamontes, Andre Csillag, Mark Farrow, Brian Griffin, Jaime Hernandez, Alan Perry, Sheila Rock, Shizu Saldamando, Donna Santisi, Graham Smith, John Stoddart, Mary Jane Valdez, and Patssi Valdez.

Paul Cassidy and Kevin Kelman have facilitated my deep love of Scotland, shared stories, and provided boundless amounts of enthusiasm. (Watching BBC documentaries and reruns of *Top of the Pops* with them is pure joy.) Our mutual friend, Joey Terrill, to whom I'm thankful for his friendship and example, connected us in Chicago when a brunch date turned into a weekend-long jaunt through the city to explore the bars, restaurants, and neighborhoods that I miss daily since my return to California. Through Kevin and Paul, I met many friends across the Atlantic. They include Hazel Mcilwraith, Gillian Farmer, Jon McNeill, Garry Taylor, Jude Taylor, Derek McKee, Graham Roberts, Susan Smith, John Lawson, Allan and Vicky Quinn, Pauline and Roger Hulme, Etty and Derek Leslie, Eric Livingston, and Richard Buchan. Pat Silva and Ana Landeros, based in LA, are part of this network of friends, and I treasure them immensely.

Holly Johnson has consistently taken time out of his schedule to answer my questions and offer bundles of support. Christos Tolera graciously met with me at the Bar Italia in Soho and answered my questions about Blue Rondo a la Turk and the London nightlife scene of which he was a part. The encouragement and generosity shown by Andy Polaris is unprecedented, and I can't begin to express how much I admire him. Matthew Worley and David Wilkinson have been enormously helpful by answering random questions and producing essential scholarship on punk and post-punk from which I've learned a great deal. Tim Lawrence listened to and encouraged my ideas during his visit to UC Riverside in 2017. For kindly and diligently answering my clarification-seeking questions, thanks go to Dave Barbarossa, Lewis Martineé, Michael Alago, Kevin Haskins, Izzy Sanabria, Brian Soto, José "Che" Bracamontes, and Cristian Nuñez. Suzan Colón generously made time for my inquiries and encouraged this project early on. Shari B. Ellis read my text messages about the book and has been nothing short of enthusiastic. Deep gratitude to Stuart Cosgrove and Shirani Sabaratnam for their long-distance care. Ian Morrison has been a cheerleader for this project from the start. Ian, Carlos Álvarez, Claire Bloxsom, Stevie Nicholl, Gordon Gray, and Iain Tough are my favorite Petheads who gift me with unshakable support from many points on the globe. Dania Herrera and Michael Wright have been superb company during my trips to London, and I cherish their friendship and our conversations over pints. Because of my travels to the UK, I've been lucky to reconnect with my cousin Bryan, who relocated with his family from Southern California to Glasgow.

My dear friend Mirelsie Velazquez accompanied me on my first trip to London and it's with her that I share common interests and politics that infuse every page of this book. Ariana Ruiz is a cherished friend and colleague who inspires me with her wit, work, and brilliance. For over twenty years now, Eugene Rodríguez has inspired and challenged many of my ideas. His art and intelligence are simply stunning. Steven Goldwater listened to me rant and rave over beers and helped provide the sonic backdrop necessary to think through many of this book's ideas. I thank him for his unrefined sense of humor and his unswerving friendship. Gina Aguillon is an ideal concert companion who always insists on waiting around after the show with hopes of meeting members of the band. My aunt, Mary Valdez, has also attended shows with me and shared her brilliant photography and enthusiasm for all things popular. I dragged my godson Anthony Valdez Jr. to gigs at the Concert Lounge in Riverside, and his love and enthusiasm for what I do means so much. Dionne Espinoza is also a concert-going friend whose criticism, political convictions, and astute assessments of culture I always learn from. Margaret Sena was my *120 Minutes* viewing partner while we were undergrads at Berkeley and continues to share my love of British popular culture. Veronica Kann encouraged me to write this book over drinks, fried broccoli, and repeated plays of the Rolling Stones, the Velvet Underground, Iggy Pop, and Elvis Costello on the Esquire Lounge digital jukebox in Champaign. I am forever thankful to her, and I miss her immensely.

John McKinn, Jerry Miller, and J. Kēhaulani Kauanui are equally colleagues and dear friends who share my musical passions. I love being able to break out into a conversation about the small details of a song lyric, a music video, or an obscure historical factoid about our favorite bands and singers. John is a delightfully incorrigible accomplice with whom I have much in common. Kēhaulani has kindly given me her unflagging support, which made this book a reality. Jerry listens carefully to my incoherent ideas and helps makes sense of them. He also continues to enthusiastically support my bad object-choices. My ride-or-dies, Richard Villegas Jr. and Milton Sánchez, keep all my secrets and always have my back.

Michael Jaime-Becerra identified and demanded more of the creative elements making up this project. Seeing Bauhaus with him and Elizabeth and at the Hollywood Paladium in 2020 was a majestic experience. Michael and our dear friend and UCR colleague, Jennifer Nájera, make up a writing group that never failed to breathe new life into this book. I am forever thankful for their insights, coconspiring, and camaraderie. Writing sessions with valued friends and colleagues Manuel G. Galavíz and Martin Manalansan were essential in seeing this book through completion. Heartfelt thanks to Mary Pat Brady, Deborah Vargas, and Alexandra T. Vazquez for the solidarity, laughs, brutal honesty, and frequent check-ins, all of which rescued me from writing slumps and work-related monotony. Their necessary insights and fire emojis aided in wrapping up the writing. My academic mentors, including Teresa de Lauretis, James Clifford, José David Saldívar, the late Alfred Arteaga, Kirsten Silva Gruesz, Julia Curry Rodríguez, Carlos E. Cortés, Norma Alarcón, Angela Y. Davis, and the late Nina Baym, inspire me in innumerable ways.

Numerous friends and colleagues lent me support of all kinds (including reading parts of the book and commenting on them) while cheering me on as I wrote. Among them: C. Ondine Chavoya, Alex de Guia, Ramzie Casiano, Ricardo A. Bracho, Keith M. Harris, Lilia Fernández, Constancio Arnaldo, Norma Marrun, Javier González-Rocha, Alex Espinosa, Elias Martínez, Diane Ortega, David Lloyd, Alberto Sandoval-Sánchez, José Luis Guerra, Amanda Ellis, José Dominguez, Israel X. Nery, Ray Fernández, David Orta, Ricky López, Angel Romo, David Vázquez, David Rodriguez, Beto and Arturo Del Real, Eric Téllez, Miguel Alfaro, Gustavo Colinga, Oscar Rivera, Will García, Manny and Osvaldo Torres, Osvaldo Valdes, Jesse and Joe Palencia, Jaime Olmos, Tony Ortega, David Ayento, Gabriel Corral, Horacio Avelar, Antelmo "Elmo" Quintero, Dustin Morris, Jason Toledo, Ricky Toledo, Juan López, Janet Moreno, Jerry and Esther Oseguera, Ramiro Tavares, Arlene Martin, the late John Mendez, Alexandro Gradilla, Aurora Guerrero, Carolina González, Danny Nuñez, Luis Alberto Campos, Edgar Patiño, Rick Esparza, Sam García, Erasto Avila, Rigoberto Campos, José Luis Benevides, Christian García, Dustin Shattuck, Jordan García, Ted Faust, Alberto Venegas, Chris Garza, Francesca

Royster, Lourdes Torres, Fede Aldama, Robert Ramírez, Tammy Ho, David Martínez, Sherryl Vint, Regie Peaslee, Javier Esparza, David Evans Frantz, Ernesto Chávez, Luis Alfaro, Charlene Villaseñor-Black, Rudy Aguilar, Celine Parreñas-Shimizu, Xavier Ramírez, Cindy San Miguel, Carlos Saucedo, Francisco J. Galarte, Eric Gonzales, Adrián Félix, Xóchitl Chávez, Mariam Lam, Freya Schiwy, Amalia Cabezas, Alicia Arrizón, Juliet McMullin, Earl Jackson Jr., Anne McKnight, Michelle Bloom, Michelle Raheja, Armando García, Alex Espinoza, Susan Straight, Gerald Clarke, Jonathan Mark Hall, John Kim, Ben Olguín, Cati Porter, Rodrigo Lazo, Ramón Rivera-Servera, Larry La Fountain-Stokes, Lucas Hilderbrand, Gaye Theresa Johnson, Catherine S. Ramirez, Norma E. Cantú, Esteban Elizarraras, Rosa Martínez, Arlene Torres, Wanda Pillow, Sarah Rafael García, Sarah Espinosa Romero, Carla Mireles, Joe Whitcher, Nikolay Maslov, Harry Gamboa Jr., Barbara Carrasco, Barbie Gamboa, Joelle Mendoza, Rubén Mendoza, Colin Gunckel, Tony Huizar, Brian Pérez, José Héctor Cadena, John Falk, Luis J. Rodríguez, Tony Mills, Albert Flores, Brian Montes, Scott Miller, Mike Madden, Jason Lappin, Greg Storms, Mark Sachse, Obie Leyva, Aurora Sarabia, Gabriel Guzmán, Santiago Piña, Siobhan B. Somerville, Nic Flores, Junaid Rana, Maryam Kashani, Lisa M. Cacho, David Coyoca, Kristine McDonald Parada, Justine Murrison, Francisco J. Ceja, Miguel Ramírez, Alejandro Lara, Alberto Vaca, Karen Tongson, Roy Pérez, Wendy Truran, John Musser, Michael Shetina, Alicia Kozma, Aurora Valdez, Noel Zavala, Jennifer Lozano, Jessica Easter, Frank García, Luis Román-García, Curtis Perry, Robert Dale Parker, Julie Dowling, Jonathan Inda, Javier Hurtado, Pete Sigal, Stacy Russo, Mike Luengas, Juan Fernandez, Mayra and Vicky Lagunas, Iván Ramos, Josh Guzmán, Leti Alvarado, Steven M. López, Robert Scheffrin, Teresa Camacho, David Wright, Tommy Serafin, Kate Izquierdo, and Ned Raggett.

Miguel Alcalá, Eleazar Flores Barrios, and Ana Fuentes are three UCR undergraduates who have engaged with the ideas in this book, providing invaluable insights about their own deep connections to popular music. Many thanks to Stephanie Michel for locating hidden treasures that helped solidify the book's arguments and fill in evident gaps. The students in my winter 2021 Punk and Post-Punk Cultures class—especially Eliana Buenrostro, Melissa Peykani, and Cat Rabin—taught me so much about that which I thought I already knew. Other students who have supported me and my work while in Champaign-Urbana and Riverside include Jorge Trujillo, Arlene Delacruz, Marlen Ríos-Hernández, Carolina Muñoz, Preston Waltrip, Heejoo Park, Ray Pineda, Lauren Hammond, Gennyvera Pacheco, Jonathan

Donabo, Gabby Almendarez, C. Jacob Marcos, Brandy Lewis, Jeshua Enriquez, Josh King, Zehra Qazi, Kory Chávez, Deonté Lee, Angela Olivares, Ronnae Lockette, Selena Razo, Meranda Knowles, Arman Virabov, Kishore Athreya, Mario Rangel, José Luis Pérez, Elizabeth Lourdes Morales, Jonathan González Díaz, Jessica Gutiérrez, Sergio Arroyo, Iván Montero, Joanna Aguirre, Hugo Treviño, Josette Lorig, Ryan Kelley, Osvaldo Mendez, Ezekiel Acosta, G Pineda, Cole Pofek, Hayden Petrovick, Shamus Lyons, Travis Bohall, Skyler de los Reyes, Matt Hardy, Abbot Haffar, Danny Carnazzo, Ethan Payne, Dean Miller, Anthony Russo, Connor Cannon, Aren Aghamanoukian, Rachel Graham, Ricardo Delgado-Solis, Bill Seaton, Terri Tomlinson, Angela and Dustin Williams, Jeremy Jurgens, Alex Maldonado, Luis Chun, and Martha Delgado. In the summer of 2017, Daniel Piña and Hector Servin would swing by my UCR campus apartment for coffee, books, and conversation. They helped motivate me to sit and write after a long day of teaching and meetings. Luiz Fernández and Ishmael Ramírez soon after filled their shoes and also dropped by for coffee and provided delightful conversations about life, literature, film, and music.

At UCR, Erika Suderburg and Judith Rodenbeck have been superlative department chairs. Everyone in the MDU office provides laughter, support, and camaraderie every day of the working week. Thanks to Diana Marroquin, Diane Shaw, Holly Easley, Josie Ayala, Francesca Moreira, Geneva Amador, Irene Dotson, Kristine Specht, Ryan Mariano, Victor Moreira, Dawn Viebach, Odie Jasso, Brenda Aragón, Cassie Barba, and Alicia Kofford. I am thankful to my colleagues in Media and Cultural Studies and English for the tremendous inspiration they provide. Sandra Baltazar Martínez, Toi Thibodeaux, Estella Acuña, Arlene Cano Matute, Nancy Jean Tubbs, Dennis McIver, Mayra Jones, LaToya Ambrose, Lourdes Maldonado, Nelly Cruz, Rich Cardullo, Ryan Lipinski, Nelda Thomas, Katrice Wright Calloway, Susan Brown, Beth Reynolds, Cindy Williams, and many others are members of the campus community who sustain me.

DJing at KUCR has added another dimension to this work, and my weekly show, *Dr. Ricky on the Radio*, is made possible by Elliot Wong, Louis Vandenberg, Mikaela Elson, Eddie Valencia, Sarah Bazzy, Precious Fasakin, Ismael González Jr., Aaron Grech, Deborah Wong, Conrad Talamantes, Joshua Moreno, Tina Bold, Josh Kreeger, and all of the other brilliant DJs at the station.

My sister, who accompanied me to concerts in Orange County and LA (including Culture Club, Adam Ant, Bryan Ferry, Simple Minds, Squeeze, Duran Duran, and David Sylvian), has always shared my love for music and books. My parents aided and abetted this love, and their musical tastes—reflected in records by the Beatles, Carole King, the Supremes, and Aretha Franklin, along with their love of oldies but goodies broadcast on KRLA—inspired me to write this book. Sunday visits to the Orange Circle antique stores helped me acquire records, magazines, and other memorabilia that were crucial to this project's development. My grandmother, who passed away as I completed this book and whom I miss daily, joined me on these visits and provided laughs, gossip, and essential motivation.

A Kiss across the Ocean is dedicated to my niece, Natalie Rodríguez Merino. Nat always teaches me new things about popular culture, and she never fails to elegantly explain why it matters.

A KISS ACROSS THE OCEAN

An Introduction

February 1984, one Saturday morning in Santa Ana, California. I was twelve years old, one month shy of entering my teenage years, and already feeling alienated from many of my peers because of the widening divide between us around our respective awakening identities. I also found myself enduring the constant warring of parents who had fallen out of love years ago, but frequently—and desperately—attempted to stay together for their children's sake. My mother was working long hours at the cosmetics counter at the Broadway department store, struggling to make ends meet to support my sister and me after my father decided to once again flee our frequently contentious household. Not wanting to leave us home alone, she always dropped us off at my aunt Irene's apartment on weekends, where we would arrive with an arsenal of library books and art supplies to keep us busy until retrieved hours later. Yet on this particular morning, we walked into Irene's apartment precisely as Culture Club's "Karma Chameleon," a melodically buoyant yet lyrically lovelorn song that I had recently become obsessed with, given its repeated plays on the radio, arose from the single speaker of a modest television set atop a stereo system.

> It's love in stereo.
> **Culture Club, "I'll Tumble 4 Ya"**

The song seemed to greet our arrival, and what appeared on the screen further lodged the song at the center of my heart. The band's singer—a glamorous, self-assured, and gender-ambiguous figure I would soon come to know as Boy George—captured and held my gaze for the duration of the music video, profoundly moving me and immediately influencing my lifelong attachment to popular music. Like the transformative televisual moments for Alice, the teenage protagonist of Keith English's 2018 film *The More You Ignore Me* who sits transfixed by Morrissey and the Smiths performing "This Charming Man" on *Top of the Pops* in 1983, and for gay Black British choreographer Les Child who, in the 2020 documentary *Beyond "There's Always a Black Issue, Dear,"* comes to know himself when first witnessing ballet on the small screen, I suddenly began to see the world anew. This newfound perspective manifested not only from a multicolored prism consisting of "red, gold, and green" (as discerned from Culture Club's song lyrics and music video alike), but also through a kaleidoscope of class, gender, race, sexuality, and desire.[1] "Karma Chameleon," however, was only the first in a long line of British pop songs and music videos that would touch me in affective and thought-provoking ways.[2] Be it the doubly somber and dramatic synth masterpiece "Here Comes the Rain Again" by the Eurythmics, which also seemed to play recurrently on the radio alongside "Karma Chameleon," or Soft Cell's "Tainted Love," an angst-induced self-diagnosis of a spurned lover set to an electronically enveloping sinister beat, this music shook the very foundations of my existence and brilliantly soundtracked an otherwise ordinary life.[3]

Announcing a second British Invasion, the first occurring twenty years earlier with the stateside arrival of the Beatles, the November 10, 1983, issue of American rock magazine *Rolling Stone* featured Boy George on the cover and sounded the clarion call of music artists from across the pond on the verge of taking the US by storm.[4] Featuring a host of bands symbolizing "that strange animal variously called 'New Wave' and 'new music'" (Puterbaugh 1983, 31) (or what I choose to call post-punk, as will be explained later), this special issue also spotlights the glossy magazines of the era that showcased these artists to a growing stateside fan base. While my introduction and dedication to the post-punk era were certainly facilitated by a host of media—radio stations like KROQ and the Mighty 690, an assortment of Southern California–based music video programs like *Video One* and *Request Video* and, of course, the US cable channel MTV—it was unquestionably print media that provided the information on who these fabulously made-up creatures were, how they came to be, and what made them tick. Green Gartside, singer and founding member of the sui generis post-punk band Scritti Politti, notes that he drew great inspiration from a magazine interview with John Lennon in which the eminent Liverpudlian maintained

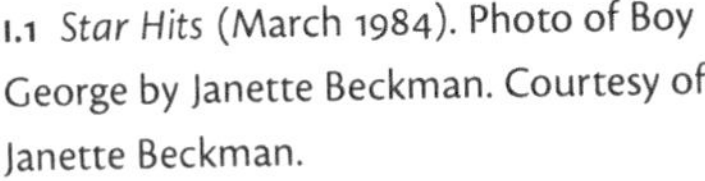

I.1 *Star Hits* (March 1984). Photo of Boy George by Janette Beckman. Courtesy of Janette Beckman.

I.2 *Smash Hits* (July 19–August 1, 1984). "Boy George and Four Close Friends." Photo by Andre Csillag. Courtesy of Andre Csillag.

that "we must make the workers aware of the really unhappy position they are in, break the dream they are surrounded by." For Gartside, "This was the stuff that I was finding out about—at eight, nine, ten years old. Apart from the power of the music itself, their musical-sophistication development really drew me towards being attracted to difficult musics and ideas. In a way, theory and politics and music were bound up for me from the very beginning. It's unimaginable to think of them as separate in any way" (2016, 196).

Star Hits magazine, discovered on a magazine rack at the local Alpha Beta supermarket, opened similar vistas and bestowed a wealth of information about a growing list of British pop stars whose singular music and relatable lives I became preoccupied with. It also served as a guide for discovering artists, writers, philosophers, and earlier musicians who not only compelled me to excel in school but also set me on the path toward an academic career and, as with Gartside, establishing an inseparable bond between theory, politics, and music.[5] Fittingly, Boy George's face was on the cover of the first issue of *Star Hits* I would purchase (fig. I.1). Shortly thereafter, I encountered *Star Hits'* predecessor and sister publication from across the Atlantic: *Smash Hits* (fig. I.2). And while it might mean something that Boy George was also on the cover of the first issue of *Smash Hits*

I'd own (purchased at Music Market in Costa Mesa), it was the interview with Sex Pistols and Public Image Limited singer John Lydon (or Johnny Rotten) inside that July 18–August 1, 1984, issue of the British publication that would impact me just like the Culture Club video. Interviewer Peter Martin, after asking Lydon what people thought of him in America after his move to Los Angeles, posed a follow-up question: "Apart from 'getting together a new band,' what have you been up to out there?" Lydon responded, "I hang around with the Chicanos (Mexicans who live in America) who are into all that cruising around in '50s cars. I've got a '57 Caddie (Cadillac). I got it for 2000 dollars. V-8 engine, the works. I've had it souped up so I'm going into races now—some serious stock car stuff. I love it" (Martin 1984, 48).[6]

It was this interview with Lydon that stuck with me throughout my teenage years when I was told this music was not meant for me. To employ a word whose recent parlance signifies recognition, I felt seen. Whether it was the aggression experienced at concerts or white peers who claimed white artists as rightfully theirs (consider the racist vitriol espoused at an X concert in Brett Easton Ellis's 1985 novel *Less Than Zero*—"'There are too many fucking Mexicans here, dude.' . . . 'Let's kill 'em all'" [184]—or when, in Depeche Mode's documentary *101*, about their historic concert at the Rose Bowl in Pasadena, a white kid calls brown kids "poseurs" to regulate their claims to music incompatible with the culture to which they are essentially consigned), musical tastes were commonly demarcated in class-structured and racially segregated ways. As much as revisionist historians and commentators assuredly argue that people of color were "always present" in alternative music scenes of this era, such information does not counter the fact that I and many others were made to believe, by both whites and peers of color alike, that we did not belong.[7] This one sentence spoken by Lydon onto which I held firmly also charges the inspiration to circle back to this era to consider the intimate transatlantic connections that manifested in myriad ways, evidencing a politics of transcultural exchange that may perhaps prove exemplary if not instructive in our current historical moment in which renewed threats of global violence match the late–Cold War 1980s of my adolescence.

Part of the impetus to write this book comes by way of motivation from an assortment of recent publications—Francesca T. Royster's (2013) *Sounding Like a No-No: Queer Sounds and Eccentric Acts in the Post-Soul Era*, Carl Stanley's (2015) *Kiss and Make Up*, Michael Jaime-Becerra's (2019) "Todo se acaba: 11950 Garvey Avenue/7305 Melrose Avenue," Pete Paphides's (2020) *Broken Greek: A Story of Chip Shops and Pop Songs*, and Phuc Tran's

(2020) *Sigh, Gone: A Misfit's Memoir of Great Books, Punk Rock, and the Fight to Fit In,* among others—which intertwine a deep love of popular music with coming-of-age memoir. As Robert Edgar, Fraser Mann, and Helen Pleasance write in the introduction to their edited collection, *Music, Memory, and Memoir,* "Our teenage years and the records we bought have irreversibly shaped who we are and how we like others to see us" (2019, 1). In *Adolescent Alternatives: Road Trips with Japan, 1978–1980,* Stephen Holden, with regard to his love for the British band Japan, reflects, "I now think that such unconditional fandom is the exclusive domain of a teenager. Yet the memories of those times are ones that will live forever and resonate within me . . . even now. As I write this, I am getting a tear in my eye, evoking my long-lost youth in the here and now" (2020, 106). Quite similarly, *A Kiss across the Ocean*—the title taken from Culture Club's 1983 London Hammersmith Odeon concert, which I saw at the house of a friend whose parents subscribed to HBO (fig. I.3)—takes up memoir for capturing and blending both my early and current status as a fan of British post-punk music with the interlocking connections between this music and Latinidad in the United States.[8] Akin to James Clifford's 1997 book *Routes,* "The personal explorations scattered throughout are not revelations from an autobiography but glimpses of a specific path among others. I include them in the belief that a degree of self-location is possible and valuable, particularly when it points beyond the individual toward ongoing webs of relationship" (15). Such webs of relationship reveal a multifaceted intimacy that flies in the perplexed faces of those writers of the tedious articles intent on cracking the code to how Latinos/as could possibly listen to music that exceeds their reductionist designation of the cultural parameters of taste.[9]

As for Clifford, "the struggle to perceive certain borders of my own perspective is not an end in itself but a precondition for efforts of attentiveness, translation, and alliance" (1997, 15). Certainly, "my own perspective" is one of many nodes for chronicling multidirectional transatlantic exchanges since the early 1980s. One such recent example in this vein is Gurinder Chadha's 2019 film *Blinded by the Light,* about British-Pakistani Muslim teenager and Bruce Springsteen fan Javed Khan in 1980s Luton. Others are found in published interviews, autobiographies and biographies, feature-length films and documentaries, magazine and newspaper articles, promotional videos, music recordings, performance footage, and written and oral memoir—such as mine here and those which one might hear recounted among middle-aged concert goers in Southern California or written and read on friends' Facebook walls or under Instagram posts. While *A Kiss*

1.3 *TV Guide* (April 28–May 4, 1984) advertisement for HBO televised Culture Club concert, "Kiss across the Ocean."

across the Ocean at times emphatically sheds light on Latina/o/x fandom for British popular music (however unusual this might initially seem to those with preconceived ideas of people's musical tastes; for who, after all, gets to decide what we listen to, or that our tastes must naturally align with, for example, rancheras, salsa, hip-hop, or reggaeton?), fandom dissolves into a multipronged reciprocity derived from musically and culturally motivated multidirectional contact.[10]

MULTIDIRECTIONAL INTIMACIES AND THE TRANSATLANTIC TOUCH

In her 2016 book *Mozlandia: Morrissey Fans in the Borderlands*, Melissa Mora Hidalgo tackles at the fore what has been identified by many journalists, filmmakers, and critics alike as the curious phenomenon that is the US Latino fandom of Steven Patrick Morrissey (known simply as Morrissey or Moz), the former frontperson of the British band the Smiths. Hidalgo explains:

> I wrote this book because I, along with many other Latina/o fans, got tired of the same ol' questions of "why" we love Moz. The question of Latino (and more specifically, Mexican and Chicano) Morrissey fandom, and what have now become stock, if not clichéd, explanations, are useful starting points, and indeed they highlight important contexts for understanding this seemingly unlikely affinity. . . . I am less interested in asking that question again and producing the same evidence to show that, yes, a lot of Mexicans, Latinos/as and Chicanos/as *do* (as do many other groups of people) love Morrissey. We know these fans and communities exist, and it's not really so strange after all. Rather, I am interested in asking the "what" and "how" questions, new questions that provide us with nuance, complexity, insight, and new ways to see, hear, and understand these fan communities in "Moz Angeles" and around the borderlands. (2016, 5)

Drawing inspiration from Hidalgo in short-circuiting the "Why do Latinos/as love this kind of music or this particular band or singer?" question for the way it upholds a "strange phenomenon" evaluation, *A Kiss across the Ocean* operates in solidarity with *Mozlandia*, given how both refuse an exclusive framing by or focus on fandom. Our related approach is instead animated by a deep investigative labor propelled by fannish investment. Like Hidalgo's book, this project involves formations of Latinidad that exceed essentialist attachments to immutable cultural identities and affiliations to instead signal how they emerge in tandem with unofficial archives, ephemeral evidence, and transnational cultural processes.[11] Emphasizing knowledges and experiences difficult to capture on traditional registers of analysis (not unlike post-punk itself, with its assorted sonic range encompassing sparse guitar jangles and electronically interwoven textures), it unapologetically takes pleasure in refusing ready-made academic and nation-based discursive frameworks.

Highlighting the varied collaborations, physical convergences, and mutual influences of British post-punk music artists and Latina/o/x communities in the US from the 1980s onward, the book explores the myriad ways seemingly disparate parties touch one another.[12] Indeed, we must not forget how this phenomenon is not only Latina/o/x fans flocking to Morrissey concerts and brandishing tattoos of their favorite Manchester crooner, but it's also Morrissey himself, who wrote about an LA-based Chicano homeboy named Héctor ("the first of the gang to die"), titled his 1999–2000 tour ¡Oye Esteban!, and declared his affection for Mexican people for being "so terribly nice" and who "have fantastic hair, and fantastic skin, and usually really good teeth" (Guerrero 2018). And as it's impossible for me not to also discuss Morrissey in this book (although this discussion is decidedly limited), I suggest an alternative angle from which to appraise his and many of his contemporaries' circulation within and impact on Latina/o/x communities. For as much as Morrissey has intimately touched Latino fans in manifold ways (as a considerable body of scholarship and journalism on the topic has insightfully shown), I argue that this touch is mutual.[13]

Karen Tongson, in *Relocations: Queer Suburban Imaginaries*, importantly comments on the way British popular music impacted youth of color (herself as well as the Latinos and Latinas among whom she grew up) in Southern California. Extending Jennifer Terry's unpublished formulation of "remote intimacies" allows Tongson to capture the temporal discontinuities between fans in Southern California and British popular music. As Tongson writes, "I have come to imagine remote intimacies describing the communities for whom intimacies cohere across virtual networks of desire through radio, music, and television, on the Internet, and now through online social networking sites. Remote intimacies account both technically and affectively for the symbiosis that can happen between disparate subjects—like the storied connection between Latinos and Morrissey, for example, or between suburban queer kids of color and Anglophilic ear candy in general" (2011, 130). Tongson's articulation of remote intimacies captures my own and many others' (urban and "suburban queer kids of color") attachment to many singers and bands from across the Atlantic. Indeed, "remote intimacy" helps charge the sense of touch on which this book focuses. But as I disclose the sweetness of this "Anglophilic ear candy" for Latina/o/x audiences (particularly relating to my own status as an adoring fan), I additionally document the allure of US Latinidad for British post-punk artists to underscore the interplay of reciprocal intimacy. Moreover, while deep connections are undoubtedly established across time and space, they often manifest in real time and thus generate a combined sensuality that is not flatly disparate but advantageous given the fortuitous opportunity of temporal and spatial alignment. As Iain Chambers notes in his book *Migrancy, Culture, Identity,* the ubiquity of popular music of the 1980s and 1990s represents "a hegemony that has simultaneously created the conditions for an international sound network that subsequently encouraged a proliferation of margins and an emergence of other voices. In the wake of these developments, surprising trajectories can emerge on the musical map, resulting in stories of unexpected influences and strange combinations" (1994, 77).

Touch, then, registers the intimate bonds examined throughout this project given music's unbounded haptic capability of animating networks of cultural, collaborative, amorous, and political affiliation. In *Touch: Sensuous Theory and Multisensory Media,* media theorist Laura U. Marks compels us to see how learning to "appreciate the materiality of our media pulls us away from a symbolic understanding and toward a shared physical existence" (2002, xii). That is, the material effects generated by the circulation of media and its makers allow us to grasp the physical proximities of cultural producers and their audiences (and an attendant mutual acknowledgment) even when temporal and spatial divergences manifest. Touch therefore registers the material and psychic energies that animate the potentialities of unbounded haptic intimacy. Here, touch is proposed as one answer to Lauren Berlant's question, "What if we saw [intimacy] emerge from much more mobile processes of attachment?" (1998, 284). The title of the book therefore metaphorically signals how British post-punk touches Latinidad and vice versa, not unlike the way that a kiss transpires as a gesture requiring a "mobile process of attachment" to intimately bring together two distinct accomplices. After all, when a kiss is blown, it must successfully meet its intended target to actualize its affective motivation.

Additionally, touch helps index encounters that are horizontally organized and orchestrated by a dual recognition of lives and histories (no matter how limited or provisional) of those parties conjoined, acknowledged, or referenced. In a 2016–2017 exhibition at the Vincent Price Art Museum in East Los Angeles titled *Tastemakers and Earthshakers: Notes from Los Angeles*

Youth Culture, 1943–2016, Morrissey was once again deployed as exemplary of the appeal British pop music has for Chicano/a youths. Yet the exhibition's narrative minimized the multidirectional influences shared by US Latina/o/x communities and UK post-punk artists, a mutual movement of traveling cultures that Ariana Ruiz identifies as constituting a Brown Atlantic.[14] And parting ways with recent scholarly efforts to decenter punk's typically assumed origins from 1970s European and Anglo-American contexts, *A Kiss across the Ocean* takes a different tack by foregrounding networks of affiliation rather than playing the game of who-beat-whom to the preliminary punch. As with the curatorial goal of C. Ondine Chavoya and David Evans Frantz's exhibition *Axis Mundo: Queer Networks in Chicano L.A.*, the book maps "a network of affinities, connections, affiliated aesthetic and conceptual practices, and political alignments" that is "promiscuous and capacious" (2017, 25). This includes Siouxsie Sioux's friendship with Kid Congo Powers; Marc Almond's affection for Chicano Scottish writer John Rechy; Adam Ant's attraction to racist and hypersexualized film and television images of Latinos; Blue Rondo a la Turk's devotion to the zoot suit and Latin music; and Holly Johnson's political awareness of the US's longstanding discriminatory practices against Mexican Americans.

At the heart of Chavoya and Frantz's exhibition is the loving bond between the late Los Angeles–based Chicano artist Mundo Meza and noted British fashion icon Simon Doonan. In an afterword to the exhibition catalog titled "Mundo Goes to Hollywood," Doonan narrates his relationship-turned-friendship with Meza prior to his death from AIDS-related complications in Los Angeles:

> We had an enormous amount in common. We were both immigrants in the land of opportunity. We also spent a great deal of time exploring each other's ethnicity. I was intrigued by his Mexican-ness, he was enthralled by everything that was trendy and English. He introduced me to Frida Kahlo's paintings and ranchera music and various artist friends from East L.A. like Cyclona and Patssi Valdez and Gronk. I introduced him to Boy George acolytes like Pinkietessa Braithwaite and the pop star Marilyn; they had recently moved from London and lived just around the corner. (2017, 367)[15]

The association established here—between Doonan and Meza, but also between Doonan, Meza, Pinkietessa, and Marilyn (Peter Robinson)—stands as one example of the Latino/British networks forged vis-à-vis friendship and mutual influence. Indeed, this is a kiss that has traversed the Atlantic Ocean and touched down on Southern California terrain.

Doonan further illustrates here and in his 2009 memoir, *Beautiful People: My Family and Other Glamorous Varmints*, how British post-punk music and fashion (with which Marilyn and Pinkietessa are also associated) helped consolidate the bond between himself and Meza. As he explains, "There was no shortage of activities for us marginalized creative misfits in Hollywood. This was the early 1980s when, if you were au courant, you were probably worshiping ABC, Bow Wow Wow, and The Thompson Twins. Every week another new band of hopefuls—Spandau Ballet, Madness, The Specials, Siouxsie Sioux—was playing at the Roxy or the Whisky A Go Go" (367). Doonan in addition details how the fashion of the early 1980s was inextricably tied to the era's music.

> When we weren't watching live music, Mundo and I were flitting about in Vivienne Westwood pirate gear at "New Romantic" clubs with names like The Veil, The Fake, and Club Lingerie. It was good old-fashioned pointless fun. We took full advantage of the vogue for costumey dress up. I have boxes of snaps of us in various guises: Mundo dressed as Valentino, me as Betty Rubble, Mundo as a goat-legged Bacchus, and me as Queen Elizabeth II. The apotheosis of our overdressed trendiness occurred in 1981 when we were recruited by director Russell Mulcahy for the Kim Carnes "Bette Davis Eyes" music video. Mundo gets more screen time than me, but that's my gloved hand in the opening shot. (2009, 367)

That the "Vivienne Westwood pirate gear," commonly linked to Bow Wow Wow and Adam Ant, also adorned Meza and Doonan further points to how British post-punk aesthetics traveled to the United States and indelibly touched a Tijuana-born and East LA–raised Chicano multidisciplinary artist like Mundo Meza.[16] Moreover, Mulcahy's recruitment of Doonan and Meza in the US was motivated by his awareness of the New Romantic scene and its unmistakable style in the UK, which he had captured not much earlier in Duran Duran's "Planet Earth" video (both videos were shot and released within the first three months of 1981). Recalling the making of the "Bette Davis Eyes" video, Mulcahy explains, "The New Romantic thing was getting started and that was bigger in England, but it was going to a degree in America, and so we pulled these kids in."[17] Although Kim Carnes's music and style in Mulcahy's video do not entirely match the New Romantic sound and look adopted by Duran Duran, the "kids" in "Bette Davis Eyes" approximate an aesthetic with the band from Birmingham, albeit refashioned for and by a scene including working-class LA Latinos and Latinas also aspiring to make art.

On the East Coast, a Puerto Rican kid from the Bronx by the name of Michael Anthony Alago became a pivotal figure in booking up-and-coming bands at noted New York City venues like the Ritz and the Red Parrot in his capacity as assistant music director. Through his stint as an A&R executive at Elektra Records (during which time his renown would increase given his role in signing the band Metallica), Alago coordinated the introduction of post-punk bands to US audiences. In his 2020 memoir, *I Am Michael Alago: Breathing Music. Signing Metallica. Beating Death,* Alago writes about his role in Public Image Limited's historic yet notorious 1981 Ritz performance that resulted in riot-induced violence. To the great excitement of the Ritz owners and concertgoers who helped sell out the show, Alago successfully booked the recently formed Bow Wow Wow to perform at the venue. However, he was soon devastated to learn that the band's infamous manager, Malcolm McLaren, had canceled their appearance due to then thirteen-year-old singer Annabella Lwin's mother's refusal to allow her daughter to travel to the States.[18] Thanks to quick thinking and acting, Alago secured in Bow Wow Wow's place Public Image Limited, who at the time were visiting New York to promote their recently released LP *The Flowers of Romance.* With disappointment shifting to renewed excitement, Public Image Limited quickly sold out two nights at the Ritz. Yet John Lydon's post–Sex Pistols outfit delivered the dubious gift of an alternative performance instead of a clichéd rock concert. Alago explains:

> Little did we know, however, that the evening would turn into a violent free-for-all. At the start of the show, the song "Flowers of Romance" blasted through the speakers, but five minutes later, you could feel that something was not right. John and the band refused to come out in front of the screen. PiL saw this event as a performance art piece, but the fans wanted to see a concert. They wanted to hear the band play and play furiously—basically, they wanted Johnny Rotten in action. But they didn't get that, and the audience went ballistic. They threw bottles at the huge video screen. Chairs flew everywhere. The crowd pulled on the screen, tearing it down, ripping holes in it and smashing bottles on the stage. John still refused to come out front, because to him, this was not a gig. (2020, 60)

One might think such a debacle would be enough to congeal a lifelong animosity between all parties involved. Quite the opposite. Alago recalls, "After the show, a bunch of us, including photographer Laura Levine, gathered in the dressing room. Scott Rubinoff, a big PiL fan, whose head was bleeding from the crowd's attack earlier, was there as well—he was so excited to meet

John. We all drank up a storm, celebrating the chaos of the show. An unpredictable but lovely thing came out of it for me as well—a close, personal, and professional friendship with John Lydon—one that lasts to this day" (60).

Soon after the infamous and fortuitous PiL show, Alago would make his way to the UK "to scout out bands to perform at The Ritz." In a few weeks he saw "Bauhaus, Altered Images, the Thompson Twins, Theatre of Hate, The Cramps, and Echo and the Bunnymen at a Festival in Leeds, as well as Depeche Mode on *Top of the Pops* in London" (2020, 60–61). Unquestionably, Michael Alago epitomizes a central link between Latinos/as in the US and British post-punk artists, given his central role in enabling the spaces where those artists performed while maintaining intimate ties with central figures like Lydon.[19]

The momentum of the second-wave British Invasion of the early 1980s was unstoppable, compelling aspiring musicians in the US to emulate the sounds—and sometimes accents—of those artistic innovators from across the ocean. One such example is the Chicago-based band Ministry, whose Cuban American lead singer Al Jourgensen (née Alejandro Ramírez Casas) is intimately connected to the now-famous Wax Trax! Records independent label and considered a prominent figure in the industrial music scene. Yet before Ministry's turn to a hard-hitting industrial sound, the band's early musical offerings—including the 1982 single "Work for Love"—may very well have been pressed by a British label like Mute alongside acts such as Depeche Mode and Fad Gadget.[20] In the July 23, 1983, issue of the British magazine *Record Mirror*, Ministry is briefly spotlighted, with an unnamed writer beginning the feature titled "Gospel Groove" in the following way: "Just fancy this: America's been invaded by waves of British electro-talent and they don't even realise they have some of their very own" (14). The writer continues, "Ministry are from Chicago and strut a mean slice of white funk stuff. They are Al Jourgensen, Chicago's answer to [New Romantic founding father and Visage member] Rusty Egan, drummer Stevo (absolutely no relation [to record label Some Bizzare owner and Soft Cell producer of the same name]) plus a girl backing vocalist with the name of Shay Jones" (14). In the write-up, Jourgensen maintains that Ministry is "very off-the-wall for Americans" (and debatably insists that "nothing's come out of Chicago since 1927 when Muddy Waters was born"); yet the "white funk" of the band, he insists, is the result of his status as a Havana-born and US Midwest-raised descendant of Cuban musicians. In his absorbing memoir, *Ministry: The Lost Gospels According to Al Jourgensen*, the Ministry frontperson writes about one of his first memories recalling his uncles playing "tribal Cuban music on congas" (2013, 8). Jourgensen explains, "That's where I got my first taste of contrapuntal beats and triplets, and it stuck with me. If you listen to Ministry, even the really old stuff like '(Every Day Is) Halloween,' 'Deity,' 'Burning Inside,' and up through 'Double Tap' from *Relapse,* you can hear the contrapuntal style blended with metal and whatever keyboard stuff I was doing" (8).

Reading and rereading my steadily mounting pile of British and American magazines and newspapers (including issues of *Star Hits, Smash Hits, Record Mirror, Melody Maker, Sounds, Creem, No. 1, New Musical Express* (NME), *Video Rock Stars,* and *Rolling Stone*), I soon found myself seeking out books, artists, and earlier influential bands and singers mentioned in pop star interviews, personal information questionnaires, and top-ten albums lists. Prompting my search for information on Jean Cocteau and Andy Warhol at the Santa Ana Public Library (noted by countless musicians—including David Sylvian, Bill Nelson, and Duran Duran's Nick Rhodes—as their favorite artists), scouring the bins at independent and mainstream record stores for vinyl by T. Rex, Roxy Music, David Bowie, the Velvet Underground, New York Dolls, and Sparks (name-checked as key influences), or learning about the everyday, working-class cultures of contemporary Britain (from which most admired performers emerged), these publications fed my intellectual curiosity and the ever-expanding musical network to which I felt intimately bound.

In the December 1984 issue of *Star Hits,* in a regular feature titled Get Smart (where readers' letters addressed to an imaginary magazine columnist named Jackie were cleverly answered), I discovered the existence of a New York City–based Japan fanzine titled *Japan: Made in the USA* (*J:MUSA*).[21] Despite disbanding two years earlier in December 1982, Japan was quickly becoming one of my favorite groups (I initially discovered them referenced as one of Duran Duran's principal influences). I clearly recall placing the requisite one-dollar bill in a folded sheet of notebook paper and sending for what "Jackie" fittingly called "an imaginative xeroxed fanzine." Not only was *J:MUSA* rich with information about Japan's former members and their musical associates (Peter Murphy from Bauhaus, Ryuichi Sakamoto, and Yellow Magic Orchestra among them), but it was also a network of fans who made up my remote yet intimate community. Along with facilitating my letter writing to fellow Japan fans based in San Antonio, Ann Arbor, and Roseville, California, I was also introduced to one of the fanzine's main contributors with a strikingly familiar (i.e., Spanish) surname: Suzan Colón.

The daughter of the late Puerto Rican comics artist Ernie Colón and an Irish mother, Suzan Colón was involved with both *J:MUSA* and *Star Hits*. Not knowing anything at the time about her personal history, her last name alone made me privy to her existence as a Latina in my imagined community of British post-punk utopia.[22] David Keeps, former editor of *Star Hits*, recounts in a 2014 interview Colón's onboarding:

> Within the first year [of *Star Hits*' existence], two crucial things happened. A girl claiming to be our biggest fan and the publisher of a magazine about David Sylvian and his band Japan called the office three times in one day and I finally gave in and told her to come up when she mentioned she could type 86 words a minute. (This was in the murky past where no one used computers.) Her name was Suzan Colón. She became our intern. Then when [founding editor] David Fricke left the magazine, I became the Editor and gave Suzan a full-time job. She was more than a co-worker. She was a cohort, a comrade, and between us we could make the ridiculous sublime. We've been friends ever since (mullets i have loved 2014).

With her name first appearing on the December 1984 masthead of *Star Hits* as the magazine's assistant editor (and becoming deputy editor), Colón's presence in *J:MUSA* was equally enthralling as a result of bridging US Japan fans with the ex–band members based in the UK. In a feature titled "A Meeting of the Minds (Part II), or MADE IN USA Crosses the Second Plateau" (1984), Colón recounts her trip to Nomis Studios, described by famed producer and manager Simon Napier-Bell as "a London centre of operations for top musicians," to (unsuccessfully) secure an interview with any of the former members of Japan—David Sylvian, Steve Jansen (Sylvian's brother), Richard Barbieri, or Mick Karn—for the fanzine.[23] Before Sylvian's 1992 marriage to Mexican American Prince protégé Ingrid Chavez, Colón was early proof of a linkage between Latinas/os in the US and post-punk artists from the UK as a Latina who actively crossed cultural and geographic plateaus.[24] In the initial stages of this project, Colón was kind enough to answer questions and chat with me about her time with *Star Hits* on Skype. I made sure to tell her that her work, including her elegant writing, was an early inspiration to me. Allow me to offer an example. In the September 1985 issue of *Star Hits*, Colón published a review in the magazine's Nights Out section of the LA traveling club called the Fetish. It concludes, "When one gets too stiff from posing, there are videos of everyone from Bauhaus to Batman to squint at, and the music of Dead or Alive and T. Rex to slink to. The main activity, however, is The Promenade, though it's so dark here tonight that the nocturnes have to use their sonar to avoid hair clashes. But if you're in Los Angeles on a Friday and you've got the hearse for the night, ask the palest person with the most hair spray where to find The Fetish. Bat's entertainment!" (Colón 1985, 45).[25]

More recently, Los Angeles–based gallerist and curator Danny Fuentes exemplifies such long-standing and enduring connections. In his 2018 *Los Angeles Times* article "For Outsiders and Outliers, Danny Fuentes' Gallery Is a Place to Call Home," journalist Andy Hermann spotlights the downtown LA gallery Lethal Amounts and its owner: "Fuentes was raised in pre-gentrification Glassell Park, a working-class Latino neighborhood under the threat of gang violence. At a young age, he discovered punk rock through an older sister. 'She was like, "OK, I'm gonna take you by the hand. Because you could either wind up a cholo and dead, or I could guide you a little bit."'" Noting how Fuentes, as a young gay man, was initially "drawn to . . . outliers like [Southern California–based band] Christian Death," Hermann remarks that "the owner of Lethal Amounts is challenging the conventional narrative of punk rock, which has tended to erase the influence gay culture had on its development." While the article almost exclusively focuses on "punk" (perhaps using it as a wide enough umbrella to encompass post-punk, not unlike calling a tangerine "citrus"), Fuentes's more recent efforts—such as exhibiting art by the late Throbbing Gristle and Psychic TV frontperson and icon Genesis Breyer P-Orridge and hosting Soft Cell singer Marc Almond (the focus of chapter 4) under the auspices of a touring party dubbed Sex Cells, both in 2019—signal a deep bond to central queer figures of British post-punk.[26]

Hermann additionally gestures to the historical gap between Fuentes and those very things he has come to appreciate and spotlight in Lethal Amounts. He writes, "Though he's far too young to remember it firsthand, Fuentes' favorite period in art and music is an even earlier era in New York's demimonde: the 1970s, when punk-rock was born at CBGB and Andy Warhol's Factory was in full swing" (2018). This gap, however, does not diminish the intimate connection cultivated by Fuentes in his work with P-Orridge and Almond, for example, nor does it minimize his ability to touch and be touched the music or art of an earlier era. Indeed, the intimacy here speaks to what queer theorist Carolyn Dinshaw identifies as a "queer historical impulse" to make "connections across time between, on the one hand, lives, texts, and other cultural phenomena left out of sexual categories back then and, on the other, those left out of current sexual categories now" (1999, 1). As her queer historical impulse is primarily concerned with cross-temporal sexual cultures, Dinshaw's formulation is correspondingly crucial for considering additional conjoint alignments established across time and space. Therefore the *post* in *post-punk,* typically granted a limited time frame and a sound purportedly more approximate to punk than pop, might be deeded a more capacious interval to account for the lasting effects of that music inspired by and following on the heels of punk, persisting in memory as much as it manifests in the present as, to extend the judicious insights of José Esteban Muñoz (2013), a post-punk "commons" aspirant for a queer futurity.

AUDIBLE ANTECEDENTS AND PUNK AFTERLIVES

What, then, counts as post-punk? In her book *What Is Post-Punk: Genre and Identity in Avant-Garde Popular Music, 1977–82,* musicologist Mimi Haddon (2020) pushes against previously narrow notions of post-punk to account for the genre's myriad influences feeding into its dynamic history. Haddon rightly argues that "the current discourse includes the following threads: post-punk is coherent as a movement or genre but is nevertheless stylistically diverse and hybrid. The music is oriented toward the radical, the new, and the experimental. It is not as mainstream as punk. The movement began in about 1978 and came to an end in 1985. And the genre displayed more 'musicianship' than punk, and assumed a kind of 'mature theatricality'" (2020, 4). Skillfully showing how such threads inevitably result in entanglement, she also reveals the impossibility of clearly differentiating categories like post-punk, punk, and new wave, which inexorably bleed into one another. And while Haddon's book is particularly useful and, in many ways, complementary to my project (especially around race and gender politics), I am less interested in genre and more invested in tracking post-punk's historical reverberations beyond the time period her book brackets (1977–82). As she importantly advocates "that the 'post' in post-punk might be an indicator of stylistic hybridity that emblematizes the symbolic capital that other genres of popular music, including punk, are seen to lack" (2020, 20), I extend Haddon's argument to suggest that the *post* heralds punk's afterlives that form a genealogy embracing the "stylistic hybridity" astutely captured in her study. As with Haddon's book, *A Kiss across the Ocean* refuses the common move to maintain a historiography of punk and post-punk that adheres to a masculinist taxonomy and upholds arbitrary brands of aesthetic purity that snub maligned categories such as the mainstream, the popular, and the spurious.[27]

But does Culture Club—with whom I began this book—qualify as post-punk (not to mention other music artists, e.g., Pet Shop Boys, whose connection to punk might appear something of a stretch)? I argue they do, especially in spite of what the title of music critic Dave Rimmer's book—*Like Punk Never Happened: Culture Club and the New Pop*—suggests.[28] In her classic work *Feminism and Youth Culture: From* Jackie *to* Just Seventeen, cultural studies scholar Angela McRobbie identifies "Boy George as [a] key figure in [the] post punk-to-pop crossover" (1991, 168). Yet Boy George and Culture Club (particularly drummer Jon Moss, who was briefly a member of the influential punk bands the Clash and the Damned) were both a part of the original British punk movement (with Boy George regularly citing Siouxsie Sioux, whom I discuss in chapter 1, as a contemporary and an exemplary figure) and formative in conceiving the New Romantic/Blitz Kids scene that arguably took the torch of its predecessors for establishing an alternative milieu for marginalized-cum-empowered youth.[29] This project is therefore attentive to how punk lives on in and metamorphoses into future movements and scenes; it simultaneously recognizes punk's passing alongside its enduring spirit. As Jayna Brown, Patrick Deer, and Tavia Nyong'o maintain, "if punk has an afterlife, it is because we are still sorting through the shards of history that cling to its edifice—and its ruins" (2013, 1).

What McRobbie writes about Culture Club and other groups that "made it big" in the early 1980s—particularly in light of their appearance in magazines like *Star Hits* and *Smash Hits*—resonates for me as in thinking about my musical interests as a queer Chicano adolescent. Drawing on the writings of Paul Morley in the *New Musical Express,* McRobbie asserts that the era served as a moment when artists producing "pure pop" had the potential to be "subversively popular instead of being critical or radical from miles out on the fringes of the independent scene" (1991, 167). She explains:

> There was a moment, at the tail end of punk, when these musical energies were re-directed back towards that sector of the music industry which was most despised by serious musicians. This was a market which consisted of a female rather than male audience. The new attitude on the part of those bands and musicians whose interests were turning profits to be made from the pocket money of 13-year-olds, as a result of soft soulful pop tunes and heart-throb good looks ("Wham" were the best example) with a new commitment to the pop mainstream. There was a kind of camp splendour about having thousands of girls screaming and crying and setting up fan clubs up and down the country. (167–68)

McRobbie further name-checks Pet Shop Boys, whose "sweet sad strains . . . could be seen as taking this trend as far as it could possibly go" since they "represent the high quality end of the pure pop spectrum" (168); fittingly, Pet Shop Boys, whose singer and songwriter Neil Tennant wrote and worked as an editor for *Smash Hits* before becoming a music star, are the focus of this book's final chapter.

In his foreword to *The Best of Smash Hits: The 80s,* Tennant recounts, "I was lucky enough to work for *Smash Hits* in a golden age for British pop, between the end of punk and Live Aid [1985]. This was the period when young, intelligent pop stars had learnt the lessons and ideas of punk and decided to link them to the glamour of pop stardom and nightlife. A stylish, thoughtful, hedonistic pop era flourished, and *Smash Hits* was its house magazine" (2006, 3). Despite the disdain for the colorful and glossy *Smash Hits* by the supposedly more sophisticated music publications in circulation at the time, *Smash Hits* had a form and function that the others could only wish to claim. Tennant explains, "To realize what made *Smash Hits* special, you have to be aware of the competition: NME, *Melody Maker* and *Sounds*; weekly newspapers whose styles ranged from the faux intellectual to leaden music criticism. In those days we used to call them 'rockist,' an ultimate term of abuse. Actually, from our Carnaby Street offices we could look right into those of the NME across the road and mock their failing circulation" (3).[30]

As noted earlier, I learned a great deal about politics—British and American—from the pages of *Smash Hits* and its US sister publication, *Star Hits*. Under that banner of politics were the antiracist struggles (Rock against Racism), the advocacy of workers' rights (Red Wedge), opposition to homophobic policies (anti–Clause 28 efforts), Caribbean and South Asian migration to Britain, the case for nuclear disarmament, and emergent discourses of gender nonconformity and nonnormative sexuality that incontestably fed into what would soon materialize as queer theory.[31] Consider by title alone Eve Kosofsky Sedgwick's (1996) essay, "Gosh, Boy George, You Must Be Awfully Secure in Your Masculinity!" While punk is often heralded as clearing space for resistance to the powers that be, the gender alternatives alone offered by post-punk British popular music were for me unparalleled, generating a reverberating effect even when, as political pop music critic Robin Denselow puts it, "the music's over" (1989, xviii). And although the 1980s categorically fomented a chilling moment of notorious conservatism, it was also a time of queer-subversive possibility. This was true for youths in both the US and the UK. In the context of the former, British music also represented an alternative to the American mainstream music scene that regularly upheld a straight white macho posturing and an antiqueer nativism, validated by mostly all-male hard rock ("cock rock") bands as well as alternative punk and post-punk artists.[32]

NOW THAT'S WHAT I CALL INTIMACY

A Kiss across the Ocean is organized into seven chapters and a conclusion that oscillate between the past and the present and from the UK to the US, simultaneously drawing on memory and relying on textual evidence held onto since the mid-1980s and recently obtained from personal, official, and unofficial archives.[33] Some of the magazines, books, and newspapers I reference in the following pages have been a part of my library for decades, weathering many moves—from Santa Ana to Berkeley and Santa Cruz, back south to Los Angeles, then on to Champaign-Urbana and Chicago, and ultimately returning to Southern California in Riverside. More recently obtained materials from libraries, used bookstores, the internet, antique and charity shops, and international sellers on eBay help fill in narrative gaps by supplementing what was initially understood or previously assumed.[34]

I regard the chapters in this book as similar to an assortment of tracks on a various artists compilation LP like the first one that made its way into my record collection: the original 1983 British volume of the long-standing worldwide marketing phenomenon known as *Now That's What I Call Music* (on which one can find a range of tracks including personal favorites like Heaven 17's "Temptation," Simple Minds' "Waterfront," the Human League's "(Keep Feeling) Fascination," and the Cure's "The Love Cats"). But because each chapter is shaped by some degree of intimacy personally held with the music artists spotlighted therein, the book as a whole might be best understood as my own greatest hits collection or an inspired mixtape (or, more recently, a Spotify playlist) consisting of bands and singers who saved my life or, at minimum, altered it. This compilation is further authorized by my self-recognition as, in the suitable words of Ariana Ruiz, "an authoritative musical cartographer" (2019, 198).

While there is to an extent a chronological linearity behind the placement of the artists introduced chapter by chapter and their appearance on the music scene, my relationship to them is best understood in the frame of the aforementioned queer temporality since my discovery of or admiration for them does not parallel nor approximate a strict historical timeline. A common move in corroborating true fandom for a band regularly comes by way of one's ability to authoritatively evince an early discovery of or encounter with that band before others' initial (or lacking) encounter. "I was there," for example, is a declarative statement sometimes heard to firmly substantiate one's presence at a historic show or some such storied moment in musical history. My status, as will be made clear, is hardly one with momentous clout for shaping, let alone being seen in, the scenes discussed throughout these pages. Indeed, I anticipate the common condescending accusation, "You weren't there!" (to riff on the title of the 2007 documentary on Chicago punk) or, as I've been asked at live performances, "What are you doing here?"[35] Yet while I was indeed at times present, thus allowing me the opportunity to provide a kind of witness testimony, other times I admittedly wasn't.[36] Despite my more than occasional absence (after all, who can be everywhere and anywhere anyway?), sitting on my bedroom floor listening to records, tapes, and CDs on the Magnavox Integrated Stereo System MX 1810 my family chipped in to purchase for my birthday, while also reading assorted issues of periodicals and fanzines, provided that indispensable intimate touch.

In a letter titled "Out of the Closet" and published in the March 1982 issue of *New Sounds New Styles,* a reader named Maze from across the Atlantic—in Enfield, Middlesex, to be exact—writes in to stake a similar claim:

> I am truly amazed by your fabulous magazine. Being black I get criticized for buying your magazine by many of my friends but that doesn't bother me—they even laugh at the way I dress. I am sure there are many other black people who get looked down on because they want to express themselves through their clothes, and many more who are too scared to try it. Well, it's time we all came out of our closets, black and white, and wore the clothes we want to wear, not those our friends or parents like or even just those that are in fashion. (60)

As I began this introduction with my first encounters with the magazines *Star Hits* and *Smash Hits,* throughout the chapters I incorporate information gleaned from a host of music-based publications stemming from the early 1980s to the present. Not only do these print sources help chart a historical narrative of post-punk bands and singers featured here, but they also exist as resonant sources through which readers like Green Gartside develop a stronger familiarity with the artists to whom they become attached.

Indeed, getting to know one's favorite performers—a dynamic also predicated upon the act of touching—is often established through print media as well as chance encounters with songs played on the radio, music videos, posters, T-shirts, and other cultural ephemera. In a discussion of

Richard Hoggart's *The Uses of Literacy* ([1957] 2009), Stuart Hall queries "relations between attitudes in the popular papers and magazines and the working-class readers to whom they were typically addressed" ([2007] 2019, 36).[37] Serving as a medium for transatlantic cultural exchange (particularly before the advent of the internet), popular newspapers and magazines functioned as sites of ideological struggle whereby repudiated "low cultural forms" might directly or implicitly communicate potentially mobilizing knowledges and catalyze relations between ostensibly dissimilar social actors. As previously noted, magazines like *Star Hits* and *Smash Hits* (and even the Neil Tennant–identified "rockist" newspapers) are illustrative given how they simultaneously tender critical information about local and global politics and, for the project at hand, chart a range of Latina/o/x and British associations—manifesting in myriad and often inextricably intertwined ways—that contour post-punk cultures.

Chapter 1, "Red over White," considers a singer and her band that got their start as part of an early roster of acts emerging from the mid-1970s British punk scene: Siouxsie and the Banshees. Although singer Siouxsie Sioux early on cultivated a reputation for her standoffish and irreverent persona (hence her nickname "the Ice Queen"), she and the band would be claimed by Latina/o/x fans in the US for both their wickedly stunning musical oeuvre and their razor-sharp, formidable image. Purveyors of a recalcitrantly aggressive punk sound that, true to post-punk musical sensibility, soon blossomed into an elaborate soundscape crafted by haunting synthesizers, intricate string arrangements, and psychedelic-tinged melodies, Siouxsie and the Banshees were also attuned to Latina/o artists—Kid Congo Powers and Vaginal Davis, for example—with whom they cultivated intimate ties. The chapter shows how Siouxsie's touch extends from the stage to the everyday, documented in an array of sources such as literature, television, visual art, and memoir.

Adam Ant, a contemporary of Siouxsie Sioux's, rose to prominence with his band the Ants after their formation in 1977. Chapter 2, "Touching Prince Charming," examines the charge of racism against Ant by the organization Rock against Racism (RAR) in the band's eroticization of Nazi fascism. While Adam and the Ants would make a concerted effort to deny their alignment with racist projects, I nonetheless suggest a critical examination of songs like "Puerto-Rican" and "Juanito the Bandito" to signal the way Latinos, for better or worse, have served as a source of inspiration in Ant's musical repertoire. For as much as the anthem-like "Prince Charming" grants an aural force field for the disempowered ("Ridicule is nothing to be scared of"), the two aforementioned tracks reveal the racial discrepancies underscoring a resonant repertoire known as "Ant Music for Sex People." The chapter therefore ponders the predicament in which a Latino fan is placed when he finds himself questionably reflected in the lyrics of a beloved music artist.

Chapter 3, "Darker Entries," examines a band inspired by the energy of punk but shifting the aesthetic in a direction that additionally incorporated an early glam style (consider, for example, their grippingly frenetic cover of T. Rex's "Telegram Sam") that catalyzed the movement identified as goth. Indeed, Bauhaus, whose first single from 1979 was "Bela Lugosi's Dead," would cultivate a following that took to the band's darker yet highly sexualized image. Not unlike Siouxsie and the Banshees, Bauhaus would deny their categorization as goth but nevertheless inspired a movement of individuals embracing their music and identifying as such. Contesting the taken-for-granted whiteness of goth style and sound (in terms of a seemingly requisite pallid visage as well as an Anglocentric cultural impulse fueling what counts as the genre's musical origins), the chapter points up the band's acknowledgment of its Black and US Latina/o influences and audiences and thus compels one to rethink the title of their last album as something of a declaration: *Go Away White.*

One of the most recognizable British post-punk pop songs in the United States is arguably Soft Cell's 1981 "Tainted Love," a cover of the 1964 Northern Soul classic originally recorded by Gloria Jones.[38] While Soft Cell is often granted the dubious recognition of a "one-hit wonder" (the song ranked number 5 on VH1's *100 Greatest One Hit Wonders of the 1980s*), this debatable if not nativist honor ignores the prodigious outpouring of this creative duo composed of singer Marc Almond and keyboardist Dave Ball. Chapter 4, "The Shining Sinners," examines how Soft Cell's and Almond's solo work is stimulated by a strong familiarity with and lasting attachment to Latina/o/x sexual cultures. From the work of Chicano Scottish writer John Rechy to the deliciously seedy hotspots of pre-Disneyfied New York City, Almond's and Soft Cell's seductively perverse lyrical and sonic reveries are acutely attuned to the vibrancy of queer Latinidad.

Chapter 5, "Zoot Suits and Secondhand Knowledge," is distinct in contrast to the other book chapters, as the band on which it focuses—Blue Rondo a la Turk—did not receive playtime on my teenager turntable or Walkman cassette player. Yet my embrace of the band, as I explain, came by way of my entrance into Chicano/a studies and British cultural studies through an early interest in the zoot suit subcultures to which my grandparents and their peers belonged in 1940s Southern California. Unpacking the secondhand adoption of the zoot suit and Latin music by the short-lived but notable ensemble, I examine not only their chosen aesthetic, which in some ways complemented while standing in sharp contrast to their contemporaries and collaborators in the New Romantic scene, but also their studied and distinctly animated Latin sound that significantly impacted and shifted the aesthetic contours of early 1980s post-punk culture.

Like Soft Cell, Frankie Goes to Hollywood is often considered a one-hit wonder in the United States given the remarkable success of their first single, "Relax" (although their second single, "Two Tribes," nearly cracked the Billboard Top 40 but rarely registers as a hit thanks to the selective amnesia feeding into the mind-numbing 1980s nostalgia machine). And similar to the Leeds duo of Almond and Ball, the Liverpudlian quintuplet embodied an eye-opening and politically stimulating sexuality—often in the form of an infectiously pulsating queer disco beat—that appealed to many a young queer kid like me. Chapter 6, "Mexican Americanos," traces and links the appeal of Frankie's assertively queer stance in the midst of Reagan/Thatcher Cold War conservatism to lead singer Holly Johnson's solo hit "Americanos," an homage to Chicanos and their incessant historical erasure from the grand narrative of American history. Looking across the ocean for inspiration (although with an idea initially incubated in Pittsburgh, Pennsylvania), Johnson's song—a great success in Britain but failing to chart and circulate widely in the US—communicates a profound political investment by a gay man from England to utilize one's unflinching queer boldness to direct attention to a regularly maligned racial/ethnic population on the opposite side of the Atlantic.

With its title influenced by the words on a van parked at a Miami beach and spotted by Neil Tennant and Chris Lowe (who in turn posed for a photo in front of the van for the cover image of their single "Domino Dancing"), chapter 7, "Latin/o American Party," takes as its subject the indelible influence of Latin freestyle on the Pet Shop Boys' variegated musical sensibilities. Focusing in particular on the track "Domino Dancing," the chapter challenges the commonly held belief that the video for this distinctive and memorable first single from 1998's *Introspective* was largely responsible—in its courtship of homoerotic imagery—for short-circuiting the band's heretofore escalating commercial success. This chapter, however, argues that the ability of "Domino Dancing" to absorb a seemingly uncharacteristic sound—one that flies in the face of those who may see freestyle as too poppy for serious consideration and a lesser-than offshoot of hip-hop—served as a touchstone moment for Pet Shop Boys Neil Tennant and Chris Lowe to flesh out their potential for moving in sonically innovative directions, no small thanks to the influence of Latin musical styles and cultural aesthetics.

Spotlighting three Los Angeles–based tribute bands—Strangelove (which pays homage to Depeche Mode), the Curse (a nod to the Cure), and Sweet and Tender Hooligans (a band honoring the Smiths)—and the Anaheim-based DJ/selector collective Ghostown, the book's conclusion registers the emergence of Latino-fronted music acts and activist networks that pay homage to British bands that have, since the 1980s, made a lasting impact on US Latina/o/x communities. Refusing to regard the tribute band and subsequent generations of music fans as engaged in a simplistic performance of mimicry and woefully mired in uncritical nostalgia, I position these artists and activists as partaking in uncompromising acts of resignification while considering the historical and cultural politics of the enduring appeal of British post-punk music. Since mainstream popular culture's frequent attempts to revisit "The 80s" are laced with romanticism and flimsy grabs at reviving the decade's frivolous (not to mention reactionary) elements, the Latina/o/x fans and members of Strangelove, Sweet and Tender Hooligans, the Curse, and Ghostown take seriously the foundational songs from the past that both made us cry and saved our lives. I ultimately show how popular music facilitates understanding of the intimate connections between foundational British bands and successive generations of fans.

Allow me to offer some points of clarification regarding this project—and in many ways to address questions my reader may have pertaining to the book's significance, questions that have been posed to me at bars, before concerts, over collegial dinners, or during after-lecture Q&As by often perplexed strangers or colleagues. First, this book is not an uncritical fetishization of British culture, particularly as some monolithic entity. On the contrary, I hope to reveal the deep connections between working-class, racialized, queer, and historically marginalized individuals and communities from the trajectory of popular music.[39] Indeed, when I began discovering more about the British bands I was drawn to, I realized and appreciated that they, too, were—as Danny Fuentes and the patrons of Lethal Amounts are described by the *Los Angeles Times* (Hermann 2018)—the "outcasts and outliers" of the dominant culture. As should go without saying, reading "British" and "American" strictly on the surface forecloses the ability to ascertain the nuances of and interruptions within national histories and cultures while ignoring the way networks of affiliation always manifest in complex and ostensibly paradoxical ways. Second, I realize that my youthful dislike of most US punk and post-punk bands (Blondie was one of the few exceptions) had to do with the fact that they reminded me of peers with whom I held an antagonistic relationship, those very kids whose "possessive investment in whiteness" and upper-/middle-class entitlement extended to forms of cultural expression they assumed were theirs merely based on surface-level perception of rightful ownership.[40] And third, this project is best understood as embracing cultural hybridity rather than endorsing cultural appropriation. Nestor García Canclini's classic formulation of cultural hybridity—which, to my mind, stands in stark contrast to the recently resuscitated and often sanctimonious indictment of cultural appropriation—is useful for understanding the bilateral transatlantic dispatches mapped in this book. To be sure, the charge of cultural appropriation too easily shuts down deliberation on the ways disparately situated people and histories indelibly move and touch one other. I maintain throughout *A Kiss across the Ocean* that the charge of appropriation bars recognition of mutual exchange and give-and-take dynamics, elements that are indeed at work in the encounters between British post-punk artists and US Latinas/os. Overall, the book follows the lead of Frances Aparicio and Cándida Jáquez (2003), who draw on the idea of cultural hybridity to explore the impact of transnational "Latino/a American musical migrations," and extends the analytic parameters of their important book *Musical Migrations* to consider the multidirectional, transatlantic intimacies in popular music cultures.

The multidirectional "kiss across the ocean" spotlighted in the forthcoming pages represents more than an act of, once again riffing on Culture Club vis-à-vis the title of their 1982 debut album, "kissing to be clever," but rather traces a number of sensuous connections involving listeners, lovers, spectators, collaborators, friends, fans, and exemplars. Let's begin, then, with one of the many bands with which I became familiar from the pages of *Star Hits* and *Smash Hits*: Siouxsie and the Banshees. The inimitable influence of the band's singer—namely the Banshees' iconic frontwoman Siouxsie Sioux—extends to almost every other artist discussed in this book, not to mention generations of Latina/o/x musicians and fans. Notwithstanding the nocturnal setting in which the band's edgy music and overall shadowy aura are often comfortably cast, the first chapter ardently aims to throw light on Sioux's formidable transatlantic touch.

One

RED OVER WHITE

Many friends whose teenage years have been marked by some form of trauma—induced, for instance, by bullying, alienation, divorce, or poverty—have told me there's a particular album that helped them weather their distress. Mine is the Cure's *The Head on the Door* (1985), which helped me cope with a combination of the abovementioned hardships. Initially led to the band by three songs in particular ("The Walk," "The Love Cats," and "Let's Go to Bed," all featured on the 1983 singles compilation *Japanese Whispers* that I received as a Christmas gift), *The Head on the Door,* purchased with lunch money banked for buying music in lieu of cafeteria food, tapped into and assisted in making sense of the despair that preoccupied me at the time. It was also the Cure, particularly the band's lead singer Robert Smith, whom I credit for leading me to Siouxsie and the Banshees. Indeed, I was thrilled to spot Smith in the video for the Banshees' cover version of the Beatles' "Dear Prudence" I fortuitously caught one day after school on *Video One,* the music video program airing weekdays at 5 p.m. on KHJ-TV channel 9 and hosted by LA-based British DJ Richard Blade.[1] Directed by Tim Pope and shot in Venice, Italy, the video showcased a band whose name I had stumbled upon in magazines and eventually read on T-shirts and stickers plastered on my peers' notebooks (Regie

Into the light / Our hearts entwine

Siouxsie and the Banshees, "Into the Light"

in geometry, Javier in biology) but which I had not until then considered investigating.[2]

In a preinternet era, investigating music often entailed blindly purchasing a record or cassette based on the band's name alone with the hope that the music, heretofore unheard on the radio or some other media platform, might personally reverberate after hitting the turntable or the tape deck.[3] Alternatively, one's entryway into a band's musical oeuvre was made possible by a friend generously dubbing on cassette the records they or their siblings owned or borrowed. In some instances, a second-generation dubbed tape sufficed for securing one's fandom of an artist whose work wasn't easily obtainable due to difficulty in procuring based on lack of money or record store availability (Music Plus around the corner couldn't compete with the selection at Tower Records in faraway El Toro).

While my obsession with the Cure began to wane after *The Head on the Door* (to be quite honest, 1987's *Kiss Me, Kiss Me, Kiss Me*, with its much too jaunty first single "Why Can't I Be You?," left me cold), it did, however, get transferred onto Siouxsie and the Banshees for my deep appreciation of *Hyaena* (the American version of the LP on which "Dear Prudence" appears) and their back catalog into which I subsequently dived. Moreover, I was drawn to Siouxsie Sioux herself, in no small part due to her unapologetic display of unshaved armpits and icy disaffection in the "Dear Prudence" video, a visual analogy of sorts to the directive, "Fuck off!"[4] Furthermore, the range and exuberance of her singing voice—enlivening but sarcastic on "Slow Dive," distressed and breathless on "Obsession," or frenzied yet bold on "Monitor"—resonated as a force that was as aggressive as it was empowering. Siouxsie, in short, appeared to me at the right place and at the right time. As if recounting my own personal history, Benjamin Harper, in his essay "Black Eyeliner and Dark Dreams," writes, "As a chubby, alienated gay teen, I was searching for someone—anyone—who could tell me being different was okay. When I saw Siouxsie in her signature thick eyeliner and hair teased as if she had just stuck her finger in an electrical outlet, something clicked. This woman was a weirdo—and completely unrepentant about it. I knew she was the one for me" (2009, 230).[5] In a similar vein, feminist journalist and music historian Lucy O'Brien corroborates: "To me then, an idealistic sixth form innocent, timorous yet aching to enter the wild, strange, androgynous world she and her coterie seemed to signify, Siouxsie was the One Who Knew, a woman who had surely been to the edge, nay, was living on it, study of which would somehow give us access. Although she was a lone woman among men, Siouxsie, to me, symbolized a kind of sisterhood" (1994, 88). And while drawn to the likes of the Jam and the Clash, Chicana punk icon Teresa Covarrubias, lead singer of the East LA band the Brat, notes that "immediately the most striking . . . were the women: Poly Styrene, Siouxsie Sioux, The Slits—these really wild women. To me that was so encouraging. . . . To see this whole wave of new music coming out with all these women was just amazing. That was what first got me to thinking, *Hey, I can do that too*" (2016, 112).[6] It is precisely this rousing, outsider connection to Siouxsie, a bond shared by many women, queers, Latinas/os, and Latinx queers ("We are entranced / Spellbound!"), that elucidates the post-punk transatlantic touch guiding this book.

Recruited by the Sex Pistols' manager Malcolm McLaren, Siouxsie and the Banshees first took to the stage at the historic two-day 100 Club Punk Special on September 20, 1976. Organized by concert promoter Ron Watts, the festival's lineup featured a number of punk luminaries—including the Clash, Subway Sect, Buzzcocks, the Vibrators, the Damned, and the Sex Pistols (the event's headliners)—most of whom were then unsigned to a record label.[7] While none of the bands had rehearsed before their performances, the fact that they were the only act fronted by a woman distinguished the Banshees from the others. Wanting to "come across as all powerful" and "painful for people," Siouxsie—along with Marco Pirroni on guitar, Steven Severin on bass, and Sid Vicious on drums—improvised a close to twenty-five-minute set that consisted of a one-song mashup (or rather a "song which wasn't even a song," as Pirroni insists) of "The Lord's Prayer," which included lyrical sampling of and chords from "Twist and Shout," "Deutschland über Alles," "Knockin' on Heaven's Door," "(I Can't Get No) Satisfaction," "Tomorrow Belongs to Me," and "Smoke on the Water."[8] Although well-known in the burgeoning London punk scene as a member of the Bromley Contingent, the name given by journalist Caroline Coon to the trendsetting group of Pistols fans from the suburb of Bromley, Sioux had not previously performed live until the historic 100 Club gig.[9] Indeed, in his classic study *Subculture: The Meaning of Style*, Dick Hebdige writes that punk artists "succeed[ed] in subverting the conventions of concert and nightclub entertainment" given how "'ordinary fans' (Siouxsie and the Banshees, Sid Vicious of the Sex Pistols, Mark P of [the zine] *Sniffin Glue*, Jordan of [Adam and] the Ants) . . . made the symbolic crossing from the dance floor to the stage" (1979, 110–11).

Sioux, whose given name is Susan Janet Ballion, is the daughter of an English/Scottish mother who worked as a bilingual English/French secretary and a French-speaking Belgian bacteriologist father who milked snakes. Growing up middle-class, Sioux was clearly aware early on that neither she nor her family blended into their neighborhood. She explains, "I grew up in a suburban, residential district with seemingly perfect lives and neat lawns, though our house stuck out like a sore thumb. Everything was overgrown and, as a young girl, I hated the fact that, although it wasn't deliberate, we seemed to draw attention to ourselves, that as a family we were opposed to that correct, middle-class way of being seen to behave" (Paytress 2003, 16). While she later "felt proud of the difference," Sioux maintains that "when you're young you're desperate to conform." Indeed, "When my name was called out in class, I wished I was a Jones or a Smith. No one could pronounce Ballion, and often I wouldn't own up that it was my name" (17). Bringing to mind Mexican American students in Southern California schools who were made to feel embarrassed by their ethnic names and their inability to assimilate into middle-class white America (an enduring historical legacy that encompasses my teen years in the 1980s when friends and classmates were expected to modify their names in the service of monolingual teachers, e.g., Javier to Harvey, Gerardo to Jerry, María to Mary, or José to Joe), this shame would often serve as a catalyst for self-empowerment to in turn establish a communal sense of solidarity with others maligned for the difference they represented.[10]

A victim of sexual assault at age nine and losing her father at fourteen from alcoholism, Sioux's traumatic childhood and adolescence were made more bearable, as she notes in Mark Paytress's biography *Siouxsie and the Banshees,* with the help of music and movies. And it was her cinematic exposure to Native Americans that led, as she has declared on more than one occasion, to her name change from Susan to Siouxsie. More than a simple respelling of her name, Siouxsie's identification with the "Indians" over the cowboys in Western films serves as a significant motivating force in the creation of her bold and unabashedly defiant persona.[11] As she notes, "I just loved Indians! I'd always hated the cowboys, even though we were told that the Indians were the baddies. They were too easily the scapegoat, and were always being attacked, and yet they looked so much better, so much sexier" (Paytress 2003, 18). Refusing the effortless inclination to do so, Sioux's alignment with Indians—a championing of "red over white"—should not be flatly read as an appropriation of indigeneity as much as a declaration of solidarity with the underdog, here the vilified Indians who must, in the conventional order of things, succumb to historical and silver-screened defeat by the white colonizer cowboys.[12] Furthermore, in the context of 1960s and 1970s Britain, the temporal moment framing the young Susan Ballion's experience with misogyny and social estrangement, rebellion against the norm—not unlike my own gravitation toward Siouxsie—took shape through identifying with popular culture exemplars standing in defiance to the norm.[13]

As with the other artists I discuss throughout this book, Siouxsie is not cast here as a flawless exemplar when ascertaining her significance for US Latinas and Latinos, particularly from some requisite point of view governed by essentialist political virtuousness. By situating the significance of popular music and its attendant icons for disenfranchised youths (especially for those refusing to conform to sanctimonious ideologies or sacrosanct symbolic gestures), the value and impact of cultural forms on identity formations (whose origins are never pure to begin with) becomes crystal clear. Conjoining the omnipresent sway of Siouxsie and the Banshees' music on Latinas and Latinos as reflected in memoir and fiction with an assortment of face-to-face encounters with Siouxsie facilitates a necessary departure from the simple tallying of distant relations to instead underscore how deep moments of intimacy—mediated by a shared sense of outsiderness—bind together Sioux, her fellow artists, and a legion of admirers.

A FRIEND NAMED SIOUX

In their introduction to the anthology *Goth: Undead Subculture,* Lauren M. E. Goodlad and Michael Bibby identify Sioux as one of goth's founding figures. They write that Sioux, "who began her career as a gothic doyenne in the Sex Pistols' scene, helped to popularize a look characterized by deathly pallor, dark makeup, Weimar-era decadence, and Nazi chic" (2007, 1). While one might take issue with their conflation of Sioux's styles that span a significant period of time (particularly when her adoption of "Nazi chic" was an early, brief, and much regretted move that assented to the miscalculated punk attempt at subversiveness by wielding the swastika on an armband or T-shirt), Goodlad and Bibby are right to note her significant role in popularizing what we now understand as goth.[14] However, on numerous occasions, Sioux and Banshees bassist Steven Severin have commented on their association with goth, often times referring to it as "goff" to signal a clichéd performance that has flattened rather than highlighted the nuances underscoring the band's music. As Sioux asserts, "Gothic in its purest sense is actually a very powerful, twisted genre, but the way it was being used by journalists—'goff' with a double 'f'—always seemed to me to be about tacky harum scarum horror and I find that anything but scary. That wasn't what we were about at all. There was something hippie about it too. *Juju* [the Banshees' fourth and undeniably most critically acclaimed album] did have a horror theme to it, but it was *psychological horror*, nothing to do with ghosts and ghouls" (Paytress 2003, 106, emphasis added). Noting that they were "reading a lot of Edgar Allan Poe at the time" (107), Severin admits that while the band indeed described *Juju* as "gothic" upon the album's release, journalists had not picked up on or immediately classified the music and the band as such. Cited as a key influence on subsequent artists, Sioux clarifies that the "strong identity" of *Juju* was diluted: "The goth bands that came in our wake tried to mimic [us]. They were using horror as the basis for stupid rock 'n' roll pantomime" (107).

While the "psychological horror" characteristic of the album and much of the band's music runs more in the vein of *The Twilight Zone* than *Dracula* (or as one-time Banshees guitarist John McGeoch recalls, "More blood dripping on a daisy than scary beast sinking its fangs into its victim" (Paytress 2003, 107), it is also about the everyday alienation experienced by those on the periphery. Indeed, Severin notes that the track "Halloween," which based on title alone may seem to conjure that yearly celebration's attendant ghosts and ghouls, is based on a revelation the bassist had as a six-year-old: "I suddenly realised that I was a separate person. I was no longer simply a part of things. And once you realise that, you've lost a certain innocence."[15] As the lyrics substantiate, "'Trick or treat' / The bitter and the sweet / The carefree days / Are distant now." And while Siouxsie became, as Mark Paytress points out, "a style icon for a generation of ambitious, thrill-seeking young women" who visually emulated their rebellious idol, she and the Banshees sounded a marshaling call for outsiders everywhere to stand and be counted.[16] Recounting how she was bullied daily at school as a child, Garbage lead singer Shirley Manson saw in Siouxsie a rebel with whom she could identify, and the Banshees' music provided the stimulus for converting her disenfranchisement into the feeling that she could rule the world.[17] Moreover, in her foreword to Paytress's biography, Manson reasons that miscategorizing the band as goth dulls the "real edge" of Siouxsie and the Banshees. Their music, she maintains, reveals "so much articulated spite, humour and politics with a small 'p'" while refusing to perambulate "down that simple, gloomy path" (Paytress 2003, 9).

In the band's assessment of *Juju* and its contested gothic impulse, what I find most remarkable is Severin's following confession: "If there was a band that influenced what we did on *Juju* it was The Cramps. Not musically, because they were much more rooted in straightforward rock 'n' roll, but in terms of some of their imagery and the way they came across" (Paytress 2003, 107). The Cramps—described by one journalist as "the scariest band of all time" (Tashjian 2018)—were an American punk band that began to take shape in Akron, Ohio, in 1974 and took flight the following year in New York City. Consisting of the husband-and-wife combo of vocalist Lux Interior and bassist Poison Ivy, along with guitarist Bryan Gregory and numerous drummers in their early years, the Cramps—after making a momentous impact on the formative New York punk scene and playing noted venues like CBGB and Max's Kansas City—relocated to Los Angeles in 1980. According to Ivy, "We didn't move to LA because the scene was in LA, it was because there was no scene any more that there was no reason to stay in New York" (Porter 2015, 163). And at that time, Lux notes, "New York [was] concentrating on British bands or out of town bands" (163). Indeed, 1980 was the year Siouxsie and the Banshees would first tour the United States.

Severin's aforementioned comment that the Banshees drew influence from the Cramps makes sense for how the former crafted their persona after the latter, based not on their music but on their "imagery" and "how they came across." When comparing the image of the Cramps and Siouxsie and the Banshees, what becomes apparent at this particular moment is that they both boasted an undeniable psychedelic aesthetic that flew in the face of an assumed perpetual adornment of all-black gear. One might also point to Ivy's and Siouxsie's teased big hair or both bands' affinity for classic horror and psychological thriller films (which, despite each group's distinct musical styles noted by Severin, is titularly registered by the Banshees' "Spellbound" and the Cramps' "I Was a Teenage Werewolf").[18] And like the Banshees, "The Cramps were a fully formed vision. People think, 'Ooh horror movies, and ooh black.' But no, it's so much more than that. . . . It was a whole lifestyle. A manifesto" ("Kid Congo Powers Oral History" 2005). In view of their association, I want to signal another link between the two bands: the bond shared by Siouxsie and the Cramps' one-time guitarist, Kid Congo Powers.

The same year Siouxsie and the Banshees first toured the States, Kid (né Brian Tristan), a third-generation Mexican American born in La Puente, California, joined the Cramps to replace Bryan Gregory on guitar. Introduced to a variety of musical traditions and genres from his family, Kid recalls hearing Mexican *rancheras* at weekend family parties and bands like the Beatles and the Rolling Stones (and "low-rider music, doo wop, oldies, a lot of soul and funk music, a lot of Santana, Jimi Hendrix, and Black Sabbath") while growing up.[19] A thirteen-year-old "big magazine hound" who pored over the pages of *Creem* and *Rock Scene,* he learned of Lou Reed, Iggy Pop, the New York Dolls, Television, Patti Smith, and others defining the 1970s New York City glam and emergent punk scene, eventually becoming the Ramones fan club president. In 1977, the seventeen-year-old Brian traveled with a school group to Europe. With London as one stop on the trip, he and a friend split off from their peers "and just went to concerts the whole time and sought out punk rock record stores." As he recalls, "I went to this club, the Vortex Club, and I saw the Slits play and different bands. And the Clash were hanging out and Siouxsie and it was all very very very exciting. I was like seventeen—not even eighteen yet. And I got a punk rock haircut and came back to NY at the time and saw the Dead Boys and the Heartbreakers and went to CBGB's and went back to LA quite informed with what was going on" ("Kid Congo Powers Oral History" 2005).[20]

A devoted fan of the Cramps, the twenty-year-old Kid was beyond elated when invited to join the band as their guitarist upon Gregory's departure.[21] Renamed "Kid Congo Powers" by Poison Ivy and Lux Interior from a Santeria candle with the inscription "When you light this candle, Congo powers will be revealed to you," Tristan added "Kid" because he "thought it sounded like a boxer or a pirate" (Porter 2007, 87–88). Appearing on two of the band's signature releases—*Psychedelic Jungle* (1981) and the live mini-album *Smell of Female* (1984)—he remained with the Cramps until September 1983. In an illuminating 2005 oral history with the online publication *New York Night Train,* Kid details his abiding relationship with Siouxsie over the duration of his membership with the Cramps, the Gun Club (the LA-based country/cow punk/post-punk band to which he was recruited by longtime El Monte friend and collaborator Jeffrey Lee Pierce, who in his book *Go Tell the Mountain* identifies Siouxsie and the Banshees as "friends more or less" [(1998) 2017, 45]), and Fur Bible (a collaborative endeavor with Patricia Morrison—bassist and cofounder of the Bags and later a member of the Sisters of Mercy—and drummer Desperate). In Kid's words:

> We had been friends with Siouxsie for a long time. I had actually met Siouxsie and the Banshees, the whole band, when I was in the Cramps and we did some shows together and I befriended them. Billy Holston, who was their assistant, right-hand man—he's the guy who made the Fur Bible cover, the artwork on that—he was a champion of our band. And he suggested it to them. And the Gun Club had played some shows with the Banshees as well and they were big fans of the Gun Club. And so they asked

> us to go on a tour with them and of course we said yes. And that was good because they were really popular at the time. We played at the Royal Albert Hall, where Bob Dylan played, and we played at big theaters everywhere in England. I guess we went over OK. I don't remember. ("Kid Congo Powers Oral History" 2005)

After the Gun Club's split in 1984, Fur Bible lent their support to the Banshees, opening a number of shows for the Tinderbox tour. From their reformation two years later in 1986 until their final days in 1996, Siouxsie remained a fan and friend to both the band and Kid.

In Donna Santisi's landmark book of photographs, *Ask the Angels* (originally published in 1978 and redistributed in 2010), Kid and Siouxsie are captured together during a 1982 visit to Disneyland in Anaheim, California.[22] Santisi provides the backstory:

> One day Siouxsie Sioux wanted to go to Disneyland. It was Sioux, Kid Congo, Marcy Blaustein, Randy Kaye, and me. Sioux was really excited when we got there but once we were on Main Street, two security men came up to her and told her she had to leave. They said that she looked like an attraction and it would confuse the people in the park. Siouxsie was telling the men that she just wanted to see everything and go on the rides. They finally agreed that Sioux could stay if she covered up with Randy's raincoat. We were followed all day by several security people with walkie talkies.[23]

Capturing Sioux's delight in absorbing the sights and attractions of Disneyland, Santisi's photography, as Kid keenly notes, "catches the subject matter at ease, casual, yet exciting" (Santisi [1978] 2010, 32). Since encountering these photos, I have diligently studied their details. Not only do they index the globally recognized theme park I've visited since childhood, given its location in the next city over from where I grew up, but they register an unmistakable intimacy between Siouxsie Sioux and Kid Congo Powers.

In the two photos reproduced in Santisi's book—one in which they flank the walkaround character Br'er Fox culled from the animated sequences of the Disney film *Song of the South* (Foster and Jackson 1946) and the other capturing the two sharing a ride on the Tomorrowland Rocket Jets (fig. 1.1)—Kid and Siouxsie, with their almost identical big, black manes, recall Severin's comparison of the Banshees and the Cramps. In this instance, though, the Cramps are represented by this Chicano from the Los Angeles suburb of El Monte whose discernable brownness contrasts with his

1.1 Donna Santisi, *Siouxsie Sioux and Kid Congo Powers at Disneyland*, 1982. Courtesy of Donna Santisi.

friend's pallid complexion, yet his chosen aesthetic categorically matches that of the former suburban Bromley recluse turned Ice Queen. With Disneyland—a wider-scale Wonderland of sorts—serving as one spatial point of contact, Kid and Siouxsie's post-punk transatlantic intimacy manifests in Santisi's photos that connote unequivocal joy and affection. Apparent in the discernable touch shared by Siouxsie and Kid in the small space of the jet, one may also, following Tina Campt (2017), listen to this image to hear their respective bands' sonic intimacy. And I can't help but imagine my ten-year-old self at nearby Disneyland on the same day as Siouxsie and Kid, admiring these outcast and defiant figures whose names I would learn three years later from music magazines, not unlike those publications the young Brian Tristan, also as a thirteen-year-old queer Chicano Southern California kid, intently read with the information discovered on their pages solidly committed to memory.[24]

Troy Andreas Araiza Kokinis, in his poignant essay "El Monte's Wildweed: Biraciality and the Punk Ethos of the Gun Club's Jeffrey Lee Pierce," writes about the "otherness" uniquely experienced by Kid and Pierce (whose mother was Mexican and who felt at home in Southern California Mexican American culture) in relation to the punk and alternative music scenes. For Kid, Kokinis writes, "the Hollywood punk scene" was "a site of refuge for weirdos and outsiders of all types, including racialized people and gender queers," whereas Pierce, despite "being a white-passing biracial

Chicano," "remained uncomfortable with whiteness throughout his life" (2020, 237, 238). Yet Kid, noting his inability to pass as white, concedes his incessant outcast status: "America is white culture and Anglo culture. No matter how I do not even speak Spanish; I was raised as anyone would be in LA. But you still feel like an outsider" (238). With the combined dimension of his queer sexuality, Kid declares a "built-in otherness and built-in bucking the system," thus prompting his ability to "shine and belong, to others" (238). Given her history as a social outcast and her alliances forged with kindred outsiders like those making up "the Bromley Contingent," Siouxsie's bond with Kid Congo Powers makes complete sense not only with respect to their mutual admiration as artists but also based on the affinitive alignment of a gay Chicano man in a predominantly white subculture and a woman fronting an all-male band in a mostly male music scene. And while the body of writing about the participation of queers and people of color in punk contexts in either the US or the UK has exponentially grown, there's also much to be said about the relationships cultivated between American musicians of color and British post-punk artists in these often-overlapping music scenes.[25]

IF YOU TOUCHED MY HEART

After many failed attempts due to lack of money or a wrong place, wrong time situation, I was lucky to finally see Siouxsie and the Banshees perform live at the Hollywood Palladium on August 11, 2002. The show was part of the Seven Year Itch tour, and it was thrilling to finally see them in concert, especially before the band officially disbanded that same year.[26] To my great surprise, the band's two opening acts were none other than Bauhaus bassist David J (discussed in chapter 3) and artist and singer—to name only two of her many roles—Vaginal Davis.[27] While at first David J made more sense than Davis, deeper reflection gave way to the logical comprehension of this more-than-compatible lineup due to Siouxsie's deep familiarity with key players like Davis and Kid Congo Powers hailing from the Southern California punk and post-punk scenes.[28] Davis, according to José Esteban Muñoz, "first rose to prominence in the Los Angeles punk scene through her infamous zine *Fertile Latoya Jackson* and her performances at punk shows with her Supremes-like backup singers, the Afro Sisters" (1999, 95). The singular-encounter offspring of a twenty-year-old Mexican American father and a forty-five-year-old Black Creole mother, Davis is, as is evident on her blog *Speaking from the Diaphragm*, as brilliantly blunt as she is thoroughly detailed in quotidian documentation. In an entry dated "Monday Mid-August 2002" on her blog, Davis writes: "In more pleasant news [and this is after Davis discusses the increasing gentrification in LA which led to her displacement and relocation to Berlin]: It was wonderful opening up for Siouxsie and the Banshees at the Hollywood Palladium where I was conceived 3000 years ago. Siouxsie looked divine—radiant youth and Budgie was his charming self. They were complete angels to me."[29] The relationship between Davis and Siouxsie (and Budgie) pivots on their mutual admiration and, undoubtedly, their capacity to identify with one another's history of embodied otherness. Furthermore, the Banshees' invitation to Davis to support their performance at the Hollywood Palladium, where Davis was conceived under a table, indeed signals the long-standing acknowledgment of and intimacy between Siouxsie and the Banshees and an array of queer Latina/o/x artists including, of course, Kid Congo Powers.[30]

"Queer bonds," according to Joshua J. Weiner and Damon Young, "are what come into view through the isometric tension between queer world-making and world-shattering, naming a togetherness in failures to properly intersect, the social hailing named by recognition as well as its radical occlusion" (2011, 223–24). The queer bonds between Siouxsie and her US Latina/o/x followers, as with her artistic colleagues, run deep given her ability to touch a legion of "outsider" fans aligned by their failure "to properly intersect" with the norm. Consider, for example, an episode of *Request Video*, a music video program broadcast from Southern California and hosted by KROQ DJ Jim "The Poorman" Trenton featuring Siouxsie and Budgie. Shot in 1990 during Banshees offshoot project the Creatures' tour for their second album, *Boomerang*, the episode not only includes a rather extensive interview with the two but additionally introduces the winner of a contest to meet Siouxsie and Budgie. Receiving over 1,400 letters for the chance to meet the duo (with the selected individual allowed to bring along a friend), *Request Video*'s winning letter was submitted by a young Latino named Martin. Accompanying Martin is his aunt Myra, identified as "a Siouxsie fanatic."

While Martin appears both nervous and indifferent about the encounter (his question to Siouxsie and Budgie about their favorite place to play concerts is somewhat underwhelming), Myra is evidently elated and asks an intriguing question about the influence of world events on Siouxsie's songwriting, particularly with regard to the Creatures' song "Manchild." Siouxsie then provides a detailed account of the inspiration for the song, a

1.2 Screenshot of Siouxsie touching Martin on *Request Video*, 1990.

young Colombian boy named Nelsito marked for death at the age of eighteen but assassinated sooner as a result of being caught in the crossfire of a drug cartel–inspired feud. The exchange between Siouxsie, Budgie, Martin, and Myra, which is tellingly not mediated by the Poorman, is quite touching, especially when one watches other interviews with Siouxsie where she clearly despises the interview situation and obviously wishes she was elsewhere. Indeed, the Poorman appears out of place during this moment of queer bonding roused by a mutual recognition and an awareness of their shared social occlusion. I find it additionally delightful when Siouxsie jumps out of her seat, lunges at Martin, and touches him all over, thus inducing an intimate encounter with the winner who only submitted one letter for a competition that would give way to a personally momentous experience (fig. 1.2).[31]

Beholding this encounter, it's difficult not to focus on Myra's Siouxsie-like aesthetic: wild black hair, black eyeliner and eyeshadow, and black clothes. Yet what I find striking about the onscreen juxtaposition of Siouxsie and Myra is how Myra's style—unquestionably modeled after Siouxsie's from an earlier stage in her career—also recalls the fashion sense of Southern California Latinas who, over the course of many generations, take seriously their stylistic presentation. Although largely known as a painter, the photographic work of artist Patssi Valdez has vividly captured these women who were, as Leticia Alvarado writes, "bearers of an

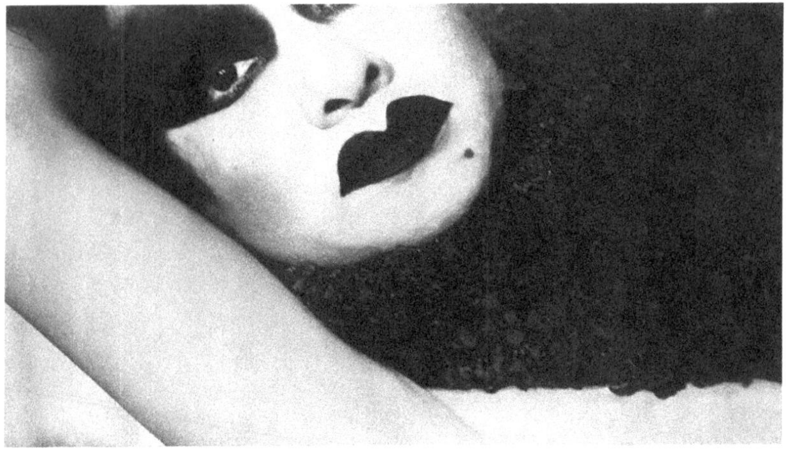

1.3 Patssi Valdez, *Portrait of Sylvia Delgado*, c. early 1980s. Hand-painted photograph with ink and pastel, 20 × 36 in. (50.8 × 91.4 cm). Collection of Joel Wachs. Courtesy of Patssi Valdez. Photo by Ian Byers-Gamber.

edgy beauty and incredible talent who existed as art themselves, though without strategic artistic career goals" (2017, 97). Taking as her subjects those "on display on weekends in [Los Angeles] clubs, including Circus, The Outer Limits, and Rodney Bingenheimer's English Disco," Valdez, Alvarado notes, focused on such "spaces that reflected an open fearlessness marked by creativity and fluidity of gender expression, relations, and regard for societal expectation" (97).[32] One such photo is *Portrait of Sylvia Delgado* (fig. 1.3). Produced in the early 1980s, this "hand-painted photograph" applies "ink and pastel *as* makeup." Alvarado continues, "Captured in black and white, but altered to emphasize Valdez's signature femme presentation, the pallor of the recumbent Delgado is cooled to a macabre stillness by rich purple and blue hues. The compositional framing that cuts her countenance across the corner of her eye, eliminating the upper-left corner of her face, enhances a sense of femme aggression as the other eye, unaffected by the 'cut,' gazes out at the viewer" (101).

This "femme aggression," embodied by the Chicanas in Valdez's photographs, might also be attributed to Siouxsie Sioux. And Chicanas like Myra. Thus, while the nominal subject of *Portrait of Sylvia Delgado* may at first blush appear to be Sioux, the second blush gives way to the possibility that Siouxsie and the Chicanas and Latinas with whom she no doubt interfaced in Southern California in the early 1980s may have borrowed makeup tips from one other (fig. 1.4).

1.4 Alan Perry, *Siouxsie Playing Coventry*, 1981. Courtesy of Alan Perry.

1.5 Lola, a Siouxsie and the Banshees fan. Copyright © Jaime Hernandez. Courtesy of Fantagraphics Books (https://www.fantagraphics.com).

A common misperception about the influence of British post-punk on Latina/o/x fans is that the phenomenon is specific to Southern California (again, the overdetermined example of Morrissey encourages such belief). Yet Siouxsie's influence surfaces in Latinx expressive culture from varied geographic locations. In chapter 2, "Wildwood 1982–1985," of Junot Diaz's (2007a) Pulitzer Prize–winning novel *The Brief Wondrous Life of Oscar Wao*, the reader is introduced to Lola, the sister of the book's eponymous protagonist. As a young Dominican woman whose musical and aesthetic sensibilities clash with those around her, she is ridiculed for defying the cultural codes assumed to be the norm for a Paterson, New Jersey, Latina. According to Lola, she was rendered a "punk chick. That's what I became. A Siouxsie and the Banshees-loving punk chick. The puertorican kids on the block couldn't stop laughing when they saw my hair, they called me Blacula, and the morenos, they didn't know what to say: they just called me devil-bitch. Yo, devil-bitch, yo, yo!" (Diaz 2007a, 54). Excerpted as a short story titled "Wildwood: Teen-age Dominican Runaway" for the June 11, 2007, issue of the *New Yorker*, Díaz's piece is accompanied by a full-color drawing by Chicano artist Jaime Hernandez, one of Los Bros Hernandez and creators of the noted graphic novel *Love and Rockets* (fig. 1.5). In it we see Hernandez's rendition of Lola, here an Afro-Latina with a pink-streaked mohawk sporting a T-shirt emblazoned with "Siouxsie and the Banshees." Complete with a snarl, Lola hands her mother, reclining on a sofa, an ice-cold drink. In Hernandez's image, one recalls the cool punk women—Esperanza Leticia

"Hopey" Glass, Perla Luisa "Maggie" Chascarillo, Theresa Leeanne "Terry" Downe, Daphne "Daffy" Matsumoto, and Isabel "Izzy" Ortíz Reubens—residing in the Southern California town of Hoppers. But here, the defiant style previously captured by Hernandez is tailored for a young Dominican girl who, given her outsider status, no doubt finds solace in Siouxsie and the Banshees's music.

In a midwestern context, Erika L. Sánchez, in her bestselling 2017 novel *I Am Not Your Perfect Mexican Daughter*, writes about a rebellious young woman named Julia coming of age in Chicago and in the shadow of her deceased sister, Olga. Feeling "like a fat sausage in this tight and tacky dress covered in frills, ruffles, and sequins," Julia repeatedly proves inadequate in contrast to Olga, as she sees herself as "the bad daughter who didn't deserve a quinceañera, but my parents wanted to throw a party for my dead sister" (Sánchez 2017, 153). Fittingly, her musical tastes correspond with her misfit standing: "With these majestic violins, you'd think we were in some castle on the English moor instead of a dingy church basement in Chicago. If I'm going to be forced to dance, I want to do it to the Smiths or Siouxsie and the Banshees, but Amá refused, of course. What would the family think? And why do I have to always listen to Satan music?" (153). Like Lola, Julia's tastes not only bedevil those immediate purveyors of the norm but also represent an unapologetic assertion of unconventional sensibilities.

Commenting on Myriam Gurba's identification of her stories as "Chicanx gothic," Carribean Fragoza (2021), author of *Eat the Mouth That Feeds You*, responds to her fellow Los Angeles–based Chicana writer in the following way:

> I don't know exactly what Chicanx gothic is, but I do believe that as a genre, it's something that is being invented and shaped and evolved as more Latinx and Chicanx writers engage publicly in literary conversations. It's very exciting to imagine what we'll come up with that will be relevant and resonant with our lived experiences. When I think of Chicanx gothic, I don't immediately think of a literary genre. I think of a Chicana wearing a lot of eyeliner listening to Siouxsie and the Banshees and The Cure somewhere in Southeast Los Angeles or in the San Gabriel Valley. (Eng 2021)

Further in a West Coast context, one may additionally point to a Central American Latina from South LA like Sandy, appearing in Chicana/Japanese American artist Shizu Saldamando's 2007 drawing *Sandy and Siouxsie* (fig. 1.6). Saldamando, originally from San Francisco's Mission District but relocating to Los Angeles to attend UCLA and CalArts, would discover

1.6 Shizu Saldamando, *Sandy and Siouxsie*, 2007. Courtesy of Shizu Saldamando.

others in Southern California who, as Elina Shatkin writes in her *Los Angeles Times* article "Chicano Portraiture Meets Siouxsie Sioux," "found others who shared her background and her interest in British shoegazer rock" (2007, E12).[33] According to Saldamando's biography on the Self Help Graphics and Art website, her "portraiture employs painting and drawing on canvas, wood, paper and cloth, and functions as homage, as well as documentation, of subcultures within and around the Los Angeles metropolitan area."[34]

Sandy and Siouxsie captures a Latina wearing a Bauhaus T-shirt who is not formulaically goth yet wears a pink streak in her hair like Lola in Jaime Hernández's drawing and undeniably fuses aesthetic sensibilities attributable to both the Southern California Latinas who came before her (recall Sylvia Delgado in Patssi Valdez's abovementioned painted photo) and Siouxsie, who appears in the form of a tattoo on Sandy's arm. Drawn from mid-1990s LA clubs like "Club Bang, Perversion, Satellite—which was Dark Wave . . . and Club London at Vertigo," which "were predominately Latinx" (Miranda 2020), Sandy visually indexes a palpable and enduring transatlantic bond between working-class US Latinx communities and the post-punk artists from whom they draw inspiration. In her astute reading of *Sandy and Siouxsie,* art historian Julia Bryan-Wilson writes that Saldamando's drawing "suggests that the affective communities created through musical taste and other cultural affiliations can shape our identifications and sense of belonging as much as racial or ethnic ties do" (2008, 432). Such affiliations enliven the transatlantic intimacy shared by British post-punk and US Latinidad.

Not the spoiled rich white surfer kids in Southern California who insisted that bands like Siouxsie and the Banshees belonged to them (as I was often told growing up in racially and economically segregated Orange County, California), the bond between the three aforementioned Latinas and Siouxsie materializes as a transatlantic intimacy arising from a distinctly situated yet mutual sense of otherness. To be sure, they are not the fans the band met in California who, according to Budgie, "looked terrible"; such fans were, as the Banshees drummer puts it, "the ones who were trying to be punks [but] were just spoiled rich kids wearing bin liners and safety pins. They'd pretend they were really into us then, when we met them they'd say, 'Hey guys, you wanna come to the beach with us tomorrow? We can score some grass!' Terrible people" (Paytress 2003, 103). Quite the opposite, Martin, Myra, Lola and Sandy sharply contrast with these "terrible people." Drawing influence from Siouxsie and the Banshees as a way to navigate the normative terrain shot through with social hierarchies, their esteem of Siouxsie derives from outsider identification.

Siouxsie's status as a figure with whom such identifications are formed is most recently evident in the music video for LA feminist punk icon Alice Bag's "Modern Day Virgin Sacrifice" (2016). Here we witness a young Latina contending with body image concerns as she fails to see herself reflected in the women who appear on the pages of fashion and celebrity tabloid magazines. Siouxsie makes a brief yet strategic cameo appearance on a poster pinned to the bedroom wall of the video's protagonist. As Bag and a group of women with distinctive backgrounds and body sizes exuberantly cavort to affirm their refusal to play the role of "modern-day virgin sacrifice," the young protagonist ultimately comes to affirm what makes her different from the likes of Kim Kardashian, who appears on the cover of the *Star* magazine she conclusively rips in half. As she gazes from the poster above the protagonist's bed, one can't help but recall Siouxsie's self-declared inability to approximate a standardized body image—"blond, suntanned, and smiling"—common in the *Jackie* magazines she read as a young woman. And it is this recognizable difference, bleeding into the sense of shame those incapable of assimilating into the norm customarily experience, that would serve as a catalyst for her own self-empowerment. As Siouxsie affirms, "Growing up in the suburbs you're always very aware of being different. You want desperately to just not stick out. Thankfully as I grew older I kind of appreciated the difference and, I guess, accentuated it."[35]

FACE TO FACE

Following the path of other Latinos and Latinas touched by Siouxsie, I close this chapter with a personal account that extends beyond my undying love for the Banshees and predates my attendance at the Banshees' Hollywood Palladium show. In 1994, I took time off from graduate school, thinking I was going to drop out after becoming disillusioned with my graduate program—a "psychological horror" of a different kind. I moved back to Santa Ana from Santa Cruz to live with my grandparents, and for about six months I could not pick up a book, let alone read one, after experiencing a self-diagnosed nervous breakdown. Alex, my best friend from high school, called me one evening to invite me out for an evening in Hollywood. Although familiar with Alex's growing interest in the S/M scene, I did not consider that our destination was a fetish club. This club was admittedly more distressing than enticing. Unmoved by the sea of flesh spilling from ass-less leather chaps and club attendees bound and gagged or walked on leashes (Soft Cell's "Sex Dwarf"—"I would like you on a black leash, / I will parade you down the high streets"—seemed to play on an endless loop in my head), I was admittedly perplexed by the streams of blood induced by the onstage acts of crucifixion and self-mutilation. But instead of evoking within me a feeling of fright, what I was witnessing came across as a mere performance—not unlike the way goth might easily slide into "goff"—that could hardly approximate the psychological horror through which, at the moment, I was working through.

With my gaze transfixed on the stage, however, at one point I glanced to my left, toward the person who had briefly brushed up against me. In doing so I found myself staring into the eyes of Siouxsie Sioux, who stood alongside Budgie. Stopped in my tracks, my speechlessness immediately gave way to a noticeable head nod. To my jubilant surprise, Siouxsie nodded back. To this day I wonder what she would have said to me had I introduced myself. But that moment and her acknowledgment captured therein proved more than enough. Siouxsie had not only physically touched me for a split second, but seeing her in the flesh was a reminder of how since my early teenage years the Banshees' music and her singing voice have served, as Licia Fiol-Matta says of Puerto Rican singer Lucecita Benítez's stunning command of volume, to "cement the bond between the listener's ear and the discursive register of intimacy" (2017, 219). The animating force behind propelling one's ability to move into the light during dark times—indubitably in effect that one night at the S/M club—Siouxsie endures in rousing a host of intimate bonds with her Latina/o/x artistic peers and fans, the latter category in which I situate both my younger self and the entranced devotee I remain.

Two

TOUCHING PRINCE CHARMING

During the summer of 1984 I began my first real job. Before this I had frequently earned a few dollars by raking leaves or crushing aluminum cans for my grandfather. But thanks to my father's connections, I soon found myself working at the Orange County Fairgrounds weekend swap meet where I earned twenty dollars for spending a ten-hour day stacking crates in the back of a large box truck at a fruit and vegetable stand. I absolutely hated the job. Just as it was physically exhausting (especially on excruciatingly hot Southern California summer days), it also opened my eyes to the racial division of labor. While there were others my age working at the stand, their responsibilities consisted of weighing, bagging, and selling the produce. The only Mexican kid in the group (the others were white), it was clear to me that I was not to interface with the customers but only indiscernibly perform the behind-the-scenes duties for which I was strictly hired. I tried to quickly finish my responsibilities, however, so I could leave the truck as soon as possible to walk over, with twenty dollars in hand, to the nearby music stand that sold British imports on vinyl and cassette.

> I want the touch of your charms.
> **Adam and the Ants, "Physical (You're So)"**

I distinctly recall that it was at this music stand that I purchased my first Adam Ant seven-inch single, "Vive le Rock" (the incomplete version I tape-recorded from the radio no longer satisfied me, not to mention that I was seduced by the image of Adam and his band on the back of the sleeve). Although I had heard my peers talking about him since the start of middle school, I was only now compelled to listen carefully after being drawn in by the lyrics for "Vive le Rock" and its accompanying music video. In particular, the following lyrics served as a kind of empowerment for an alienated and often-bullied fourteen-year-old kid: "And if the enemy don't see it your way / Be smart, play dead, live to fight a new day." Watching Adam in the song's video was perhaps the bigger draw. With a series of seductive poses, wearing red fringed and flared leather pants with a muscle-exposing black short-sleeved shirt in one sequence and jeans and a black leather jacket in another, Adam's look, on par with the one established in the video for his previous single, "Apollo 9," turned me into an admiring fan (fig. 2.1).[1] A few years later, my first viewing of Kenneth Anger's *Scorpio Rising* (1963)—the film inspiring the track "Scorpio Rising" (and including the line "Leather jackets, big packets") on Adam's 1985 *Vive le Rock* LP—would befittingly register a parallel homoerotic biker aesthetic gleaned from the videos for "Apollo 9" and "Vive le Rock."

The track on the B-side of "Vive le Rock," however, would soon receive more playtime on my turntable. This track, "Greta X," was eye opening for me. Although I can't claim to have instantly known what "T.V." (that is, transvestite) meant when I first heard it, I was well aware that gender codes were being scrambled in this song, and Adam was singing about his embrace of the feminine vis-à-vis a drag persona. As he sang: "In femininity there's pride / We'll marry soon / I'll be the bride . . . What's your gender? / No one knows." Long before philosopher Judith Butler apprised me (after anthropologist Esther Newton did the same for her) that "drag is not an imitation or a copy of some prior or true gender," but rather "drag enacts the very structure of impersonation by which *any gender* is assumed" (1991, 21), Adam Ant taught me that one need not subscribe to only one of two presumed genders. Indeed, by claiming the name Greta in "Greta X," Adam rejected the hard-and-fast expectation of masculinity while adopting the X—a move signaled by the recent use of the term "Latinx"—as a sign of gender-liberating ambiguity. Thus, "What's your gender? / No one knows."[2]

Hardly an unblemished example of gender nonconformity but one that I needed at the time, the song indexes a moment in my adolescent life when the X—that is, the one in "Greta X"—signified a refusal of gender conventions while at the same time upholding the typically denigrated elements of femininity ("In femininity there's pride," Adam insists). This has much to do with music's capacity to build intimacy with its listener—through

2.1 Adam Ant, 1984. Photo by Dave Hogan/Hulton Archive/Getty Images.

its combined rhythmic and lyrical potency, its spatiotemporal entry onto one's subjective mis-en-scène—and thus qualifying one to believe, "This song is about me!" Yet aside from those tracks that suffuse one with self-assuredness, there are others that register, through a different sort of identification, in not-so-empowering ways. Although discovering an artist at a later stage in their career allows a freshly smitten fan to unearth the treasures of their back catalog (including "Prince Charming," one of my all-time favorites with the Ants before Adam went solo, with its queer-empowering and affirming lyrics, particularly for a gay boy constantly reminded he wasn't masculine enough—"Ridicule is nothing to be scared of / Don't you ever, don't you ever / Stop being dandy, showing me you're handsome"), learning of the songs "Puerto-Rican" and "Juanito the Bandito" (another B-side, this one for the 1982 single "Friend or Foe") stopped me dead in my tracks. These often-buried songs in the Adam/Ants discography evince a complex racial history of an all-time favorite artist whose visual and musical appeal has largely proved empowering.

In this chapter, I reflect upon this history to illustrate—in some ways similar to, yet in other ways distinct from, the previous chapter on Siouxsie and the Banshees—the knotty politics of representation and negotiation entailed in embracing expressive cultural forms that are and are not about (and for and not for) the receiver of these forms. On the back of three promotional photos of Adam Ant taken by Brian Aris (presumably from 1983, given that Ant's particular look coincides with the release of his second solo album, *Strip*, from that year), the following quote from Adam appears: "The heart of the record—the heart of the people, is what matters; to make people tingle. I want to touch people with the record, with the videos, with the performance and with the ideas." Yet while such erotic energy may indeed manifest between the performer and "the people," I wish to inquire here into the vagaries of tingle and touch based on my encounter with various discordant representations in the pantheon of figures constituting this British Prince Charming's expressive oeuvre.

A SHADE TOO WHITE

Growing up in a working-class area of North London, Adam Ant (née Stuart Leslie Goddard) endured a difficult childhood, with his parents divorcing when he was seven years old. Living with his mother, who worked as a seamstress and domestic (at one point hired to clean Paul McCartney's

London home), his relationship with his father remained nothing short of estranged.[3] His artistic talent was identified and encouraged early on by his teacher, Joanna Saloman, at Robinsfield School. Such skills proved essential in cultivating his pop star persona as well as the overall visual semblance for which Adam and his Ants would later become known.[4] Close to completing a degree at Hornsey College of Art in graphic design, he dropped out in 1977 to pursue a career in music. That same year, a victorious battle with anorexia saw him rise from the ashes of Stuart Leslie Goddard like the mythical phoenix, giving way to the arrival of "Adam Ant." His new name, aiming to complement his refashioned persona, stemmed from the reasoning that Adam "was the first man" and Ant "because, if there's a nuclear explosion, the ants will survive" ("Adam Ant on Fame" 2011).

Like other post-punk luminaries of his generation, Adam would cultivate his distinct musical sound after drawing inspiration from the Sex Pistols. Remarkably, it would turn out that the Pistols played their first-ever gig at St. Martin's College in November 1975 as the opening act for Bazooka Joe, Adam's first band in which he played guitar. Taking mental note of the support band's sonic innovation, Ant's subsequent group the B-Sides would reform in 1977 as the Ants in the audience at a Siouxsie and the Banshees show in London. Performing their first-ever live show on Cinco de Mayo that year, Adam and the Ants were hardly the beneficiaries of instant success. John Tobler recounts that while their early shows' audience included Poly Styrene of X-Ray Spex and Styrene's manager Falcon Stuart, the latter—with whom Adam had hoped to work—regarded the aspiring star's "leather-clad image a little too uncommercial" (Tobler 1982a, 11). Even in an otherwise affirmative review of a September 1977 performance at the Nashville in London, reporter Jane Suck (the nom de plume of Jane Solanas) writes, "The Ants, with their barbed sound—guitar, bass drums (now, a second guitar or keyboards would *really* be nice)—and jugular attack are not an 'immediate' band, but the best bands never are. Unplug the jukebox, kids, and learn about addiction" (Suck 1977).

Although the Ants had garnered a significant cult following, inspiring Adam's casting in Derek Jarman's infamous 1978 punk film *Jubilee* (which also featured punk celebrity and early Ants manager Jordan (Pamela Rooke/Jordan Mooney), the band was not satisfied with their inability to crack the code for unlocking mainstream success.[5] An admirer of the managerial virtuosity of Malcolm McLaren (as well as a dedicated patron of McLaren and Vivienne Westwood's Sex Shop on the Kings Road), Adam commissioned the former Pistols manager to assist him over the course of a month to shore up his potential for major success.[6] Undoubtedly a curious move for abetting this success, McLaren had the Ants fire Adam to in turn defect to the band the notorious punk Svengali was presently managing: Bow Wow Wow. This move, albeit initially confounding for Adam, facilitated a fortuitous shift on the road toward his commercial ascendency. Though the band's debut album, *Dirk Wears White Socks*, made a substantial impact when released in late 1979 (reaching number one on the UK Independent Albums Chart), the LP that would catapult Adam and the Ants to celebrity status was 1980's *Kings of the Wild Frontier*. With Dave Barbarossa (also known as Dave Barbe), Matthew Ashman, and Leigh Gorman leaving him high and dry after the release of the first LP, Adam was subsequently joined by guitarist Marco Pirroni, a longtime collaborator who was part of the initial lineup of Siouxsie and the Banshees at their first performance at the historic 100 Club punk festival. Yet before McLaren's unintended assistance in their achievement of worldwide notoriety, Adam and the Ants straddled a punk/post-punk line that lacked the flash of their subsequent persona. Such flash, without a doubt, had a great deal to do with the shift in their presentation that entailed the adoption of a distinct tribal sound and look.

Steve Taylor's article "Anti-Hero" in the October 30–November 12, 1980, issue of *Smash Hits* charts the shift from the early Ants persona to their new image, citing Adam's declaration that "leather has had it—as fashion—and that it's purely practical" (40). What is decreed fashionable, Taylor notes, "is more nouveau Red Indian," "the sort of thing he'll be modelling on the upcoming tour" (40). In his *New York Times* feature "The Pop Life; Latest British Invasion: 'The New Tribalism,'" journalist Robert Palmer succinctly encapsulates this fresh and entwined visual and musical aesthetic: "War paint, Mohawk haircuts, three-cornered admirals' hats, pirate garb and rhythms copied from a field recording of African tribal music are some of the unlikely components of Britain's latest contribution to pop music" (1981, 13). The incorporation of a Burundi-style drumbeat was precisely the "catharsis of energy, grace and athleticism" (Jacquemin, Sezirahigha, and Trillo 1999, 610) required for the band's sonic rebranding as "Antmusic." As Adam himself notes in the liner notes to the 2016 remastered rerelease of *Kings of the Wild Frontier*:

> The most important element of the new sound would be the drums. The idea of having two drummers had come about after seeing the great James Brown at Hammersmith Apollo, pounding out the funk, the drums complimenting [*sic*] each other and hitting you in the chest like a cannonball. I

> began to research, beginning with the famous Burundi beat. I spent weeks listening to as many albums of tribal and ethnic music as I could lay my hands on. African, Asian, Maori, Native American, Aboriginal, of course these beats and unique rhythms were accompanied by a wide range of chants and choruses using the voice in a way removed from the western grain. (Ant 2016)[7]

Aspiring to "a 'hybrid' sound matched by an equally individual look" (Ant 2016), Adam simultaneously "concentrated on a new look for the stage, deciding that [he] would go for an Apache/gypsy warrior look, with knee bells to make [his] moves percussive, kilt flying and a white stripe across [his] nose" (Ant 2006, 146). I return to this white stripe shortly.

"Kings of the Wild Frontier," the first single released from Adam and the Ants' eponymously titled second album, captures the two-pronged musical and visual aesthetic the band decided to "go for" and which in turn brought to life Adam's well-known iconographic "Indian" image. While the pirate aesthetic, prominently featured in McLaren's and Westwood's Sex Shop, was likewise embraced by Bow Wow Wow, the patent adoption of American Indian symbolism was uniquely Adam's.[8] In an interview with Mark Ellen in the June 25–July 8, 1981, issue of *Smash Hits*, Adam identifies two films and a television miniseries—*Soldier Blue* (Nelson 1970), *Little Big Man* (Penn 1970), and *Roots* (Chomsky et al. 1977)—that "set the cogs in motion for the Red Indian image, all three having a strong emphasis on an ethnic culture oppressed by White Western Man" (Ellen 1981, 40).

In addition, Ellen notes that these media representations "led him to discover some more explicit and accurate accounts of Indian philosophy by reading *Black Elk Speaks*, *Bury My Heart at Wounded Knee*, and *The Gospel of the Red Man*" (41). Thus, Adam's cultivation of an image that took from indigenous traditions was further charged by the lyrics of "Kings of the Wild Frontier" with the assertion that one's true native self lies concealed within, yet yearns to break free from, a suffocating white body. That is, beneath a lamentable huelessness resides one's true "redsk*n" self to which a kinship of followers—"A New Royal Family, a wild nobility, we are the family"—stirred and roused by "Antmusic," might lay claim.[9] In a declarative manner, Adam sings, "I feel beneath the white / There is a [redsk*n] suffering / From centuries of taming." To fully extricate this concealed "redsk*n," the denunciation of a civilized and trendy dandy-draped exterior (perhaps a reference to Westwood and McLaren Sex Shop garb), as the means to properly channel the inner noble yet wild savage, is required. Adam sings:

And even when you're healthy
And your colour schemes delight
Down below those dandy clothes
You're just a shade too white
Shade too white!
Shade too white!

The lyrics to "Kings of the Wild Frontier"—sounding a rallying cry for a newfound legion of Adam and the Ants followers—make clear the unharnessed potential for aligning with a "New Royal Family" that stands against civility, refinement, and sexual constraint. Indeed, along with lyrically substantiating to its listeners that "Antpeople are the warriors" for whom "Antmusic is the banner," the *Kings of the Wild Frontier* album as a whole fortifies yet another popular catchphrase, taken from the track "Don't Be Square (Be There)," with which Adam—both with the Ants and in his subsequent solo career—is commonly associated: "Ant music for sex people."[10] Recalling Siouxsie's spectatorial identification with televisual and cinematic Indians, Adam's rapport with Native American culture also derives from the contrast between red and white. Aligning himself with the former over the latter (arguably because of his marked difference from his peers as the child of Roma parents and the influential reverberations of the enduring American Indian Movement), this point is lyrically articulated when Adam wishes to discard the white to in turn decolonize the long-suffering red from the forces of genocide and oppression. This alignment, however, derives value in the cultivation of an anticivility politics inextricably bound up with an unbridled sexuality.

Aside from the use of the Indian headdress in a logo prominently featured on Adam and the Ants record sleeves and merchandise (and around which the phrase "Ant music for sex people" is circumscribed), another significant symbol associated with Adam points to his absorption of American Indian cultural traditions: the aforementioned white stripe painted across his face, which is prominently featured on the cover of *Kings of the Wild Frontier*. In Dylan Jones's *Sweet Dreams: The Story of the New Romantics*, Malcolm McLaren takes credit for Adam's white stripe as part of a concerted effort to counteract punk's "black and chrome" tint with some (ethnic) color. According to McLaren:

> There was a sense that in order to reinvent the cultural spirit of punk, you needed to create something not black, but colourful. At the time, it was more to do with gold; a little bit more theatrical, the opposite of all the

> black and chrome that was so strong with punk rock. I happened to notice some pictures of Geronimo, and apparently when the Apaches used to go to war, they would paint this white line across their face, and that looked very powerful, and I liked the marriage of that with the black look of Adam. I thought, "This boy is really going to be a big hit." I could sense it then. When he put that on, he was made, really. My job ended right there. (Jones 2020, 245–46)[11]

Adam's newfound image of, in the words of historian Philip J. Deloria (1999), "playing Indian" soon came to the attention of Native activists and leaders in the United States. As James Maw writes regarding their concern over Adam's incorporation of indigenous traditions for fashioning his stage persona: "One of the interesting reactions to the enormous publicity that the band were receiving was from the North American Indian community. They were very concerned about Adam's stripe. They wrote to the offices of CBS and declared their disapproval saying that it was a sacred Apache warsign and he should abandon it. Instead of dismissing it, Adam decided to go and meet them personally, rather like the American generals would go unarmed on a horse up into the hill country for a pow wow" (1981, 145).

Maw tells us, however, that Adam's meeting with Native American leaders led to a more affirmative understanding of his adoption of indigenous symbolism:

> Adam arranged a meeting with them and he found himself going through the door of a very ordinary office of the North American Community Indian Association in New York. All the people there were wearing smart business suits but had names like George Stonefish and Rudi Martin. After he had talked to them for a while they could see that he wasn't using their culture as a gimmick at all. His love of it stemmed from a genuine interest in their culture and a personal identification with them. He invited them to see a show, ten came in all, and from then on they gave him not only approval but applause. They agreed that he had won his stripes, and in effect accepted him as an Indian brave. (145)[12]

There are many cringeworthy rhetorical moves in Maw's account of Adam's meeting with representatives of the Native community (like the assumption that meeting with stripped-down and not smart-suit-wearing American Indians might be conducted on a reservation as opposed to "a very ordinary office . . . in New York," for example). What I particularly wish to take issue with, however, is how initial concerns that Adam might be "using their culture as a gimmick" dissipate not simply because Adam "had won his stripes" but most likely given the Native leaders' adroit negotiation of his indubitably imperfect "Indian" performance. As Michelle Raheja argues in a cinematic context, for Native spectators, "films with Native American plots and subplots capture the imagination by signifying at least some sort of *presence*, however vexed, in a representational field defined by *absence*" (2010, xi). That is, as with the spectator in Stuart Hall's ([1973] 2019) influential "encoding/decoding" model who is capable of shifting the intended meaning of a text to one customized in accord with their social positioning and interpretive desires, the Native Americans in attendance at Adam's concert were capable of negotiating the vexed figure of Adam-as-Indian.

Nonetheless, using the example of the ten Native Americans enjoying his show does not preclude competing interpretations of Adam and his white stripe. So, how might others—including other Native Americans and those not "a shade too white"—read Adam's Indian image with regard to racial representation? At an Adam Ant concert I attended at the Greek Theater in Los Angeles on September 30, 2017, seeing white fans wearing both T-shirts with the image of Indian headdress and a white stripe painted across their faces stirred within me a sense of discomfort, recalling the fans at my previous university who dressed in Indian mascot gear to cheer on "The Chief" during sporting events' half-time shows.[13] Thus, while racial or ethnic imagery taken up by an artist (often for the imagery's ability to signify a "primitive"-suffused insubordination) invariably evokes a range of discrepant readings, I am unwilling to let go of naggingly conflicted responses by those (myself included) who cannot help but see their reflection in the mirror upheld by the artist trafficking in racialized performances. Indeed, Adam's playing Indian, a move that helps fuel the sexual energy consistently promoted from the early days of the Ants to his later solo efforts, is part and parcel of the gallery of racial and ethnic others underpinning the history of his career. This libidinal current charging these racialized performances (recalling what film scholar Celine Parreñas Shimizu [2007] identifies as "the hypersexuality of race") additionally stimulates Adam's references to Latinos—Puerto Ricans and Mexicans in particular—on two early tracks that on the one hand rely on elements of caricature while on the other hand assist, quite like the figure of the Native American "noble savage," in delivering the sticky-sweet sex music to which Ant people are drawn.

BEACON-LIT RICANS AND RANDY BANDITOS

Prior to Adam's foray onto indigenous territory, charges of pro-fascism and racism underscored the early emergence of the Ants. The summer 1978 issue of *Temporary Hoarding,* the noted zine associated with Britain's Rock against Racism (RAR) movement, published an interview between Lucy Toothpaste (Lucy Whitman) and Adam and then-Ants drummer Dave Barbarossa (who eventually departed for Bow Wow Wow), focusing principally on the band's courtship of Nazi symbolism. Exemplifying this point is the song "Deustcher Girls," the lyrics of which were inspired by Liliana Cavani's *The Night Porter,* the hotly contested 1974 film about an enduring sadomasochistic relationship between a former Nazi prison guard (played by Dirk Bogarde, one of Adam's longtime heroes and after whom Adam and the Ants' first LP is named) and a concentration camp detainee (played by Charlotte Rampling) once under his captive surveillance.[14] In the interview, Toothpaste challenges Ant (and to a lesser degree Barbarossa) about his flirtation with Nazism alongside an attendant obsession with young German girls.

Explaining that the Ants' music functions purely as an escape from everyday life, Adam adamantly declares, "I'm not a fucking nazi, I hate nazis. I mean, my parents are Romany Gypsies you know, and there's this fallacy that only Jews got knocked off in the war, but there was lots of other people got it, Slavs, gypsies and blacks were on the list too. I've probably got more reason to hate them than anybody else" (Toothpaste 1978). With further reinforcement from Barbarossa—registering his fear of the National Front, having grown up a "darkie" with a Jewish mother and a Black father in the "posh conservative area" of Winchmore Hill, Enfield—who couldn't possibly be playing for a band advocating fascism or racism, Toothpaste concedes that Adam and the Ants do not "believe in fascism."[15]

Although "Deustcher Girls" would have remained a distant memory as performed on stage and as a part of the soundtrack for Jarman's *Jubilee,* the song was released as a single by his previous record company, EG, hot on the heels of *Kings of the Wild Frontier*'s stunning success. In the 1982 second issue of *News of Adam: Adam Ant's Own Monthly Fanmag,* Adam expresses his dismay over EG's release of the track with "Plastic Surgery" on the B-side. Offering EG £50,000 to buy back the rights to the song given that it conflicted with his recent makeover, he notes that his frustration has nothing to do with the track's age but rather the fact that "the song is a Nazi send-up, which may have been OK then, but now, with the National Front,

Texteth and everything, it just isn't funny anymore" ("Adam's Antics," 7). We're further told by the uncredited author of the fanzine write-up that "he did manage to persuade the company to change a line he found particularly offensive. 'You're so Nazi' has been wiped out, and 'You're so nasty' substituted" (7–8). In spite of his dismay over EG's opportunistic move, the transition from "Nazi" to "nasty" not only serves as a way to eschew early accusations of the band's promotion of fascism but also fittingly feeds into Adam's persistent and uninhibited sex advocacy.

Following Barbarossa's personal account regarding his everyday life experiences with racism, Adam offers the song "Puerto-Rican" as an example of his antiracist politics.[16] He asserts:

> There's one other number in the set that I must tell you about. I do a song, "Light up a beacon on a Puerto Rican," and I'll tell you why I called it that. The Puerto Ricans in New York are on the bottom, on the floor, and lowest. You've only got to see *West Side Story* to know that number. If you get robbed by a Puerto Rican he nicks all your shoes and everything, they're really desperate people cos they're treated like fucking shit, by the whites. Anyway, in my song, the story is about a white woman who has actually got a *pet* Puerto Rican. (Toothpaste 1978)

Similar to how he was drawn to the figure of the American Indian, Adam's inspiration to write about Puerto Rican subjugation by a white woman, he explains, draws from his exposure to the television miniseries *Roots*, based on Alex Haley's 1976 novel of the same name. He clarifies:

> I saw *Roots*, and what shocked me in that wasn't the slavery, wasn't the conditions, it was when that guy went into the black slave community, and they said to him, "Look, we're animals"—*they'd accepted being fucking animals!* The old black guys were going "Don't do nothing, don't react," because it had been drummed into them. And that really made me sick, that really got to me. The fact that a human being can accept that he's garbage! So my song is about a white woman who has reduced a human being to dog status—because I thought that was a damn sight more powerful in a lyric than saying "Look at the poor Puerto Ricans." I've sung that song to Puerto Ricans from New York, and they loved it, man. Because it was singing about Puerto Ricans, and they just don't get sung about. (Toothpaste 1978)

While the track operates along lines parallel to others in the early pages of the Ants' songbook regarding sadomasochism—along with "Deustcher Girls," consider "Lady," "Whip in My Valise," "Beat My Guest," and "Physical

(You're So)"—"Puerto-Rican," according to Ant, stands as a critique of the racial economy of sadism, exposing how reducing a Black or Puerto Rican man "to dog status" cannot be identified as an act of pain-inducing pleasure given the histories of slavery and other acts of racialized subordination involving bodies of color.

Yet in the *Temporary Hoarding* interview, Adam contradictorily notes that his music does not touch on the heavy side of S/M:

> I do a number about transvestism, which is the result of a thesis I did at college. I did a thesis on all sexual deviancy, it took me two fucking years, and I must have read every book there is, and I became intrigued by it, and I also became shocked by it, and I also realised that after the first week of getting into the medical side of it, the thrill of it—like you described, the decadent appeal—soon loses its flavour, cos it's very fucking heavy. S/M is not funny—there's a funny side to it, and I bring that out—but if I were to deal with the heavy side of it, it would be disgusting, it would be really frightening. (Toothpaste 1978)

Although Adam could explain his authorial intent behind "Puerto-Rican"—not to mention consigning the song to the burial ground of an embarrassingly checkered past (its absence on commercial releases speaks volumes)—scholars like Roger Sabin have pointed to the track as representative of racism in punk, calling it a "cringeworthy example of anti-Hispanicism" (1999, 208). In his essay "'I Won't Let That Dago By': Rethinking Punk and Racism" (the title culling a line from "Puerto-Rican"), Sabin quotes from the song's lyrics, identified as "tongue-in-cheek," and proceeds to note that "the Ants were another band who messed with swastikas, and who never really threw off criticisms of what Adam called 'the Nazi thing'" (1999, 208).

The flirtation with Nazism aside and without Adam's explanation of the song's intended meaning, the lyrics are unquestionably contoured by how one might perceive Latinos as fashioned within the history of popular film and media. The track begins with "Uno, dos, tres, quatro"—recalling the opening line of Sam the Sham and the Pharaohs' 1965 hit "Wooly Bully"—but quickly reverts to an otherwise impressive tongue-rolling "¡Arriba!" and the following lines:

> A chick like you it's oh so rare
> You get off on his greasy hair
> You got a smart apartment, you got central heating

Why go waste it on a Puerto Rican?
I'm gonna light up a beacon on a Puerto Rican
Strike a matchstick on his head
Light up a beacon on a Puerto Rican
You gonna watch me smile if he drops down dead (yeah!)
Me and the boys don't think it's right
That you stayed out with him all night
But don't go making such a fuss
Come and burn him up with us
Well I'm here standing at Tierra del Fuego
While you're out, playing with that dago
With that girl I'm gonna make him cry
I won't let that dago by
¡Arriba!

While the song's opening lines—"I've seen you walking down the street / What's that big dog by your feet?"—substantiate Adam's explanation of the song's meaning, the following lines—"Whatever it is, it could do with a beating / It looks to mean like a Puerto Rican"—beg questions about it. Who longs to beat the Puerto Rican in this song? Is it the purportedly "white woman who has actually got a pet Puerto Rican"? Or is it the narrator who's incensed (based on jealousy, it seems) that this white woman is wasting her central heating on a Puerto Rican?

Another Ants track trafficking in debatable Latino representations is 1977's "Juanito the Bandito."[17] Like "Puerto-Rican," the song was an early live favorite that might have easily gone the divagated route of "Puerto-Rican" given the off-putting lyrics and their embellished delivery. "Juanito the Bandito," however, resurfaced on the B-side to the 1982 single "Friend or Foe" from the eponymously titled LP released the same year. One might argue that being "buried" on the B-side makes a song less momentous; B-sides, though, have always played a significant role in Adam's musical history, as reflected by the release of the 1994 collection *B-Side Babies* (and on which "Juanito the Bandito" fittingly turns up). Classified by writer Pete Scott for issue 12 of the fanzine *Vague* as one song that "has undoubtedly offended a lot of people" (Vague Rants 2018), the vocal performance on "Juanito the Bandito" finds Adam assuming an exaggerated Mexican accent while speaking broken and slurred English that approximates the voice of the infamous Mexican bandit punctuating the history of Hollywood film and manifesting as both the Fritos corn chips mascot the Frito Bandito, and the cartoon character Speedy Gonzales.[18]

> Lock up your shed because Juanito's coming
> Just crossed over into Mexico
> Lock up your pigsties and your daughters
> 'Cause if it moves, you know old Juanito
>
> Young ladies, he likes to ravish
> He knows how to make them wet
> And if he can't, he know he'll dig himself a hole
> Or go looking for your favorite pet, olé
>
> They call him Juanito the Bandito
> Lock up your things, you'll be robbed
> They call him Juanito, the randy bandito
> Oh, how many people have sobbed his name?
>
> He wears a soft sun-soaked sombrero
> A droopy mustache to his chin
> He will hold up, stab or shoot you
> So that he can get it in, okay
>
> They call him Juanito the Bandito
> Lock up your things, you'll be robbed
> They call him Juanito, the randy bandito
> Oh, how many people have sobbed his name?
>
> They call him Juanito the Bandito
> Lock up your things, you'll be robbed
> They call him Juanito, the randy bandito
> Oh, how many people have sobbed his name?
>
> My son, I tell you, don't bother
> I'm going downtown with the guys, okay?

With lines that read like they were lifted from a hackneyed mid-twentieth-century Hollywood film script requiring Mexicans for comic relief, bound-to-fail villainy, or both, the song's pace—largely stirred by an acoustic guitar and ringing bells—parallels the laziness ostensibly embodied by Juanito, the track's protagonist. Furthermore, Juanito, like most familiar banditos, predictably possesses an insatiable thirst to fuck anyone or anything from pigs to "young ladies." Not unlike the eponymous character of Pat Boone's popular 1962 single "Speedy Gonzales," Juanito's infidelity is one of many elements composing a conveniently constructed treacherous subject to contrast with white Western civility.

Listening to "Juanito the Bandito" is hardly an enjoyable experience despite my otherwise deep admiration for Adam's music. Indeed, whenever the track plays on my antiquated iPod (surfacing only via shuffle mode), I skip to the next track, given how I find it insufferable hearing Adam (as I do voice actor Mel Blanc on Boone's track) imitate Speedy Gonzales. Nonetheless, this comparison between Adam and Speedy makes sense when one considers the history of the animated Warner Brothers Mexican mouse who made his first appearance in 1953. According to cultural studies scholar William Anthony Nericcio: "What you may not know is that the famous Speedy Gonzales, our wonderful mascot of clever Mexican banditry, is named after the punch line of a 'dirty joke,' a joke overheard by director Bob McKimson and retold to a largely Anglo crew of animators on the Warner Brothers backlot; my research suggests that the joke, and variations thereof, was making the rounds of Southern California after 1950, the time when Speedy's name was being tossed around the Warner lot" (2007, 139). Mimicking the voice of a cartoon mouse modeled after a joke about a Mexican man suffering from "a chronic case of premature ejaculation" (Nericcio 2007, 139) befits a performer like Adam so deeply invested in a hypersexuality animated by race. In a 1978 interview reprinted in issue 7 of *Vague* titled the "Antzine" issue, Adam maintained the belief "that a writer has the right to draw upon any source material, however offensive or distasteful it might seem, in pursuance of his work" (Vague Rants 2018). Yet commenting on previously embraced "offensive or distasteful songs," Pete Scott writes: "When I look back over the lyrics to songs like 'Juanito the Bandito,' 'Cleopatra,' and 'Day I Met God,' I find it hard to understand what I ever saw in them. They seem cheap and nasty somehow, almost like the kind of thing a naughty schoolboy might write to amuse his friends during a rainy dinner hour" (Vague Rants 2018). I suspect, however, that Adam saw such "cheap and nasty" lyrics, not unlike the humor-inducing repetition of a dirty joke akin to the one that gave rise to Speedy Gonzales, were meant for presumably white audiences with no cultural or historical attachments to the racialized caricatures on which the distasteful jest hinged.

One could easily write off these songs as promoting racist representations of Latinos. Yet for me they reveal the way such representations, lifted from mass-mediated "source material," had impacted Adam—like Siouxsie—as a young outsider rebelling against the class-oppressive moment of 1970s Britain. These representations—though distorted and greatly

2.2 Screenshot of Adam Ant with English comedy duo Tommy Cannon and Bobby Ball as the Three Caballeros on *The Cannon and Ball Show*, May 29, 1982.

limited in dimension—not only reveal how Latinos discernably touched Adam but also served to generate the racially informed sexual personae on which his image was modeled. In this vein, one might also consider how in 1982, Adam appeared on the British comedy show *Cannon and Ball* playing a revolutionary toreador cum Latin lover opposite the show's nominal hosts dressed as Mexican peasants with serapes, sombreros, and exaggerated accents (fig. 2.2). They also (predictably) perform the song "The Three Caballeros" from Disney's 1944 Good Neighbor policy film of the same name.[19] And just as *The Night Porter* influenced Adam's nastiness, a selection of seedy and lustful Puerto Ricans and Mexicans also served to generate Ant music for sex people. For even though he may have declared himself a "Goody Two Shoes," Adam has persistently aspired to cast himself as the object of his fans' desires.[20]

In Richard Belfield's 2006 documentary *Stand and Deliver*, Adam makes clear that Ant music was intended for everyone (even if the motivation behind this declaration was to garner as many consumers of his product as possible) and thus snubs the early punk-elite fanbase who sought to exclusively claim the band as theirs alone. One person who took this declaration to heart was Ruth Marie Torres, a woman who notoriously came to be known as Adam's stalker after his relocation to Southern California for a career in Hollywood. While he was living in East LA, Torres would obsessively show up at Adam's door, convinced that his songs were written for her and that she was meant to be his wife (Ant 2006). By no means do I wish to make light of this episode, which added to Adam's lifelong struggle with suicidal depression and bipolar disorder. I find it striking, however, that an LA Chicana would be so touched by Adam's music that it would provoke a grievous obsession that might have made up the thematic stuff of an early Ants song.[21]

NEVER FORGETTING ALL YOUR STANDARDS

Since relocating to Southern California from the Midwest in 2016, I've seen Adam Ant perform live four different times: in Santa Ana, Anaheim, Los Angeles, and Cincinnati. Although my first Adam concert was on October 19, 1985, at the Pacific Amphitheater in Costa Mesa for the Strip tour, the show on February 17, 2017, at the Observatory in my hometown of Santa Ana, almost thirty-two years after the Costa Mesa show, was particularly significant, as he would be playing *Kings of the Wild Frontier* in its entirety. In anticipation of the show, I repeatedly played the album, paying closer attention to the lyrics and rediscovering favorite tracks (among them "Dog Eat Dog," "Jolly Roger," and "'Antmusic'"). Although "Los Rancheros" reminded me, even if only metonymically, of "Juanito the Bandito" (most likely given my discomfort with the song's peculiar citations of the Kiowa Indian tribe and Clint Eastwood), in my mind I placed the album in its historical context, thinking about how Adam and many of his songs had nonetheless lifted my spirits, ignited my desires, and contributed to an indispensable soundtrack for both teenage subsistence and middle-age everyday life diversion.

During the Observatory show, a seemingly kind white man, most likely in his fifties, out of the blue started chatting me up. The conversation began when he asked me if I could see (he was standing in front of me; it's always been my luck to find myself behind the tallest person at a show). As the lights began to dim, the woman accompanying him winked at me and began smoking an imaginary joint. I was confused at first but then realized she was asking if I had marijuana or was selling any. I shook my head to indicate "no" and looked toward the stage, opting not to further engage her so as to catch Adam making his grand appearance. To my annoyance, the white man then leaned over and asked me, "Do you *really* like Adam Ant?" At first puzzled by his inquiry, I quickly realized that he wasn't asking about the extent of my fandom (*How many times have you seen Adam before?*) but rather how I could possibly be a fan. Indeed, "I wouldn't think *you'd* be a fan," he told me. Although cordial in a way that many of the white fans with whom I'd share space at concerts performed by my favorite music artists weren't, he still reminded me of the racial politics influencing one's understanding of particular music tastes and their audiences. The incident also reminded me of the spoiled white kids in Bret Easton Ellis's novel *Less Than Zero* who were not only fans of the Los Angeles band X and Adam Ant (recall one of the teens in the book demanding that her Hollywood-connected father hire him to star in a film) but as a result felt compelled to claim these music artists as solely theirs.[22] Perhaps in their minds, this music did not belong to the "spics" annoyingly present at the concert; indeed, they were solely to be written and sung about.

With much to recall about Adam's performance in this small venue, the most memorable moment that night (perhaps as a form of reprisal) was when Adam greeted us as "Santa Ana" and not "Orange County," a distinction that was noticeably not lost on those in the audience who very well knew the difference between naming a historically reviled Mexican-majority city and the larger geographical region notoriously known for its white, politically conservative populace. This minor gesture was what I needed to remind me why I was at the show, and how Adam has at key moments come to my desirous rescue to serve as my and others'—such as the Black woman who approached me that evening to confess, "Adam drives me crazy!"—Prince Charming. Yet despite those crucial moments of eros-inflected liberation, there remains the nagging recollection of the provisional status of a reciprocally aligned transatlantic intimacy. Writing about the S/M-loving protagonist of E. L. James's *Fifty Shades of Grey*, the Black feminist writer Roxane Gay notes that the allure of Christian Grey in his role as "Prince Charming" can be hard to resist. But in the fantasy of wanting his touching charms, a fantasy that may indeed yield an attendant tingle, one must never forget, as Gay asserts, "just how much trouble Prince Charming can be" (2014, 194).

Three

DARKER ENTRIES

> With this darkness . . . go away white.
>
> **Bauhaus, "Black Stone Heart"**

One of the most memorable and undoubtedly useful classes I took in high school was typewriting. Providing me with the advantageous ability to move fairly quickly on the keyboard for the lifelong purpose of writing (along with an attendant praise garnered from witnessing friends who missed out on the chance of enrolling in such a course), this ninth-grade elective additionally helped facilitate the introduction to one of my all-time favorite bands: Bauhaus (fig. 3.1). It was one particular person also taking Ms. Smartt's typewriting class—a peer, an upperclassman, and, at least in my eyes, an on-campus celebrity—who brought the post-punk band from England into a room filled with antiquated metal typewriters as well as into my record collection. Sean was rail-thin with short, black, and spiky hair. He wore tight-fitting black jeans tapered at the ankles and traded daily between Midnight Blue Velvet Creepers and black Oxford Doc Martens. His self-assured posture and carefree attitude also contrasted with my painfully insecure and inhibited character. Sean also regularly sported T-shirts announcing his favorite bands. One of his favorite shirts, evidently so given that he wore it at least twice or sometimes three times a week, was white with black lowercase letters spelling out "bauhaus." Beneath the lettering was a thin figure correspondingly in black. Vampire-like, this figure held a woman who was either dead or unconscious and closely matched Sean's adopted look (fig. 3.2). It

3.1 Bauhaus (L–R, Daniel Ash, David J, Peter Murphy, and Kevin Haskins), 1982. Photo by Fin Costello/Redferns. Used by permission.

3.2 "Bela Lugosi's Dead" image taken from *The Cabinet of Dr. Caligari* (Robert Wiene, 1920).

also reminded me of the friends with whom he kept company at lunch and whom I admired from afar. This figure, I would later learn, was one that Bauhaus's lead singer Peter Murphy would identify as his mirror image.[1]

The "deathrockers," as they were known at the time (goth was not a commonly used descriptor then, at least by those outside their social sphere), were a group of teenage kids of varied ethnicities and races.[2] Yet the pale-skinned ones were more capable of crystallizing a seemingly mandated pallor aesthetic.[3] Sean, however, diverged from the rest. While the light-skinned Latinos and Latinas could "whiten up" with a layer of white face powder, Sean was distinctly and, I soon discovered, unapologetically brown. Indeed, he spoke Spanglish, had no qualms with cultivating friendships beyond the deathrocker crowd, and often mentioned his Mexicanness to me and in overheard conversations. And if turning white was even a possibility, I recall how he'd oftentimes roll up the short sleeves of his Bauhaus shirt, a move which I read as the need to avoid the dreaded farmer's tan.

I don't remember how he entered into my orbit to the point where we began talking (Was the introduction facilitated through a mutual friend? Did he finally respond to my incessant and probably obvious staring?). In any case, Sean eventually gave me the name "Smiley," and we would chat from time to time during class, after school, and even once at the South Coast Plaza while I was shopping with my mom. Although my familiarity with Bauhaus increased after reading about them in the pages of the Japan fanzine to which I subscribed (due to Murphy's post-Bauhaus collaboration with former Japan bassist Mick Karn under the name Dali's Car), it was the adornment of the T-shirt—with its stunning image lifted from Robert Wiene's 1920 German silent horror film *The Cabinet of Dr. Caligari*—on Sean's brown Mexican body that prompted my entry into the Bauhaus sound world. Indeed, the affectionate rapport I established with Sean ("Hey, Smiley!") helped facilitate Bauhaus's profound impression upon me. Not unlike the image on the T-shirt, the band and its music potently fused sexy and sleek with sinister defiance. Whether it was the emboldening "Double Dare" ("I dare you to be proud / To dare to shout aloud / For convictions that you feel / Like sound from bells to peal") or the melancholic "All We Ever Wanted Was Everything" ("Flash of youth / Shoot out of darkness"), Bauhaus's music stirred a range of emotions and materialized as an arsenal of auditory weaponry for navigating the rutted working-class and racialized terrain of a Mexican American–majority city forty miles southeast of Los Angeles. And comparable to the sway this band from Northampton, a city seventy miles northwest of London, would have over two Mexican American kids like us, members of Bauhaus—including singer Murphy, bassist David J, guitarist Daniel Ash, and drummer Kevin Haskins—would likewise derive influence from Latinos and Latinas during their stateside visits and eventual Southern California relocation.

Taking its title from Bauhaus's 1980 "Dark Entries," the single following on the heels of their signature debut release "Bela Lugosi's Dead" from the previous year, this chapter examines the role of racial otherness as it relates to this sui generis post-punk group and the gothic subculture to which it's more broadly tethered. While "Bela" would intimately link Bauhaus with the undead (further congealed by the band's contribution to the soundtrack for Tony Scott's 1983 vampire film *The Hunger*), Bauhaus's catalog befittingly lent musical accompaniment to those clad in black clothing, to cite from the band's homage to the eminent actor cast as Dracula in the eponymously titled 1931 film, "bereft in deathly bloom." Intended to contrast with the "dark" in the title, I draw attention to the typical and presumed whiteness underpinning goth along with the subculture's occasional obsession with the racialized, exotic other. In many ways, to prop up goth's whiteness requires a ghosted racial difference. As a means to exorcise this difference, I will show how whiteness in turn manifests as it is at once embraced, exoticized, and dislodged by interlocutors and corroborators of color, especially Latinas/os, in various gothic milieus.

Remaining in tune with the others in this book by tracking the various points of mutual attraction and influence between British music artists and US Latina/o/x communities, a singular feature of this chapter is the ambition to undo conventional understandings of *darkness* and *black* as nodal points for assessing goth aesthetics predisposed to champion whiteness—even if by default—and in turn eclipse an ability to recognize such attractions and influences. In her book *Fashioning Gothic Bodies*, Catherine Spooner writes, "Led by post-punk bands such as Bauhaus, the Birthday Party, Siouxsie and the Banshees, and The Sisters of Mercy, adherents to 'Goth' style combined the nihilism of Punk, the perverse sexuality of fetish wear and the graveyard exoticism of nineteenth-century mourning costume to create a macabre aesthetic" (2004, 162). To fully capture this aesthetic necessitated an embodied chiaroscuro of black and white, methodically manifesting in the form of black clothes and white skin. As Spooner maintains, "Garments were predominantly black, accessorised with 'vamp' makeup and *memento mori* motifs" (162). Yet what happens when race is deeded attention and not, as it were, buried alive? For despite what Spooner and many other commentators have argued about goth musical and visual aesthetics, these presumed obligatory garments were not the only referential signs of blackness shaping this late 1970s-awoken scene.

A PALER SHADE OF WHITE

Offering an astute historical appraisal that sets the stage for their edited collection *Goth: Undead Subculture*, Lauren M. E. Goodlad and Michael Bibby assert:

> Goth subculture emerged in the socioeconomic decline and Thatcherite politics of late 1970s Britain, on the heels of punk's infamous rebellion. Drawing on diverse fringe cultures, from Dada to garage rock, punk had catalyzed a generation of youth with its DIY attitude toward music, fashion preference for safety pins and thrift shops, and contempt for mass-marketed music culture. By the late 1970s punk was itself being exploited for commercial potential. Yet punk had also energized a surge of new styles such as new romantic, industrial, new wave, and hardcore. Amid this dizzying subcultural effulgence, a number of bands and personalities began cultivating what would soon become known as goth. (2007, 1)

Including the bands named above by Spooner, the list might very well include others like the Damned, Joy Division, Alien Sex Fiend, and the Cure. Although Bauhaus would time and again flatly refuse their categorization as goth, the band would become undeniably foundational for the formation of that unmistakable subculture known for its obsession with vampires in particular and horror in general. Fittingly, on the back cover of Bauhaus bassist David J. Haskins's 2014 autobiography, *Who Killed Mister Moonlight: Bauhaus, Black Magick, and Benediction*, the reader is told that "in a breathtaking ride along a flume of ink and sequins" he "plots the delirious trajectory of a band who sparked the gothic movement's second extraordinary emergence from among the cut-throat history and thousand-year churches of Northampton." Moreover, Bauhaus are time and again referred to as, in the words of a 2018 National Public Radio feature, "the godfathers of goth" (Bordal 2018).[4]

Goodlad and Bibby's discussion of goth includes an insightful engagement with music critic Simon Price, who argues that goth "was the first form of rock which couldn't be traced back to rhythm and blues. There is no line connecting Sisters of Mercy to the Mississippi swamps." Suggesting goth's detachment from Black musical influence as indexed by the US South,

Price maintains that "the likes of Bauhaus, Sisters and Sex Gang Children imagined themselves as heirs to both Wagnerian/Teutonic classical lineage and the Arabic mysticist tradition" (cited in Goodlad and Bibby 2007, 24). Further citing Price, who claims that "as 'the first form' of music allegedly to transcend rock's African descent, goth appropriates the symbolic capital of racialized others through romantic strategies of self-invention, avowing and disavowing what it chooses" (24), Goodlad and Bibby correctly argue that "in this as in several other respects goth is complicit with the normative status of whiteness in mainstream culture" (25). Yet this complicity has much to do with the ceaseless shrouding of the racialized bodies and expressive forms upon which it feeds.

If Bauhaus are indeed the godfathers of goth, then the multidimensional facets sustaining their musical style and overall aesthetic hardly render that category as one untouched by an array of nonwhite influences. In an essay by Craig Roseberry for a special edition of the band's second LP, *Mask*, Peter Murphy observes, "There was a lot more to Bauhaus than a bit of lipstick and eye shadow. Our legacy has often been misconstrued by being mucked in with the latter-day gothic thing which we may have sparked off, but we never took part in that movement. It was enough to be ourselves" (Roseberry 2009, 7).[5] And, drawing from Murphy's declaration of individual incentive, Roseberry perceptively argues that "the band appropriated the propulsive fury of punk—infusing it with the liberal musical cross-fertilization of the No Wave movement—to author their own magnetic soundscape" (7–8).[6] Similar to how the "fury of punk" is inseparable from what Don Letts calls "the radical and political side to reggae music" (2021, 50), Bauhaus's "magnetic soundscape" would remain nonexistent without Black influence.

The particular influences underpinning Bauhaus's "Bela Lugosi's Dead"—often considered, according to Nick Groom (2018), "the inaugural Goth single" (or as another writer puts it, a "'Freebird,' or 'Stairway to Heaven' for goths")—make clear that this foundational goth musical masterpiece comes complete with African influences, including dub and reggae.[7] Indeed, linking "Bela Lugosi's Dead" to these genres originating in Jamaica then traveling to England alongside an accompanying Caribbean diaspora assists in contesting the claim of goth's lack of Black roots.[8] Recalling Bauhaus's first recording session at Beck Studios in Wellingborough in 1979, David J describes the band's work with studio owner Derek Tompkins in first laying down "Bela":

> When it came to the recording of "Bela," Derek quickly miked up the drum kit and amps and then simply rolled the tape as we played the track through—one live take, vocals and all, and that take was The One. (It was the first time Peter had ever sung into a studio mic.) Derek then showed Daniel how to use his marvelous analogue delay unit, which was operated by a slider that increased or decreased the effect. Derek had recorded several reggae artists, and he was correct in recognizing that there was a dub aspect to "Bela." He told us that when it came to recording reggae artists, he would just leave them to it, and he decided to do the same with us. (Haskins 2014, 30)

J would recount in many interviews, including one as recent as 2019, that "'Bela' is an interpretation of dub" ("40 Years of Bauhaus' Bela Lugosi's Dead" 2019). In *Bauhaus Undead*, Kevin Haskins corroborates the entwinement of reggae with Bauhaus's history. In this case, it involves legendary reggae DJ, punk filmmaker, and musician Don Letts.[9] He writes, "We were shooting our first video, directed by Mick Calvert and punk dread Don Letts, for our fourth single, a cover of 'Telegram Sam,' originally by T. Rex. I was excited to work with Don, as he was an icon in the early punk rock scene, which had been such a huge influence on me. Don went on to make several music videos and award-winning documentaries as well as forming Big Audio Dynamite with Mick Jones, formerly of The Clash" (Haskins 2018, 97).

While Haskins and J were in the audience at the legendary 1976 punk festival organized by Malcom McLaren at the 100 Club in London (featuring the Sex Pistols and the first-ever live performance by Siouxsie and the Banshees), Haskins's recollection of punk's influence extends beyond the commonly cited (white) stars of the scene to center Letts. As he explains:

> It wasn't the first time that I would have met Don. That was at his very cool clothing store called Acme Attractions on The Kings Road in London. As a sixteen year old kid, I would take the train on a monthly pilgrimage to London to acquire new punk rock threads. At that time I wasn't aware of Don's involvement with the Punk movement, so to me he was just the cool looking Rastafarian guy behind the counter. Coming from a very closeted small town upbringing, it was a big deal to me back then to go down to "The Smoke" on my own. When I would enter a clothing store I used to feel overwhelmed by all the choices and would have no idea what to buy. I would spend ages trying on this and trying on that, but on this trip I eventually settled on a pair of vintage turquoise wrap around shades and multi

> colored flecked zoot suit trousers. Don was probably glad to see the back of me. I relayed this story to Don when we all visited his high-rise flat in London for a pre-production meeting for the video. (Haskins 2018, 97)[10]

Haskins's personal narrative, which also chronicles the historical shift from punk to post-punk, is insightful for its spotlighting not only of a pivotal figure who introduced reggae to many a white punk but also of the zoot suit aesthetic adopted by many fashion-conscious British youths in the early 1980s (a phenomenon I discuss in chapter 5, on Blue Rondo a la Turk). The history of the band shows that its members have never distanced themselves from Black music. On the contrary, Bauhaus has embraced many of its distinctive genres to forge a sound shored up by an unlikely, if not for some implausible, "romantic strategy of self-invention," as Price puts it.

Thus, while self-fashioned goths invested in policing the racial borders of what counts as gothic may uphold a normative whiteness in racial and aesthetic terms, the Northampton band's musical influences acutely contradict any supposition of a possessive investment in it. As further substantiation, one may consider David J's comments on *Mask*'s musical influences and objectives: "We were into this idea of deconstructing disco and funk. It was twisted disco with a surrealist bent! More rhythms, more drums and percussion. The title track was the obvious 'epic' centerpiece" (Roseberry 2009, 10). Then there's the band's ska/reggae track "Harry" (named after Blondie lead singer Debbie Harry), appearing on the B-side of their disco/funk-influenced single "Kick in the Eye." Also, on the B-side of that twelve-inch single (subtitled the "Searching for Satori EP") is the track "Earwax," which, before being given its official name, was referred to by the band as "Reggae Tune."[11] In addition, it's hard to ignore the obvious nod granted in the title of "In Fear of Dub," also on the EP. The dub/reggae influence hardly stops here. On the band's third and fourth albums, *The Sky's Gone Out* (1982) and *Burning from the Inside* (1983), it's hard to miss the recurring nods to the Caribbean sound popular with many British punks-turned-post-punks on tracks like "Exquisite Corpse," "She's in Parties," and "Here's the Dub," the B-side remix of "She's in Parties." And in an interview with LA-based British expatriate DJ Richard Blade, Boy George, a self-professed "big Bauhaus fan," maintains that "She's in Parties," one of his favorite Bauhaus tunes, is "almost a reggae record. Because sometimes Bauhaus were like funk punk" (Blade 2021, 486).[12]

Similar to the tendency to cast Bauhaus as a lily-white goth band was the incessant need—particularly by British journalists—to compare the band's sound and image to David Bowie.[13] While Bauhaus never denied Bowie's indelible influence—evident alone in their cover of "Ziggy Stardust" in large part to spite their critics—one might even argue that the bond between Bauhaus and Bowie exceeds their linkage solely as white artists to instead recognize their status as performers likewise swayed by the stimulus of Black and Latino cultural and musical styles. It therefore makes more sense to view Bauhaus's inspiration drawn from the Thin White Duke's soul stylings on an album like 1975's *Young Americans* and his instrumental reliance on the handiwork of Puerto Rican guitarist Carlos Alomar than solely as sonic "heirs to both Wagnerian/Teutonic classical lineage and the Arabic mysticist tradition." Furthermore, one might also point to the cover of the Temptations' "Ball of Confusion" by Love and Rockets—the band formed by Ash, Haskins, and J from the ashes of both Bauhaus and Tones on Tail—and, most illustrative for the context at hand, Ash's writing credit to Tito Puente on his solo single "Walk This Way" for its striking similarity to Puente's—and Santana's cover of—"Oye Como Va."[14] Thus, when Deborah Pacini Hernandez tracks the deep historical significance of "Oye Como Va" by noting that "it was an immigrant Mexican rocker who, in pioneering the subgenre Latin rock, introduced the U.S.-born Puente's Afro-Cuban dance music to mainstream U.S. rock audiences" (2010, 2), we might also consider how the song additionally facilitates a meeting ground between British post-punk artists and US Latina/o musical expression.

Bauhaus disbanded in 1983, reuniting a number of times thereafter. Releasing an album of new material in 2008 titled *Go Away White* (perhaps signaling the continued embrace of all things dark), the band again called it quits that same year due to irreconcilable differences. Bauhaus once again reunited in 2019, playing three nights in Southern California at the Hollywood Palladium with shows scheduled in Chicago, New York, London, and Mexico City in 2020.[15] Yet soon after they disbanded for the first time in 1983, brothers David J and Kevin Haskins and guitarist Daniel Ash started up the aforementioned Love and Rockets. Fittingly, *Love and Rockets* is the title of a long-running comic book series by three Chicano brothers—Gilbert, Jaime, and Mario Hernandez—from Oxnard, California. Given the subcultural yet still widespread popularity of *Love and Rockets* since its first issue in 1981, it's not difficult to imagine the comic falling into the hands of the former Bauhaus members. Beyond the US, the work of Los Bros. Hernandez also had a significant impact and dedicated following in the UK. As David J puts it bluntly in an interview, "We stole the name, basically. We stole the name from the comic book. I had a bunch of those comics because I was a big fan of that comic."[16]

For J, not only was the name perfect for the group, but it was also seen as a tribute given his love for Hernandez's work. While the band thought they would eventually hear from the Hernandez brothers with a cease-and-desist order for their use of the name, Jaime Hernandez reached out, however, to say that although he had also planned on adopting "Love and Rockets" for a band, Ash, Haskins, and J had the Chicano artists' blessing after being sent a record by J and liking it. On the occasion of their exchange regarding the name, both parties would come to draw explicit influence from one another. Gilbert Hernandez, for example, poked fun at the band by creating the graphic novel *Love and Rockets X*, featuring an LA band named Love and Rockets, including a member responding to the accusation that they had stolen their name "from a world famous new music band" (complete with a member possessing a "dreamy English accent" named Daniel Ash) with the fact that "a couple of Mexican guys turned us on to the name" (Hernandez 1999, 4).

Taking seriously Simon Price's claim that goth often "appropriates the symbolic capital of racialized others" (cited in Goodlad and Bibby 2007, 24), I nevertheless insist that, in line with the argument maintained throughout this book, flippantly denouncing cultural exchanges—even those politically difficult and affectively incensing—as appropriation often preemptively forecloses recognition of the unharnessed vitality of reciprocity. Like J's admitted fandom for Los Bros. Hernandez's comic, a multitude of adoring Latina/o fans—particularly from Southern California—have been following Bauhaus and its consequent reincarnations since they and their music arrived stateside. As one may glean this fact in conversations with fans at concerts, in record stores, and in online forums, this is also evident in the various writings by David J and Kevin Haskins.

PARTY GIRL

Haskins—who would go on to work with Ash and former Bauhaus roadie Glenn Campling under the name Tones on Tail, and subsequently with Ash and J as Love and Rockets—published *Bauhaus Undead* in 2018, an elegantly conceived book meticulously documenting the band's history through photographs and reflective vignettes. Often recognized as Bauhaus's archivist ("There is one in every group. The one who slavishly collects all the scraps and ephemeral bits that make up this wonderful crazy business of ours" (Haskins 2018, 7), as Joy Division and New Order bassist

Peter Hook puts it in the book's foreword), Haskins provides many eye-opening accounts of Bauhaus's history, from meeting their heroes David Bowie and Iggy Pop to their initial visit to the United States.

In one of the book's vignettes, "The City of Angels," Haskins recounts Bauhaus's first trip to Los Angeles, where they played three nights at the Roxy Club on Sunset Boulevard. Upon landing in Southern California, Haskins notes the contrast between himself and his bandmates and this heretofore unfamiliar landscape: "After a smooth landing at LAX I looked out of the window of the plane and saw palm trees. I motioned to the band, 'Look, there's palm trees!' We were all surprised at seeing such exotic vegetation and more so when we felt the warm Californian sun kiss our skinny pale white arms" (2018, 231). For Haskins, "This was the moment that my love affair with LA began" (231). But despite the marked contrast between LA and Northampton with respect to warm weather and exotic vegetation, this first visit also entailed an encounter with young Bauhaus fans who would—and would not—remind Haskins of himself back home in Britain. He notes:

> The Roxy's parking lot resembled a German car dealership as the BMW's and Mercedes pulled in to park, the drivers of which were not middle aged as one would expect, but the kids coming to our show! This sort of affluence was very alien to us coming from a small factory town. Not every attendee was born with a silver spoon though, as was illustrated by a knock knock on our dressing room window. This was odd because we were two flights up! On opening the window I discovered about ten kids who had climbed the fire escape. They explained that they couldn't afford to buy tickets and could they come in? I felt a strong pang of compassion and so I pulled a "Joe Strummer" and let them all in. On exiting our dressing room the security guard shot me a confused look, so I lied that they were our friends who had shown up before he did. I guess that word got around as we ended up repeating this favour the following two nights. (231)

Puzzled at first by the Bauhaus fandom that found people lined up for the band's autograph at the legendary record store Vinyl Fetish, Haskins recalls what it meant to him as a teenager to meet the Clash's Joe Strummer. But more than simply identifying with these young Americans based on a shared fan-based identity, Haskins's bond with them was largely based on class background, for it was the kids who couldn't afford to pay for tickets who recalled his Northampton upbringing. In a personal communication, Haskins informed me that this group of kids was indeed diverse, reflective of the group's multiracial and working-class Southern California Latina/o/x fanbase.[17]

The significance of this incident, as well as the enthusiastic response received by the band, would endear Haskins, J, and Ash in particular to the region, as they would come to relocate there. As Haskins writes, "LA audiences were very attentive and I remember us firing on all fours. We tapped into 'The Spirit' and delivered a very intense performance. It was a marvelous introduction to the city that I would eventually call my home" (2018, 231). Based on their intimate coupling in Haskins's narrative, one might very well surmise that the fans' entry into the band's dressing room paralleled the band's entry into Los Angeles.

Four years earlier, David J would publish his aforementioned memoir *Who Killed Mister Moonlight? Bauhaus, Black Magick, and Benediction* (Haskins 2014), which would also recount the group's introduction to Los Angeles in 1982.[18] Rich with details about the band's tumultuous history since its formation in 1978, J, like his brother, recalls playing a sold-out, three-night stand at the Roxy on Sunset Boulevard. After the first of these three shows, he writes that the band "sauntered over to the Rainbow Bar & Grill," the infamous spot frequented by what he calls the "trashy hair-metal bands of the time" (111). The bar scene, populated by "disturbing spray-on spandex pants, rat's-nest hair, and chunky spiked jewelry," is suddenly interrupted by "a very pretty little Mexican girl." J writes:

> All of a sudden a very pretty little Mexican girl slid in [the large booth] beside me. Close. We said hello and I ordered her a drink. This Latino coquette was dressed appealingly in satin, lace, and black leather, with a short ruffle skirt over her fishnet tights and five-inch stilettos. When I got up to leave she slipped her arm through mine and we strolled back to the hotel. The night was soft and balmy, and as we walked we chatted about Tex-Mex music, Hollywood, and herpes. (There was a big scare about the disease at the time, which in retrospect, and in the shadow of AIDS, now seems almost quaint.) She also told me that she was from a very poor neighborhood in East LA, and that she wanted to get a machine gun to protect herself in the ghetto. Quite a gal! (Haskins 2014, 111)

As the scene unfolds, the East LA Bauhaus fan enthralls J to the point where he books her the last remaining room in the hotel, turning it into a "party room" for him and this Latina seductress. He writes, "I poured two large glasses of tequila as she sashayed onto my knee and into my lap, and suddenly I had a dilemma on my hands" (Haskins 2014, 112). Primarily functioning as a moment for J to reflect on and question his commitment to his girlfriend, Annie, back home ("By now, I had been living with Annie for five years, and I was still head over heels in love. . . . Did I really want to jeopardize it all with a groupie?"), he is hard-pressed to refuse her advances. To be sure: "On the other hand, God, this girl was gorgeous! I poured myself another stiff one, stupidly trying to drink the problem away. The girl rubbed her slim thighs together, rustling with electric sex. She stuck her tongue deep into my ear and started to whisper: 'I'll let you into a secret. I'm shaved down there, like the Indian women. I think you'll like it'" (112).[19]

While such descriptions are quoted from the seductress by J, his own description of the "Latino coquette" proves equally revealing, as she is cast in terms that draw attention to her racial and ethnic difference, sometimes trafficking in caricatured fashion similar to how one might perceive Latinas in classic Hollywood cinema or within white mainstream popular culture more broadly. In J's words, "she came up to me with that same sad puppy dog look in her huge brown eyes" (112), and "then came more pillow talk whispers, this time in Spanish. I had no idea what she was saying, but the words sounded beautiful as they rolled off her hot little darting tongue" (113).

Ultimately prohibiting her from slipping into his room—"*What if this chica has herpes—or worse?*" and "I can't do this, sorry"—J's ultimate sexual rejection of the desiring Latina hinges on her perceived threat to both his physical health and his commitment to monogamy. ("Five days and I would be home. Five fuckin' days!" [113].) The denial of her entry into his hotel room is, however, much more complex than what a surface-level reading might reveal. Indeed, we cannot simply view the Latina here as one who is misrepresented or taken advantage of; in fact, it is she who demands to be let in despite her refused entry. Furthermore, J represents for this Latina a ticket out, a star with the ability—no doubt also through his recourse to whiteness—to take her away. "'No!' she cried. 'Don't send me back there, please let me stay with you. Please!'" (112). The mutuality here, although not without complication given J's authorial privilege and his decisive upper hand, precisely exhibits how desire regularly manifests in messy, multidirectional ways.

In view of the Latina represented in J's narrative, I want to read the lifting of the name Love and Rockets as more than an homage to Los Bros. Hernandez but also a direct nod to Latinas represented in the pages of their work, especially Jaime's character Isabel "Izzy" Ortiz Reubens. Although significantly older than Maggie and Hopey, the two women on whom Jaime's work has chiefly focused, Izzy is a goth whose outcast status in the working-class Southern California city of Hoppers has much to do with her adornment of black clothes, her entwinement with the occult, and her status as a writer. Given the name "The Witch Lady" by the neighborhood kids, Izzy—whose additional last name "Reubens" is taken from the English professor whom she marries but quickly divorces—is hit hard by patriarchal violence, drug addiction, the death of her brother Speedy, and multiple suicide attempts.[20] And although the working-class punk identities of, and the on-again, off-again relationship between, Maggie and Hopey are regularly spotlighted and lauded by academics and cultural commentators, Izzy's goth status sets her apart from the other women in the pantheon of Hernandez personalities. On this note, we may turn to a more recent track by David J—"Goth Girls in Southern California," from his 2002 EP *Mess Up*—to illustrate how to understand Izzy. As the lyrics establish:

> Goth girls in Southern California
> So pale in the carcinogenic sun
> The pool is anathema
> The beach is a bitch and no fun
> Goth girls don't like that California
> Goth girls don't need that California
> Goth girls don't want that California sun
> Goth girls in Southern California
> Oh, leave them alone!

Moreover, I maintain that Izzy Ortíz Reubens has a writer-double in the queer Chicana writer Myriam Gurba, who in her debut book *Dahlia Season: Stories and a Novella* compellingly grapples with whiteness and desire as they relate to those unmistakable "goth girls in Southern California."[21] Bauhaus's influence on these goth girls is certainly not lost on Gurba. In fact, the soundtrack accompanying their everyday lives to tunefully narrate their dark desires appropriately demands it.

SHE'S A WHITE GIRL

Gurba's short story "White Girl" represents a Chicana goth who understands the racial underpinnings of whiteness and desire and yet is fully capable of understanding their more often than not hierarchical arrangements. In Gurba's story, the Chicana narrator recounts the course through which she "turned goth" alongside her friend Mickey: "We both turned goth at the same time. We both went and bought combat boots but I also got pointy-toed witch boots with buckles and we also shared Wet'n'Wild black lipstick. We bought records and put black lace up over the windows and played 'Bela Lugosi's Dead' over and over until it drove our parents crazy. We painted our nails black and gave each other fucked-up haircuts. We were twins in everything for an entire summer. It was hot and dry and it was like our honeymoon" (2007, 43). This summer of intimacy additionally finds the narrator watching *The Hunger*—featuring David Bowie and Bauhaus, whose performance of "Bela Lugosi's Dead" is famously known for opening the film—"for the twenty-fifth time" (44). While their relationship achieves the status of "best friends," the narrator ultimately redirects her attention away from Mickey and onto her older sister Gabriella. As the narrative unfolds, the narrator and Gabriella enter into an erotic relationship, complete with blood-drawing, that approximates *The Hunger* scene featuring two women "licking blood from each other's wounds" (44).

Through Gabriella we ascertain the allure for the narrator for things not only gothic but also white. Indeed, "Gabriella was exotic. She came from another world. Pale skin, green eyes, and casseroles for dinner. She spoke nothing but English. She was raised to fear the macabre and there was nothing dark about her except for what she invented and that made her powerful. It wasn't forced on her. I liked her for that and loved her for so much more" (49). "White Girl," however, tacitly exposes the vacuity of goth culture, casting light on its whiteness—its paleness—in contrast to Mexicanidad. Like Haskins's admirer, the protagonist of Gurba's story is a Chicana. She, too, desires the white gothic figure albeit in another woman. Furthermore, the goth music that would presumably set the mood for the highly charged erotic exchange between the two women is both unidentified and described by the narrator as "something painful and whiny." Throughout the story, Gurba's Chicana is wise to the racism and racial politics of goth, its blandness and presumed cultural disaffectedness (Gabriella makes fun of the narrator's mother's food because "it wasn't bland enough"). And, not unlike the Latina banging on David J's hotel room door, her desire isn't simply pining for whiteness to save her as much as it is finding sexual satisfaction in what is different from her brown self, thus casting the presumed pallid and artificial disposition of goth in contrast to Mexican culture's characteristic embrace of death.

Here I read the narrator of Gurba's story alongside Leila Taylor who, in her memoir/cultural history titled *Darkly: Black History and America's*

Gothic Soul, writes of her love for Siouxsie Sioux, the Cure's Robert Smith, Joy Division, and Bauhaus as a Black teenager growing up in the United States:

> I'd look at the photos of my idols in *Smash Hits* and my white friends with their vampiric pale skin, and I will admit that I was sometimes envious at how effortlessly they could *present* as goth. Mark Fisher called Siouxsie's look a "replicable cosmetic mask, a form of white tribalism." I never wanted to be white. Whiteness was never something I aspired to, but I considered myself a member of this tribe, and that mask never fit me. I'll admit, I sometimes felt a bit *Blacula*-ish in their presence—a Black version of a white story. (2019, 12)

Like Taylor, Gurba's Chicana possesses a deep love for the goth aesthetic but knows full well that embracing it does not require an essential or uncritical embrace of the whiteness assumed to charge its authenticity. On the contrary, both uphold the belief that the history of this aesthetic flies in the face of any assumed imperative to whiteness given its indebtedness to the cultural influences that lie at the heart of its formation and endurance. As Taylor powerfully writes at the conclusion to *Darkly*:

> I am anticipating that one-true goths will disagree with me; that cultural purists will say that goth(ic) is British and white, hands down; that music critics will complain that I haven't mentioned Christian Death, Fields of the Nephilim, or Militia Vox; that gate-keepers will question my credibility. But just as there is no one-true American, there is no one-true goth. In all its variation of fashion and music, its essence is an ineffable sublimity, and the harder you try to solidify it, the more liquid it gets. But it can be distilled to one common point, the axiom by which all goths and the gothic is understood: **Black.** (2019, 184)

Taylor accordingly returns us to the Black roots of goth—which of course includes the dub/reggae roots of "Bela Lugosi's Dead," as mentioned at the start of this chapter—that many proponents of goth have struggled to acknowledge in their undying attempt to keep goth white. Moreover, Taylor's exposure of the fiction that belies the "one-true" enables us to see that goth—whatever that might be anymore—epitomized by Bauhaus and its members is indelibly influenced by the US Latina/o/x communities and cultures, particularly in Southern California, by which they're indubitably touched.

GO AWAY, WHITE

Since my return to Southern California in 2016, my adoration of Bauhaus, the band's members, and their combined music catalog has been retrofitted for new tales to tell. One reason behind this is the frequency with which I have encountered them both onstage and in settings beyond it. For example, in July 2019 I took in a DJ set by David J at Decades Bar in Anaheim. Arriving early, I found a small, two-seater table tucked away at the back of the bar. It also afforded the opportunity to order beers and food while observing those filing in for the event. Not long after I arrived, I witnessed J enter the space, also in search of ideal seating. At one point he stood next to me, scanning the bar for options. Without much thought, I rose to my feet and addressed him: "David, you can have this table if you'd like." He looked me in the eye, put his hand on my back, and told me, "Thank you very much but it's fine. That's your table." I realize I could have asked for an autograph, engaged him in a conversation, but for me his touching response was enough to sustain, if not bolster, my admiration.

And as an alternative to goth absorbing difference into whiteness as it sees fit, I think of the fellow Latinos and Latinas with whom I share admiration for Bauhaus, from Sean in my high school typewriting class to my present-day friend and colleague Michael. But more specifically, I want to nod to those Latinas—some of whom might very well qualify as "goth girls from Southern California"—with a mutual passion for the band. I think here of the women in whose presence I've been fortunate to find myself at Bauhaus and Bauhaus-associated gigs, the latter including performances by individual members of the band and various offshoot projects: Stacie at Love and Rockets in Irvine in 1987; Teresa at Peter Murphy and Bauhaus, respectively, in 1990 and 1998 in San Francisco; Claudia at Poptone in Los Angeles in 2017; Sharlynn at Peter Murphy and David J in Anaheim in early 2019; and Dionne, Elizabeth, and Angelica at Bauhaus on two separate evenings in Hollywood in late 2019.[22] Then there are Dania and Renée—always contented to hold one of the many elegantly designed Bauhaus record sleeves while aurally absorbing the sounds encased therein—similarly finding bliss in the band's unmatched ability to strike with a deliciously scathing two-pronged visual and musical force. These spirited companions and associates have shared with me not only the pleasure of the live event and the undying bliss of the band's recorded genius but also reasons for, through teenage memories and other varieties of personal recounting, the long-standing and abiding ("undead, undead, undead") resonance of Bauhaus.

Just like this music, which cannot be adequately labeled as cursorily goth, each of these women has without provocation detailed the assumed racial dynamics of goth's whiteness that is more often than not naturalized as—to riff on the lyrics of the Bauhaus track "Lagartija Nick"—"a code of play, a nocturne rite." For while Bauhaus's sonically "cruel garden of dark delights" may prove enticing for an attendant pale subculture, it is also distinctly alluring when setting the stage for a desiring Latina, not unlike those I've acknowledged above, seeking to set the terms for her own dark entry.

Four

THE SHINING SINNERS

> Just like Johnny Rio, baby /
> I need to be desired.
>
> **Marc Almond, "Ruby Red"**

On April 24, 1989—a few weeks shy of graduating from high school and packing my personal belongings to travel four hundred miles to the Bay Area to attend the University of California, Berkeley—a group of friends and I took in the only Orange County appearance by Marc Almond (né Peter Mark Sinclair Almond) on his tour for the 1988 *The Stars We Are* album. The four of us met up after school at my parents' house in Santa Ana and left for the Celebrity Theater in Anaheim a few hours before the scheduled showtime. We were all excited about the show given that, although we didn't have the best seats, we knew the venue was small enough to guarantee a more intimate experience than we were used to—namely the free lawn seats ensured by my dad who smuggled us into concerts at the Pacific Amphitheater in Costa Mesa on the nights he worked security. This group of friends—three women, two daughters of Vietnamese refugees and the other of Yugoslavian migrants—composed the vital social network that sustained me during the last two years of high school and shared my taste for British popular music. (Our friend David—a Mexican American like myself obsessed with the Smiths and who early on emulated Morrissey's dressed-down yet sharp sense of style—unfortunately couldn't attend the show due to his minimum-wage job.) Hardly the school's acclaimed star students yet all college bound, we'd pile into Laurie's car, off to complete homework and study at the main branch of the Santa Ana Public Library while singing along to the tapes playing on the deck ("Driving in your car . . ."). Among them: the Cure's *The Head on the Door*; New Order's *Low-Life*; Scritti Politti's *Cupid & Psyche 85*; the Smiths' *The Queen Is Dead*; Depeche Mode's *Music for the Masses*; Aztec Camera's *Love*; and Marc Almond's *The Stars We Are*.

After waiting patiently outside the Celebrity, we excitedly filed into the venue as the doors opened. As expected, we located our seats at the very back of the theater, but this would not obstruct the thrill the evening promised. Although we noticed quite a few empty seats ahead, the great excitement filling the air left little possibility for granting them ample attention. As Almond and his band La Magia were due to take the stage, a venue security guard approached us. At first, we couldn't make sense of what he was saying, given the blaring music sounding Marc's entrance. Yet when he gestured for us to rise from our seats, we each thought were being asked to leave the venue—but for what reason? Instead, we found ourselves escorted not to the exit but rather to the front of the theater and reseated in row 2, presumably to fill out the vacant rows near the stage. The four of us were elated beyond belief, and almost every five minutes one of us would comment to another that this was nothing short of a dream come true.

The moment Marc began to sing the opening lines of "The Stars We Are," my eyes were drawn to a fabulous figure in the front row, an even luckier stage-proximate Latinx fan who was equally enthralling as the singer we had all come to see. Decked out in a flowing red lamé jacket and made up to perfection, they were indeed a sight to behold. Before *transgender* and *nonbinary* were in wide circulation to assert the refusal of sex/gender convention, this concertgoer—whom I affectionately dubbed "Diana" for striking Ms. Ross–like diva poses while vivaciously whipping a mane of shoulder-length black hair—was draped over a characteristically handsome muscular jock and sang along to each and every song Almond performed. From "Do you remember those hazy amber days?" of "The Stars We Are" to "Please don't go away," the closing line of Almond's cover of Jacques Brel's "If You Go Away," this was one of those unforgettable shows where each song stirred a collectively infectious jubilation. Undoubtedly, Almond was also absorbed by the euphoria as he repeatedly reached into the audience, brushing hands with those nearby—myself, my friends, and Diana included—to congeal a lovingly corroborated rapport. As songs performed that evening—including "There Is a Bed," "Tenderness Is a Weakness," "Only the Moment," "Melancholy Rose," "Ruby Red," "Black Heart," and "Something's Gotten Hold of My Heart"—would come to hold an even more profound significance in my adult life, I also regard Marc and Diana as early exemplars for disclosing a sense of intimate queer attachment—in terms of both enduring friendship and what Michael Warner (2002) identifies as "stranger sociability"—after this concert in Anaheim.

Along with the social networks of which I became a part that introduced me to vibrant spaces of queer congregation like the Bench and Bar and the White Horse Inn in Oakland and the Castro Street Fair and Josie's Cabaret and Juice Joint in San Francisco, another attachment fostered in the Bay Area was with literature penned by lesbians and gay men (mostly of color). One writer I'd soon learn about—described by more than one professor as the gay pioneer of Mexican American letters—was John Rechy. Although this Chicano/Scottish writer's surname did not make him readily legible as a Mexican American writer, it was most likely the homosexual scenarios unapologetically featured in most of his books that ostracized him from rigidly contoured ethnic literary canons. Less concerned with his questionable commitment to ethnic solidarity than with the fact that his books bald-facedly contained, as one classmate memorably put it, "cum on almost every page," an initially vague familiarity with the themes (public sex) and names (Johnny Rio) in Rechy eventually triggered a recollection of previously acquired knowledge in a musical context. As it turns out, the Soft Cell and Marc Almond LPs on my earlier teenage turntable had brought Rechy into my bedroom, albeit as nameless as one of the anonymous tricks in his gloriously promiscuous novels. While I didn't know of Rechy until a few years later, I was nonetheless acquainted with the sordid yet carnally familiar scenarios he induced Marc Almond and his Soft Cell partner-in-crime Dave Ball (David James Ball) to document with equally stimulating adulation.

I'VE GOT TO HAVE A MEMORY

Casual mention of Soft Cell's name never fails to elicit reference to the band's most recognized hit single, "Tainted Love," be it from the general fan or the most novice historian of 1980s popular music. Notwithstanding the pervasiveness and infectious force of this Northern Soul cover version written by Ed Cobb and initially performed by Gloria Jones, the duo commands a rather complex history with a music catalog that, since 1978, consistently penetrates a tainted surface and scales the depths of assorted sleazy underworlds.[1] As Jonathan Bernstein rightly argues, given how "in

4.1 Soft Cell (L–R, Dave Ball and Marc Almond), 1981. Photo by Fin Costello/ Redferns. Used by permission.

the U.K., Soft Cell were on every kiddie TV show, every preteen wall, and every radio station" with their major hit, "for a lot of that audience, 'Tainted Love' was the gateway drug that led them to hearing Almond singing about seedy films and sex dwarves" (Majewski and Bernstein 2014, 212).[2]

The genesis of Soft Cell (fig. 4.1) reaches back to 1977, when Almond and Ball met as students at Leeds Polytechnic (now Leeds Beckett University).[3] The previous year, Almond would encounter an emergent music scene that would forever alter his life: "I became curious about a development I was reading about in the music papers—a new music movement heralded by the Sex Pistols. The movement was punk. It was 1976, and I was nineteen years old. This new movement was about to change all our lives, to blow musical tastes apart, and make me throw out much of my old record collection" (Almond 1999b, 50).

Along with punk as a newfound stimulating force, Almond applied and was accepted to study performance art at Leeds. His first encounter with his future collaborator transpired when Ball asked Almond for directions to the art department. "We couldn't have been more contrasting: Dave in a denim jacket, jeans and desert wellies, tall and stocky with black curly hair; me in gold-lamé trousers, a leopard-skin T-shirt on a small skinny frame with a blonde crop" (Almond 1999b, 75). Yet despite their differences in presentation, Almond and Ball shared many things in common.

> Both of us hailed from north-west coastal towns—Dave was from Blackpool, a town you could see from Southport [Almond's hometown] beach on a clear day. We both shared a love of the bizarre, the kitsch and the seedy. But more importantly we both loved electronic music, and between two poles of musical tastes we met in a shared love for Kraftwerk and the New Industrial sounds that were emerging. Throbbing Gristle, Cabaret Voltaire

> and the early Human League had evolved from the three-chord thrash of punk, and came to inspire us equally. (75)[4]

Along with the additional citation of Siouxsie and the Banshees' first album, *The Scream*, as an early major influence for its sharp ability to turn "suburban things into nightmares" (Majewski and Bernstein 2014, 214), Soft Cell was clearly intent on riding the crest of the emergent post-punk scene while uniquely contributing to it from beyond the parameters of an often taken-for-granted London epicenter.[5] In his essay "Being in a Band: Art-School Experiment and the Post-Punk Commons," art historian Gavin Butt spotlights Leeds as an often-overlooked origin point for post-punk, citing bands such as Gang of Four, Scritti Politti, and, of course, Soft Cell, which took flight from the northern English city and the public university these aspiring artists attended.[6] And while both Almond and Ball "passed with honours" at Leeds, "thus making Soft Cell one of the very few bands which could claim that 100% of its members had B.A. after their names" (Tobler 1982b, 17), the duo were not simply, as Jonathan Bernstein argues, "a total art school band" who "were pretentious . . . show-offs . . . want[ing] to shock" (Majewski and Bernstein 2014, 212) but consistently committed to maintaining connections to worlds beyond elite and mainstream institutions.

As "Tainted Love" would catapult Soft Cell to the top of the global music charts, the band's long-standing and extensive "noncommercial" networks—not to mention Almond's and Ball's post–Soft Cell work (often encompassing yet at times exceeding pop)—is routinely overlooked in surface-level accounts of the band.[7] As Almond explains to Charles Neal in an interview published in 1987, "We sort of thought of ourselves as working in the pop area, but tried to do something different with it" (Neal 1987, 76). This something different, I argue, had much to do with embracing "the bizarre, the kitsch and the seedy" elements that brought Almond and Ball together in the first place and came to define their lasting persona.[8]

Soft Cell were certainly not like most of their contemporaries "working in the pop area" given that their major public introduction on television occasioned excessive doses of antiqueer violence directed at the duo, particularly Almond. Performing "Tainted Love" on *Top of the Pops* in August 1981, Almond writes, "I frugged onto the TV screen and a nation's jaws dropped open. Immediately and from then on, it seemed girls wanted to marry me, mothers wanted to mother me, grandparents wanted to have me arrested, lads wanted to smash my face in, fathers buried their heads in their papers, and many young gay teenage sons blushed and made an excuse to leave the room so they could go upstairs and write love notes to me" (1999b, 119). Crystallizing the formative televisual moment described in this book's introduction between myself and Boy George, not to mention the many post-punk artists who first glimpsed David Bowie's 1972 performance of "Starman" on *Top of the Pops,* Almond emphatically articulates the mutuality of influential mediated encounters: "Just as with Bowie and [Marc] Bolan in the seventies, war was declared in school playgrounds the day after, when a growing army of Marc Almond fans stood up to be counted. I had been here before, except that now I was on the other side of the screen, looking out. It was now me who suddenly revealed to the lonely teenager in some remote place that there was someone out there who might understand how he or she felt" (1999b, 119).[9]

The ability of a small-screen primal scene to profoundly touch the nascent queer spectator arguably delivers the first step toward cultivating a bond between fan and performer, oftentimes extending to an in-person, hand-touching encounter such as mine with Almond in Anaheim and Almond's with David Bowie in Liverpool. Kevin Cann's *Any Day Now: David Bowie: The London Years: 1947–1974* details how during the performance of "Rock 'n' Roll Suicide" at the Sunday, June 10, 1973, David Bowie and the Spiders from Mars show in Liverpool, Almond was "one of those who [took] hold of David's hand. 'It was a moment of epiphany,' Almond said in 2007" (2010, 301).

The queer touch between music artist and adoring devotee, however, functions in a multidirectional fashion, with Almond standing as an example of how to break down sexual and gender norms. Soft Cell's rise to prominence, best described as a combination of burgeoning celebrity and persistent derision, unquestionably helped set the stage for several subsequent queer post-punk artists.[10] Almond notes, "This was still a couple of years before Boy George, before Holly Johnson and Jimmy Somerville. Though they too did their fair share of breaking down barriers, I certainly prepared the way. I took the flak then, and still am taking it today, never quite forgiven for turning many a teenage son into a studded-wrist-band-wearing, eye-liner-sporting individual. I had that loathsome thing the public hated—I had a sexuality" (1999b, 120).

While earlier pop singers no doubt also "had a sexuality" (Mick Jagger immediately comes to mind), Almond's variety was distinctively tainted given its Bowie-like entwinement with gender-subversive presentation. Indeed, Almond's queer adornments, in the form of excessive bracelets and thick eyeliner, emblematized his refusal of BBC executive Roger Aimes's command to "Tone it down!" (Almond 1999b, 119). In an ensuing discussion of gay pop stars and the politics of coming out, Almond elaborates on the changing tide that has allowed formerly closeted pop stars like Elton John and George Michael "to take the plunge" (121). However, his striking admission that the "public will only accept homosexuality up to a point" (121) tenders an acute angle for understanding the partial mainstream grasp of Almond's expressive oeuvre. To be sure, the artistic influences on Soft Cell's and Marc Almond's subsequent solo work reveal an intimate attachment to pregentrified sexual subcultures that not only bridge the Atlantic divide but link these post-punk Leeds artists to quotidian forms of queer Latinidad. To effectively grasp this link requires discerning the literary and historical contexts through which it transpires.

SLEAZY CITIES

Like other post-punk musicians whose output drew motivation from books, films, television programs, and the visual and performing arts, Almond and Ball—both together and individually—consistently nod to an array of creative figures who might very well be credited for inciting their calling. For example, in *Tainted Life* Almond recalls how before Soft Cell had formed, he happened upon a novel that compelled him to embrace the belief that the best writing is always writing about what one knows:

> I found a book called *City of Night* by the American writer John Rechy, and was greatly inspired by it. It is a personal journey through the gay half world of New York and Los Angeles. John Rechy was a hustler who writes, and a writer who hustles. Hustling—the American slang term for male prostitution—gave him the inspiration for his writing. I believe that the greatest art comes from personal experience. You have to partake in as much as you can, sample all kinds of life, explore and sensualize, and turn even the most negative experiences into positive creativity. Many of the songs I have written come from such personal experiences. You've got to live the life you sing, and sing the life you live. (1999b, 70)

The many songs Almond has written over the years, derived from personal experience and inspired by *City of Night*—which, as noted by Almond in the introduction to 1999's *Beautiful Twisted Night*, "became a bible" (1999a, 7)—have much to do with his "partaking in as much as [one] can."[11] To be sure, Almond's song lyrics and poems, oftentimes one and the same, reveal an unabashed desire to "sample all kinds of life," to "explore and sensualize, and turn even the most negative experiences into positive creativity."[12]

The impetus to "explore and sensualize," I argue, is made possible by John Rechy, evident in Almond's inextricably contextual citations. Indeed, Rechy's influence on Soft Cell's and Almond's work, an influence inseparable from the decisive cultivation of one's "personal experience," stimulates the baseline organizing principle for each of their five LPs—*Non-Stop Erotic Cabaret* (1981), *The Art of Falling Apart* (1983), *This Last Night in Sodom* (1984), *Cruelty without Beauty* (2002), and **Happiness Not Included* (2022)—along with notable tracks like "Numbers," "L'Esqualita," "Ruby Red," and "City of Nights" in their extensive repertoire. Fittingly, these tracks in particular link Soft Cell and Almond in particular to Latinx queer subcultures in the United States, subcultures eclipsed in Rechy's work despite his Mexican American background.[13]

To best understand the link between Soft Cell, Almond, and Rechy requires awareness of the histories of underground sexual cultures of pregentrified cities like London, New York, and Los Angeles. Consider, for example, the following passage from *City of Night*, told in the novel's protagonist Youngman's first-person perspective, while in the throes of cruising in New York City's famed Central Park:

> At night they sat along the benches, in the fringes of the park. Or they strolled with their leashed dogs along the walks. . . . The more courageous ones penetrated the park, around the lake, near a little hill: hoods, hobos, hustlers, homosexuals. Hunting. Young teenage gangs lurk threatening among the trees. Occasionally the cops come by, almost timidly, in pairs, flashing their lights; and the rustling of bushes precedes the quick scurrying of feet along the paths. Unexpectedly at night you may come upon scenes of crushed intimacy along the dark twisting lanes. In the eery mottled light of a distant lamp, a shadow lies on his stomach on the grass-patched ground, another straddles him: ignoring the danger of detection in the last moments of exiled excitement. (Rechy [1963] 2013, 73)

This scene, which could very well be culled from an analogous nocturnal scenario in Almond's lyrics/poems, exemplifies the overlap of shared thematic content and aesthetic engagement between the two writers. Indeed, as Almond's appropriately titled track "City of Nights" chronicles:

> Girls sell kisses to the lonely men
> Boys turn tricks with the sleight of hand

Women fear to walk where men desire
Inspiration, hope and fire

Hey, don't be a stranger
Make a friend don't let it end you
Hey don't be a stranger
There's a light burning in the city
In the city
In the city of nights[14]

Highlighting the Rechy and Almond/Soft Cell convergence helps register the "crushed intimacy," as noted by Rechy, existing between strangers and outcasts who embody what gay African American writer Samuel R. Delany understands as the "contact" that "is vital to the material politics as well as to the vision of a democratic city" (1999, 199). This "crushed intimacy" and "contact" is what (sexually) charges Soft Cell's debut album, *Non-Stop Erotic Cabaret*, a series of ten arguably linked tracks that are in many ways anchored in the red-light district of London's West End Soho neighborhood. Indeed, from the song "Seedy Films" ("Down in your alleys / Seems that anything goes") to the album cover itself—designed by Andrew Prewett with photography by Peter Ashworth and overseen by long-time Soft Cell designer and photographer Hu Feather—places Almond and Ball smack in the middle of "British low culture" (Hunt, 1998), namely Soho's triple-X neon-lit milieu.[15]

The sexually explicit culture contouring this milieu is represented on *Non-Stop Erotic Cabaret*—and its accompanying film *Non-Stop Exotic Video Show* (1982), directed by Tim Pope and composed of promotional videos and footage of Almond and Ball hobnobbing in Soho—as more than simply romanticized squalor suitable only for sporadic slumming but one where people of mixed status converge for both pleasure and communal bonding in the face of moral policing and social dejection.[16] This is not unlike the way the presanitized Times Square for Delany functioned as a location "where people, male and female, gay and straight, old and young, working class and middle class, Asian and Hispanic, black and other, rural and urban, tourist and indigene, transient and permanent, with their bodily, material, sexual, and emotional needs, might discover (and even work to set up) varied and welcoming harbors for landing on our richly variegated urban shore" (Delany 1999, xx). Almond's grasp of the city resonates with Delany's when he writes, "Some see the city as a cruel, dirty, heartless, selfish, soulless place and although some of this is true, I see the city as a beautiful romantic place—a playground of fantasy and desire. An amorphous beautiful monster pulsing with heart and soul. A complicated network of lives—some on a solitary path but many interchanging, passing in a moment, loving, working, and sometimes killing" (Almond 1999a, 7).

Rechy's work beyond *City of Night*, however, additionally impacted Soft Cell's and Almond's work, particularly his second novel, 1967's *Numbers*, and its protagonist, Johnny Rio. Indeed, not only is Johnny Rio the motivating force for Almond's 1987 song "Ruby Red" (cited as the epigraph above and which I discuss below), but unmistakably also for Soft Cell's 1983 single "Numbers," taken from their second LP, *The Art of Falling Apart*. Johnny Rio is unquestionably an ideal figure on whom to focus given his status as a hustler whose habitat is the city streets, the cruisy parks, and the homophile bars, among other places of delightful ill repute in the City of Angels. Consider Rechy's description of Rio:

> Johnny's father, now dead, was Irish. His mother is Mexican. ("Rio" is not actually his last name—it's not even his mother's maiden name, although hers is really Mexican. He assumed the name in Los Angeles because, especially in a world where no last names are given, it sounded romantic—like a gypsy's.) From them he inherited a smooth complexion which sponges the sun's rays easily, almost, one could say, adoringly: When he lies stretched under the stark gaze of the sun—and he does so religiously each summer—he feels that the heat is making love to him, licking his body with a golden tongue. Each summer his skin becomes brown velvet.
>
> Many people have told him that he's very handsome. He likes to hear that, and he never denies it. But he knows that the designation is not exactly correct. Precisely: he is much more sexual than he is handsome; and that, for Johnny, is even better. There is something about him which exudes sensuality. He knows it, he may even have cultivated it. He has been told there is a promise of "dark sex" that hovers about him. ([1967] 1984, 18)

With a keen ability to capture such hovering dark sex, Almond's lyrics reveal an intimate link to Rio—Rechy's protagonist who displays an eager attempt to reclaim his youthful sexual attraction by scoring as many anonymous men as possible (as Almond recounts, "Numbers / Don't tell me your name I don't want to know / And don't forget to take all reminders when you go")—who in turn personifies the sexual subject in Soft Cell's and Marc Almond's "sleazy city" underworlds.

Moreover, reflected in the lyrics for songs like "Numbers"—even beyond the obvious reference to Rechy in the title alone—is an unswerving attachment to abject sexual practices and spaces performed and occupied by Johnny Rio and Almond alike. As Simon Tebbutt notes in his biography of Soft Cell, "'Numbers,' a title nicked from a John Rechy novel chronicling the homosexual underworld in Los Angeles which the author visits to see how many strangers he can pick up in a weekend" is "a soundtrack of loveless sex, a theme tune to the endless parade of strangers" (1984, 112). In the way that Rechy, in the words of literary scholar Thomas Heise, "weaves together the spaces of the city and the voices of the city's sexual outlaws" by illustrating how "geography is instrumental to how human sexuality is categorized and lived under duress" (2015, 24), the music of Soft Cell and Almond skillfully soundtracks an urban mis-en-scène that helps throw (neon) light on nonnormative and outcast sexualities and desires.

As Almond sings in "Ruby Red" from his 1987 LP *Mother Fist and Her Five Daughters* (the title taken from Truman Capote's 1975 short story "Nocturnal Turnings, or How Siamese Twins Have Sex"), "just like Johnny Rio . . . I need to be desired." The desire required by Rio, and indeed by Almond's and Soft Cell's numerous protagonists (including the narrating "I" of *Non-Stop Erotic Cabaret*'s "Youth" who, like Rio, narcissistically laments his diminishing youthfulness—"Youth has gone / Though don't think / I don't cry / We let ourselves slip / And now / I ask myself why / I'm on my own / And don't think I really mind") is resolutely located in a landscape where those from multiple walks of life cavort and intermingle. But such protagonists spotlighted in these lyrics parallel Almond's own personal experiences whose motivation would, as previously mentioned, give rise to his creative output. So while one may not always readily ascertain whether the sexual subjects in Soft Cell's and Almond's sonic productions are truly autobiographical, we can, however, look to Almond's public persona in the British music press—cast by *Sounds* as "Filthy Marc" while *Gay Times* announces his consumption of "a ton of drugs" and possession of "a string of lovers" on their respective covers—along with his prodigious writing beyond his song lyrics to understand how his personal experiences indeed mirror those of Johnny Rio's as musically recorded.[17]

Despite an evident overlap, there are discernable differences between Rio (and Rechy) and Almond. Consider the lines from "Ruby Red" succeeding those cited above: "I give up looking for my past / for the ones I left behind." Thus, the narrator of Almond's "Ruby Red," unlike Rechy's Rio (who hits number thirty-seven at *Numbers*' end), gives up looking for his past—that is, his youthful self—to instead focus on those left behind. It is here where I wish to read this "looking for those left behind" (in memory and in spaces vacated or eradicated) as an effort to remember those people who made up the subterranean worlds inhabited and documented by Almond. Reading Almond's work alongside Rechy's, I maintain, allows us to understand his citations of the various sexual subcultures represented in his songs, memoirs, and poetry. Not surprisingly, Latinos and Latinas make up a significant segment of those subcultures.

Perhaps because of the fleeting references to Rechy's Latinidad in both *City of Night* and *Numbers* (primarily in the references to his hometown of El Paso and his Mexican mother), it makes sense, once again, that Almond opts to identify Rechy as an American rather than a Latino writer. Through recourse to Rechy, Almond is henceforth spurred to write about the sexual cultures similarly represented in Rechy's writing but that are explicitly named in his interactions and encounters with Latinos and Latinas. Rechy's ability to touch Almond as a writer invested in documenting one's personal experiences—alongside "the neon-lit world of hustlers, drag queens, and the denizens of their world" (as noted on the back cover of *City of Night*)—ultimately leads to a mutual touching between Almond and Latinas and Latinos whose wide-ranging, urban-intimate encounters notably surface in Almond's work. But to make sense of this intimacy, one must first travel to and linger in the US-based urban settings where it manifests.

LOCATING LATIN MANHATTAN

Because of Soft Cell's rise to US stardom in the early 1980s given the sonic ubiquity of "Tainted Love," Almond notes in his autobiography that the duo was handed "the keys to New York" (1999b, 181). This meant consuming as much of the Big Apple as possible but mostly latching on to parts of the city comparable to London's Soho that proved lyrically influential. And once Soft Cell began traveling to the US, the focus on urban sexual subcultures widened to account for aspects of a queer Latina/o/x presence within these spaces. Perhaps the earliest and most revealing example of this fact is reflected in the song "L'Esqualita" from their third album, *This Last Night in Sodom* (1984).

Even if the Midtown bar the title indexes is really (spelled) La Escuelita, the scene Almond describes matches the one provided by sociologist Manuel Guzmán in his 1997 essay "Pa' La Escuelita con Mucho Cuida'o y por la Orillita" on how the now-defunct Latino gay bar was truly a family affair, standing alongside other unconventional nightlife spots.[18] Explaining that "'L'Esqualita' is about the famous Puerto Rican drag club in New York and its characters" (1999b, 235), Almond describes the bar alongside other favorites to which he gravitated:

> My favourite places at this time were the transsexual bars, like the Grapevine; this was no more than a brothel run by the large Madame Sherry, who informed us, "This is a whorehouse where the men wear women's clothes. If you don't like it, fuck off!" No false pretenses there. Then there was L'Esqualita, a Spanish/Puerto Rican drag club where the stunning divas performed for dollars. How good they were determined how much you chose to push down their cleavages. What I loved about L'Esqualita was that Spanish families went there for a night out, clapping and cheering the impersonators. (1999b, 181)

Despite the conflation of "Spanish" and "Puerto Rican" here—a tendency noted at other moments in his representations of Latinos/as in the US—Almond is most likely signaling the language spoken by Puerto Ricans more than tallying the number of patrons from Spain in attendance at La Escuelita.

Almond would later go into more detail about La Escuelita and respell (yet still misspell) it Esquelita, in his 2004 travel memoir *In Search of the Pleasure Palace*. Detailing a night out in Manhattan with his friend Scott Ewalt in the chapter appropriately titled "New York," Almond again lavishes praise on this nightlife hotspot that stands in stark contrast to (gay and straight) sanitized spots:

> Our last port of call had to be the club Esquelita, the infamous Latin Drag Club on 39th and 8th, where, as a wide-eyed northern boy visiting New York over twenty years earlier, I felt I had found a magical pleasure palace. But first, even back then, you have to find the damn place. It's in that nether zone of warehouses and non-gentrified dwellings in the West 30s. Line-waiting time is mandatory and nobody gets round it. Once inside imagine a run-down casino with an "Evening of Tango Madness" revue as recreated by acid-casualty drag queens with unlimited access to the sequin-and-feathers. Like a Mexican theme chain restaurant, Esquelita leans heavily on salsa kitsch to draw the crowds, and ironically Latino authentico is often the flavour least evident. (2004, 57)

While the aesthetic may not approximate what Almond understands as "Latino authentico," kitsch, as Celeste Olalquiaga reminds us, nonetheless serves to facilitate in Almond's work an experience of "mythical memory" shot through with "intensity and immediacy" (1998, 296), thus bringing together a potpourri of people—from patrons to performers—who are indeed Latina/o and those who desire them. And it also enables a strong sense of affinity Almond holds with queer US Latinx communities, particularly the drag performance culture within them, with whom a sense of connection discloses a break from a cold and abhorrent drag scene back home. He explains:

> It was a million miles away from the misogynistic British impersonators, especially the northern drag I knew, ugly and clumsy and berating, a sad comedy panto kind of approach with the usual pathetic retorts about . . . well, you can guess. But the drag in New York was a celebration of women, elegant, powerful, larger than life women—women they knew and who were real. Divas with attitude that rule a world where men were mere slavish mortals—that sort of thing. I wrote a song, inspired and named after that club—Esquelita. (2004, 58)

Admittedly, as much as I am touched by Almond's antimisogynistic stance and his proximity to queer Latinx sexual cultures, there are moments in his work that raise an eyebrow, with his work reading like that of the classic anthropologist observing native otherness in its primitive habitat. Oftentimes feelings of discomfort arise when Latino groups are carelessly conflated, as when "Spanish" and "Puerto Rican" casually stand in for one another. At other moments, it manifests when Almond's description of ethnic and racial differences reads like what one might encounter in writings by white gay men thirstily cruising men of color.

An example of the former is Almond's song "Shining Sinners," from his 1984 album *Vermin in Ermine*. Akin to "L'Esqualita," the lyrics document another encounter Almond has with New York Latinos, this time a group of individuals that recall for him a New York City gang straight out of Walter Hill's 1979 film *The Warriors*. According to Almond:

> "Shining Sinners" was the opening track of the album, and set the scene. I wrote it after being on the Lower East Side in New York one day and straying into the wrong neighborhood. I was feeling very self-conscious, because I had a lot of money on me. (Usually I never displayed what streetwise people call the "V" (for victim) and if threatened I acted a little crazy—which wasn't hard.) Suddenly I was surrounded by a Chicano gang who just stood watching me. I tried to act streetwise, even though my knees were knocking and my legs were like jelly. I reached the other end of the street safely and heaved a sigh of relief. The gang had probably been more

> amused than anything else. I imagined a more colourful scenario of me having to confront a gang such as the "Warriors" from the film of the same name. (1999b, 257)

The six-minute and thirty-eight-second song that narrates Almond's encounter with a gang is a curious fusion of New York City and Los Angeles, where the conflation of populations—Chicanos and Puerto Ricans—betrays a knowledge of US Latina/o communities no doubt gleaned from gang films like *The Warriors* and Michael Pressman's *Boulevard Nights* (1979).[19] Establishing a soundscape composed of a dramatic string arrangement, a nervously thumping beat, and an Orientalist guitar riff, the tonality of "Shining Sinners" provides the ideal aura for relating the narrator's near-fatal flaw ("You gotta run muchacho, run!") of coming face to face with a "Chicano chick" whose presence, like every fetish, is both alluring and threatening. Drawing together the "wild west" with the "wild east" for conjuring a mesmerizing encounter with racial otherness on "danger street," Almond's depiction of such shining sinners from "tenement hell" evokes the pantheon of Latina/o streetwise dwellers populating his writing on New York. From his expansive oeuvre of published lyrics, verse, and narrative poems, one may exemplarily point to 1988's *The Angel of Death in the Adonis Lounge* (with selections like "The Puerto Rican GoGo Boy" and "Christopher Street Pier"), 1999's *Beautiful Twisted Night* (including "The Savoy" and "Chi Chi La Rue's Night at the Eros"), and 2001's *The End of New York* (namely "Cats" and some of the previously mentioned titles).[20]

Such representations—particularly the lyrical—frequently hinge on clichés and eye-rolling characterizations borrowed from mainstream media and pornographic narratives commonly penned and visualized by white gay men (take, for example, the "Mexico City" chapter of *In Search of the Pleasure Palace* detailing his encounter with a group of men communally soaping each other down in a Mexico City spa in which their cocks are described as "half-stiff enchiladas"). Nonetheless, Almond's work reveals a deep cultural intimacy between British post-punk artists like Almond and Latinos/as. Moreover, while one can read between Almond's lines that these Mexican men are perplexed by (and sometimes taking advantage of) this pasty white British man who has decided to enter this space, we might very well read his work as a complex ethnographic web that documents underground Latino queer sexualities that have nearly been wiped clean from the New York City streets of the past. A poem like "Cats," for example, laments the closure of the eponymously named hustler bar once "situated somewhere on 49th and Eight, in the heart of the Times Square theatre district" (Almond 2001, 12) that contrasted with the declawed Andrew Lloyd Weber Broadway musical of the same name. Furthermore, "The Show Palace/The Gaiety Theatre" recalls Delany's recollections of a Times Square scene populated by sex hot spots no longer in existence by asking, "where do the lovely lovers of the dark go now, the worshippers in the temple of flesh, the shadow people—now the show palace has closed down, the david, the adonis lounge?" (Almond 2001, 42). One must remember that multidirectional touching never takes shape unsullied. Thanks to Almond's work, no matter how riddled with exhausted metaphors and paradoxes, we are offered insight into the multiracial, polysexual, and cross-class pollination that characterizes the rapidly vanishing London and US urban neighborhoods once conducive to a distinct transatlantic subterranean intimacy.

THE BOY WHO CAME BACK

In early 1999, while in the throes of writing my doctoral dissertation, I was thrilled to discover that Marc Almond was touring to promote his latest album, *Open All Night* (1999), which I regarded as a birthday gift of sorts given its March release. A mainstay on my CD player since purchasing it at Amoeba Records on Telegraph Avenue in Berkeley, it not only featured other favorite artists like Siouxsie Sioux and Budgie but also trip-hop–inspired tracks that earned repeated plays on my morning walks around Oakland's Lake Merritt: "Tragedy (Take a Look and See)," "Black Kiss," "Scarlet Bedroom," "My Love," "Sleepwalker," and "Midnight Soul." Soon after purchasing tickets to see him perform at Bimbo's 365 Club in San Francisco on November 13, 1999, I stumbled upon a flyer at A Different Light Bookstore announcing that Almond would also be holding a meet-and-greet at the Tower Records on Market at Noe earlier that day (fig. 4.2). Thrilled at the chance to meet one of my all-time favorite singers and have him sign my copies of his books (*Tainted Life* and *Beautiful Twisted Night* had just been published that year, but how could I not bring along my tattered copy of *The Angel of Death in the Adonis Lounge* for his inscription?), that afternoon I lined up with a friend for Almond's signature, a photo, and hopefully a brief chat. Almond kindly obliged to all three (even commenting on the "library" I brought with me) and wished us well, hoping we'd enjoy the show that evening. Inspired by this brief encounter, I thought about sending him a book

Meet
Marc
Almond

The singer from Soft Cell that brought you "Tainted Love."

at

Tower Records/Video
2280 Market Street (at Noe)

Saturday, November 13
at 3pm

4.2 "Meet Marc Almond" flyer, 1999.

4.3 With Marc Almond in San Francisco, 1999. Courtesy of the author.

that he might enjoy. But recalling that he, too, was a fan of John Rechy, I doubted there was anything in my library that he didn't already own.

Meeting Marc Almond reminded me of my first in-person encounter with him, and also Diana. Indeed, Diana's repeated touches with Almond, whom I was also lucky to touch at the 1989 concert and now at the book signing in 1999, made me realize just how significant that first concert was but also its residual resonance for me as someone who derives great pleasure and inspiration from cities like Los Angeles, London, New York, Glasgow, San Francisco, and (especially) Chicago, particularly the queer nightlife cultures within them. In short, my deep affection for Almond's work does not hinge on a nostalgic pining for my teenage years ("I give up looking for my past"), a longing for the way things once were, but rather illustrative of an enduring connection to those whose indelible importance still holds.

Before parting ways, I shook hands with Almond who, after my great trepidation about asking him for one, agreed to a photograph (fig. 4.3), thus adding yet another dimension to how I've been touched—this time through visible association—by the singer and writer Jeremy Reed (1995) has called "the last star." In *City of Night*, Rechy writes, "That world, being a world of fleeting contacts, has a great attachment to photographs, as if to lend some permanence to what is usually all too impermanent" ([1963] 2013, 301). Almond's work—not unlike the function performed by those photographs—signals a lament for the seedy days of Soho and New York City and the sexual cultures that were economically, racially, and sexually mixed. And while the gentrification of global cities like New York has eradicated the presence of these sexual cultures (a point powerfully made in Samuel Delaney's [1999] *Times Square Red, Times Square Blue*), "the impermanence of a world of fleeting contacts" is—as through a photograph—rendered visible in songs and poems by artists like Almond. And although the encounters recollected in this chapter on Almond's work may hardly be unblemished, such flaws are irrefutably part and parcel of all lives and loves—tainted and otherwise. Indeed, all moments of encounter, every juncture of contact, and each opportunity to touch involves the collision of what we've previously been taught and what we come to know about one another in the messiness of our desires. How else to glean the fortuitous ability to generate history relayed from the vantage of a chance meeting, the opportunity to fulfill the need—just like Johnny Rio—to desire and be desired?

Five

ZOOT SUITS AND SECONDHAND KNOWLEDGE

> All the guys had wide ties / and dancing was an art.
>
> **Blue Rondo a la Turk, "Me and Mr. Sanchez"**

Growing up, I always imagined myself following in my mother's footsteps by working at a department store. The appeal of taking on such a job had much to do with the studied working-class stylishness she and her friends fashioned as employees at the Broadway, demonstrating an unfailing effort to always look good despite earning wages that were indeed minimal. Glimpsing her coworkers in the men's clothing section, I particularly fancied the idea of sporting a suit on the continuum extending from the working day to the leisurely evening, togged up and poised to hit the town after punching out on those often-extolled Friday or Saturday nights popularized in the music and cinema of my preteen years. The soundtrack for *Saturday Night Fever* (1977), Robert Klane's film *Thank God It's Friday* (1978), and Bell and James's 1979 single "Livin' It Up (Friday Night)" quickly come to mind.

Unlike those peers with whom I shared overlapping musical tastes but who elected to dress in, say, *Miami Vice*–inspired threads or all-black clothing, my particular choice of attire consisted of an assortment of patterned ties and solid dress shirts acquired from discount clothing stores like Mervyn's along with the one suit I owned. Handed down from my father and first worn for my Catholic Church confirmation ceremony, this black suit tailored for broad shoulders and whose name brand escapes me was sported at least twice a week. Reminding me of my father given its combined aroma of sweat and cologne that saturated the fabric's fibers, the suit never failed to provoke teachers and peers to ask why I was dressed up on a regular school day. Upon reflection, while my adopted style did not align me with the deathrock, punk, or head banger/heavy metal fashions on display at this Santa Ana public high school, it nonetheless registered a corresponding break from that temporal moment's standardization of young men's clothing that, in the context of Southern California, took the form of Quicksilver and Town and Country surfer T-shirts and beach-ready shorts. More than standing apart from my male classmates, I understood my suit-inclined fashion sense as taking cue from and—at least in my mind—approximating the observed panache flaunted by many of the British musicians I followed: Bryan Ferry, Japan, Bauhaus, Heaven 17, Ultravox, Duran Duran, Spandau Ballet, and Annie Lennox.

Although temporarily holding jobs that easily might have led in that direction, chance would have it that working retail did not figure into a longstanding career trajectory. Due in large part to a white lesbian high school guidance counselor who gleaned and championed my academic potential, I went on to attend a university four hundred miles from home to study English literature, the one subject in which I excelled and might conceivably secure a degree. The decision to study literature (particularly but not exclusively Mexican American literature) was in no small part due to two aunts who early on passed down unreturned library copies of books like Richard Vasquez's *Chicano* (1970), Edmund (Victor) Villaseñor's *Macho!* (1973), and Thomas Sanchez's *Zoot Suit Murders* (1978), and to the recently encountered professors who stood as learned exemplars enthusiastically encouraging me to pursue an advanced degree. One of these professors was the noted Chicana feminist theorist and literary studies scholar Norma Alarcón. Agreeing to serve as my advisor for a summer research program, Professor Alarcón had me search for articles and related materials on the zoot suit, and the Mexican American *pachucos* and *pachucas* who wore them, for a project she began devising. I was thrilled about this research topic, for not only did it allow me to connect to the culture of which my grandparents were a part in 1940s Southern California, but it also enabled me to investigate a style politics that, albeit in a different context, evoked my own early fashion preference. Indeed, the embrace of the suit by an earlier generation of Mexican Americans held surplus resonance, unquestionably due to the race and class dynamics charging and intertwining our singular yet genealogically tied fashion sensibilities, of which I became increasingly aware during my moment of awakening political consciousness.

As this was 1990, there were scant scholarly sources about the zoot suit. Before the plethora of books that would appear a little over a decade later, one particular article on the history and politics of the zoot suit stood as central: Stuart Cosgrove's "The Zoot Suit and Style Warfare." Originally published in a 1984 issue of the *History Workshop Journal*, my introduction to Cosgrove's piece came as the opening essay in Angela McRobbie's 1988 edited collection *Zoot Suits and Second-Hand Dresses: An Anthology of Fashion and Music*. Although at the time I had not been introduced by name to what I'd soon understand as British cultural studies, it was this simultaneous encounter with the work of Cosgrove and McRobbie that would connect my early scholarly interests in Chicano/a studies with my graduate school training in cultural studies to this current project.[1] And after all, each moment of academic inquiry noted here exemplifies a substantial link between US Latina/o and British popular and expressive cultures.

Years later, while teaching abroad in Scotland, a chance meeting with Cosgrove in Glasgow would, based on his recommendation, prompt consideration of Blue Rondo a la Turk for this book. Thanks to Cosgrove, my vague familiarity with the band was supplanted with freshly discerned realization. Intimately connected to the New Romantic scene rooted in London nightspots such as Billy's and Blitz (of which icons like Boy George, Steve Strange, Rusty Egan, and the members of Spandau Ballet were a part), Blue Rondo contrasted with their peers given both the Latin sound and the band members' adornment of zoot suits, for which they were known. Cosgrove proposed that I speak with the group's founding members, Chris Sullivan and Christos Tolera, since I'd soon be in London. Quickly responding to my message sent on Facebook, Tolera generously agreed to connect with me. Knowing I would connect with him, I brought along my copy of *Zoot Suits and Second-Hand Dresses* to revisit Cosgrove's foundational essay. Flipping through the book after spending an afternoon with Cosgrove, I soon found myself rereading McRobbie's essay, "Second-Hand Dresses and the Role of the Ragmarket" (which follows Cosgrove's) and Jon Savage's "The Age of Plunder" (originally published in the magazine the *Face*), where he harshly appraises Blue Rondo a la Turk. Living up to his name, Savage upbraids Sullivan and the band for ripping off cubist art on their record covers and ultimately bestows a sanctimonious take on Blue Rondo (as well as Bauhaus) for mining artistic traditions, bastardizing them, and ultimately promoting what he views as a hollowing out of history. McRobbie's essay, however, offers an alternative take on such aesthetic practices that, under the sign "second-hand," allows us to understand that "while pastiche and some kind of fleeting nostalgia might indeed play a role in second-hand style, these have to be seen more precisely within the evolution of post-war youth cultures" (1988, 48).

Thus, reading secondhand as an aesthetic practice animated by historical consciousness and not simply complacent with hegemonic incorporation, I understand Blue Rondo's admiration for and adoption of the zoot suit and Latin music as derived from a secondhand knowledge of these expressive forms, in turn serving as a catalyst to breathe new life into a contemporaneous cultural moment. In this regard, my own youthful adoption of the suit similarly signaled a secondhand status given not only how the garment was passed down from my father but also how it indexed the knowledge of a style displayed by those British musicians on whom I based my presentation. While *secondhand knowledge* conventionally denotes inaccurate or inauthentic information, I repurpose the term—as one might do with vintage clothing—to consider how stylistic sensibilities are remade and remodeled across an array of temporal and spatial moments, borrowing elements of an aesthetic as a way of honoring it anew.[2] In this fashion, the title of the chapter seizes upon the cultivation of secondhand knowledge—not unlike the "second-hand" in McRobbie's essay and the title of her book—which borrows from the cultural practices of the past to shape those in the present. The ambitions behind the creation of secondhand knowledge may raise concern over authenticity and overall symbolic intention (akin to Savage's critique); however, I illustrate how this knowledge manifests as a citational practice informed by social and historical discernment and not merely cultural appropriation. This view recognizes the horizontal affiliations between transnational working-class, migrant, and racialized groups that, on the surface, may not appear to have much in common but on a deeper level stand commonly galvanized by style as a means of self-expression and collective unanimity.

So, who were Blue Rondo a la Turk (fig. 5.1), and what role did they play in early 1980s British post-punk culture? In this chapter I explain how the band emerged during the famed New Romantic moment as a studied project of self-stylization influenced by an amalgamation of factors that ranged from working-class sensibility to American urban history. The central goal at hand, however, is to illuminate how both the zoot suit and the fusion of musical currents feeding into the classification "Latin music" operate as the twin currents charging Blue Rondo's linkage to a US-based Latinidad.

5.1 Blue Rondo a la Turk, 1981. Photo by Graham Smith. Courtesy of Graham Smith.

The ensemble, I maintain, demonstrates how Latino expressive forms and practices intimately touched British popular culture at a moment now distinguished for its post-punk excess and extravagance. And while a loosely contoured New Romantic movement bridged the nightclubs of London and the hot spots of Los Angeles, we can also point to a resurgent adoption of the zoot suit that linked working-class British and Mexican American communities.

A MORE SUITABLE STYLE

Blue Rondo a la Turk took flight from the late 1970s/early 1980s New Romantic scene that gave rise to prominent artists, fashion designers, and music acts including Visage, Spandau Ballet, and Duran Duran.[3] Following on the heels of punk, the New Romantics—also known as the Blitz Kids based on their association with the Blitz nightclub—were youths bonded together in their desire for nocturnal escape from routinized day jobs, hitting the streets of London and Birmingham adorned in "extravagant costumes" and congregating at spots such as the Blitz in Covent Garden and Billy's in Soho. According to a 1981 BBC television news report, "If punk was all about rebellion, the New Romantics are all about style." While style for the New Romantics was indeed fueled by rebellion, the report insisted that their claim to style alternatively served, in added contrast to the media-perceived punk promotion of anarchy, as a "positive reaction to a difficult world."[4] In the liner notes to the 2014 CD rerelease of the band's 1982 debut album *Chewing the Fat*, Blue Rondo's founder and chief mastermind Chris Sullivan explains:

> Blue Rondo a la Turk arose out of necessity. I'd sensed that a big chunk of people like myself, who frequented clubs like Billy's and The Blitz, had little truck with either the term or the reality of the so-called New Romantic movement. Most of us had cut our teeth in the Northern and Southern soul clubs of the seventies whilst dressed in peg trousers, plastic sandals and Hawaiian shirts. We'd subsequently graduated to punk while still frequenting dance clubs such as Crackers, where we danced to imported funk by the likes of The Fatback Band, James Brown, Gil Scott Heron and War whilst wearing clothing from Vivienne Westwood's and Malcolm McLaren's shop, Sex.

Like their peers who similarly adorned the signature punk styles purchased at Sex, Sullivan and his particular lot, however, stood apart from the rest by repurposing this highly sought-after gear for a decidedly updated and culturally distinct design, an endeavored reinterpretation for one's aesthetic preferences.[5] As he explains, "They called us 'funky punks!' In 1978/9, after punk was all washed up and funk had become the detestable jazz funk, many of us, owing to a mutual admiration for David Bowie and Roxy Music, ended up dressed in suits in clubs full of chaps with big hair" (C. Sullivan 2014a). Sullivan's account of Blue Rondo's emergence suitably touches on the twin features that pattern the ensemble's alignment with Latin style: the band's music (later discussed at length) and its fashion sense. In addition, Sullivan makes clear the difficulty of divorcing Blue Rondo from their punk forerunners. The designation "funky punks" thus references the band's DIY aesthetics and the group's refusal to play by the rules of proper decorum, all the while linking their sound to an array of musical contexts, not unlike how reggae served as an animating force for and punctuated the sound of the Sex Pistols, the Clash, and the Slits. And while the category *New Romantic* would prove just as contested as *punk* for those shaping and composing these scenes, it nonetheless serves as a category under which to catalog the array of stylistic expressions surfacing at this historical moment.[6]

Describing the scene at Billy's and the formation of the New Romantic movement as a post-punk phenomenon, Culture Club's Boy George insists that this emergent scene sharply contrasted with punk, which "had become a parody of itself, an anti-Establishment uniform, attracting hoards of dickheads who wanted to gob, punch, and stamp on flowers" (1995, 118). Lamenting the demise of "the energy and music of punk," George maintains that punk had once "scream[ed] at us to reject conformity but it had become a joke, right down to the £80 Anarchy T-shirts on sale at Seditionaries [Sex]. Punk was safe, we were spinning forward in a whirl of eyeliner and ruffles" (118).[7] Unlike the expensive off-the-rack punk uniform easily obtained at Sex/Seditionaries, the "ruffles," along with other New Romantic garments, were often repurposed secondhand clothes, many times unearthed at and purchased from charity shops. As Steve Strange notes, "The look was very androgynous, dripping with diamanté and laden down with eyeliner—not just smudges but works of art. And that was just the men! Well some of us. The clothes were amazing. I wore a lot of gear from PX where I was working, but most of the crowd pulled outfits together from Oxfam shops using initiative and cheek and sheer resourcefulness" (Smith 2011, 10).

Although the suit—including the zoot suit—was evident alongside the frilly shirts and other androgynous designs "dripping with diamanté" in photographic and film footage of the scene's early days, its symbolic currency not only persisted but was further charged with added value once the New Romantic scene waned. In his book *New Romantics: The Look,* Dave Rimmer tracks Chris Sullivan's movement from the distinctly New Romantic spots like Blitz, Hell, and Le Kilt to the formation of the WAG on Wardour Street. Rimmer explains that part of this movement entailed a notable shift in style, particularly when the predominant frills look commonly associated with the scene attained mainstream absorption. As he makes clear, "just as the rest of the country was beginning to pick up on the frilly shirt look, the London boys were ditching it for good. The new fashion was suits" (Rimmer 2003, 117).[8]

Arguing that this new fashion was a claim stake for heterosexuality by drawing support from Spandau Ballet's lead singer Tony Hadley (asserting that "the Blitz scene wasn't a load of pretty, effeminate things posing and talking about art and literature. Bullocks to that! Blitz was lads getting completely out of their heads and trying to pull girls. We just happened to dress differently from the people at the normal disco" [2003, 119]), Rimmer insists the embrace of the suit was also facilitated by Sullivan's insistence on warranted recognition as the entirety of attention seemed to fall on the likes of Boy George and Steve Strange. Rimmer explains, "Sullivan decided it was time to go over the top too. Now a fashion student at St. Martins, he began designing suits. Not ordinary suits. Not straight suits like Kraftwerk or cool suits like Antony Price designed for Bryan Ferry. But huge checked suits, 'like tailored versions of clown suits.' These and later designs were made up by East End bespoke tailor Bob Browning and worn with hand-painted ties and moustaches by the likes of Christos Tolera, Ollie O'Donnell and Sullivan himself" (2003, 119). Sullivan affirms the commentary by both Rimmer and Hadley, remarking in Dylan Jones's *Sweet Dreams: The Story of the New Romantics*, "With Blue Rondo, I very much wanted to do something different. I was fed up of people wandering around with make-up and big shoulder pads and frills, fed up of electro music. I wanted to do something with men with big moustaches, in suits, without a synthesizer in sight. I wanted to do something that represented the heterosexual side of the scene. It was also turning back the clock" (2020, 345).

Despite its denotation here as a sign of heterosexuality, the suit was not entirely at odds with the scene's queer element—represented both by the nonheterosexual participants themselves and their correlated spangled aesthetic preferences—from which Sullivan aimed to establish distance. Indeed, rather than seeing "frills" and "the suit" necessarily at odds with one another, I favor highlighting their coexistence and shared ability to defy categorization—a queer force energized by their circumstantial touch—contingent upon sexual or gender identity. Thus, one might observe how Steve Strange, a self-identified bisexual man and long-standing friend and fellow Welsh compatriot of Sullivan's, is frequently captured in photographs and videos of the moment draped in frills as well as sporting suits.[9] Or consider the cover of the 1982 single "The Damned Don't Cry" by Visage, the musical collective fronted by Strange, that captures a group of suit-clad women and thus feasibly nodding to those women patrons of the lesbian nightclub Louise's taken over by punks and, subsequently, New Romantics.[10]

More than placing a bid for nonheterosexual inclusion to accurately account for who adorned the suit at this particular juncture, however, I propose consideration of the zoot suit's historically queer status given the garment's long-standing ability to buck normative gender codes and temporal configurations. That is, while the zoot suit in the 1970s and '80s may indeed recall a fashion sense of the past (a "turning back of the clock"), it nonetheless gets read as "over the top" (as Rimmer puts it) and "different" (to use Sullivan's own fitting descriptor) in the present-day moment of its recuperation. And although the zoot suit may draw its signifying force from the past, its present-tense symbolic value inevitably indexes a secondhand knowledge that makes it incompatible with constraining principles regarding gender, authenticity, and ownership. In other words, not only may the suit be said to signify queerly based on how lesbian, gay, bisexual, or transgender participants in the New Romantic scene are consistently depicted as adorning it, but the suit itself, particularly the zoot suit, is best understood as existing outside the conventional fashion industry due to its characteristically adaptive secondhand disposition.

Exceeding adoption in terms that placated convention and facilitated establishmentarian acquiescence, the zoot suit in Sullivan and company's hands was fashioned through a divergent historical trajectory. As Dave Rimmer explains:

> Through Cab Calloway, they learned about the zoot suit, and the look began to move in an Afro-Cuban direction, referencing pre-rock rebellion via the southern Californian zoot suit riots of the early Forties. It was a new look but something else had snapped back into place. New Romantic had looked to the future in its music, to the past for its costumes. But the zoot suit and salsa mix was soon to be touted as the next big thing by a Sullivan looking to sell his band Blue Rondo a la Turk, had narrowed the frame of reference back into that of post-war subculture. (2003, 119)

I read Rimmer's reference to "post-war subculture" as an acknowledgment of both the zoot suit's late-1940s debut "in London's working-class districts, to the south to the east" (Breward 2016, 137) and the 1950s Teddy Boy culture which, when conjoined with "the southern Californian zoot suit riots" he mentions, establishes a historical genealogy of style that travels across the Atlantic and subsequently gives shape to Blue Rondo a la Turk. Historian Kathy Peiss, in the chapter "Zooting around the World" from her book *Zoot Suit: The Enigmatic Career of an Extreme Style*, explains how "the zoot suit arrived in England worn by African American and West Indian seamen on supply ships that docked at British ports. . . . The extreme American style made a vivid impression on some: 'Zoot suits are all reet, old chap,' wrote the black activist and intellectual George Padmore, who served as a war correspondent from London for African American newspapers in 1943. The American look particularly attracted young working-class men, although military mobilizations and rationing made it tricky for them to adopt the style until after the war" (2011, 166–67).[11]

My utilization of *queer* for discussing the zoot suit in this chapter stands in solidarity with Peiss's deployment of the word *extreme* to mark its renegade vestiture, particularly in its contested relationship with state-sanctioned institutions like the military. Indeed, a queer perspective similarly prompts consideration of the zoot suit as an extreme style while further conveying its secondhand significance in pertaining to the perpetual repurposing of the zoot suit in divergent social contexts across a number of temporal divides. Consider the lesbian communities of 1940s Buffalo, New York (as documented by historians Elizabeth Kennedy and Madeline Davis and discussed by Peiss), as well as the working-class British youths affiliated with the early 1980s New Romantic scene. Thus, when Rimmer (2003) writes that "the zoot suit and salsa mix was soon to be touted as the next big thing by a Sullivan looking to sell his band Blue Rondo a la Turk," the scrambling of the past, present, and future—not unlike my youthful aesthetics described earlier—enables concentrated consideration of the queer chronologies of the zoot suit and Latin music.

Offering a detailed genealogy of the zoot suit in Britain since the 1940s, Steve Chibnall's (1985) "Whistle and Zoot: The Changing Meaning of a Suit of Clothes" builds from Stuart Cosgrove's earlier-cited essay published a year before in the same journal. Like Cosgrove, Chibnall cites the adoption of the zoot suit by American singer August Darnell from Kid Creole and the Coconuts, but also spotlights its impact on the New Romantic scene by way of Chris Sullivan and Blue Rondo a la Turk. Citing Sullivan, who explains that "the zoots were the first time that working class youth had rebelled against their peers in a stylistic way" (Chibnall 1985, 77), Chibnall also notes how the zoot suit's 1980s revival bridged working-class style with an upwardly mobile fashion sense that was part and parcel of the New Romantic aesthetic. As he points out, the "zoot suit had never been seen on so many magazine covers," thanks to "the roles of art colleges and popular music in forming a bridge between creative members of the working class and the traditional enclaves of high society" (77–78). Yet many at the moment of its reemergence noted how the zoot suit offered a contrast with fashion easily incorporated into the mainstream (including the "proper" suit) given its secondhand status. John Duka, writing in 1981 for the *New York Times*, explains:

> The more threadbare the English economy becomes, the more fashionable everyone in London looks. A good place to see fashion ideas is King's Road, once again the center of a youthful fashion boom, where, it seems, one can

> find more tattoos and pierced ears and noses per square foot than in any other place on earth. For many, the New Romantics trend of six months ago, the Pirate look, has become passé. Now the most fashionable young people, those who listen to the music of Spandau Ballet and Steve Strange, say the trend is yet another revival, the zoot suits of the World War II years, and listening to Blue Rondo A La Turk. (1981, B12)

A year earlier, the London-based newspaper the *Evening Standard* similarly observed the zoot suit's secondhand status while further noting its gender-defying dimensions in the article's title alone: "Dandies in Hand-Me-Downs" (Smith 1980). As Monica L. Miller astutely reasons in *Slaves to Fashion: Black Dandyism and the Styling of Black Diasporic Identity*, "In that dandies of any color disrupt and destabilize conceptions of masculinity and heterosexuality, they are queer subjects who deconstruct limiting binaries in the service of transforming how one conceives of identity formation" (2009, 11). Moreover, Catherine S. Ramírez, in her foundational study of the gendered politics of the zoot suit, observes that in 1940s Los Angeles, Mexican American zoot suiters were chastised as "gamin dandies," "pathologized as effeminate precisely because they, like women, participated in consumer culture, which historically has been gendered feminine" (2009, 73).

Just as claiming the zoot suit to assert entitlement of heterosexuality proves complicated when we consider its queer histories, dislodging it from its secondhand, working-class contexts is also an unwarranted endeavor. That is, the repurposed value of the zoot suit's countercultural force may receive ample attention in publications like the *Face*, but its extreme or queer dimensions have restrained its wholesale entrance into the mainstream fashion industry. Indeed, the British youths in early 1980s London were not unlike those Mexican American youths in the United States during the 1970s and '80s who likewise embraced the zoot suit to establish its subcultural value for an emergent Chicano politics affirming a historically criminalized style taken up in previous generations by their parents and grandparents.[12] This is evident in the pages of *Lowrider Magazine*, the San José, California–based periodical that not only showcased car cultures (to which John Lydon was drawn upon his relocation to Southern California, as noted in the introduction) but also working-class Mexican American culture. Indeed, by looking at British and American print culture of the 1980s, one clearly identifies the overlapping ways youths on both sides of the Atlantic were similarly drawing from a decades-earlier shared sense of style derived from secondhand knowledge.

It makes fashion sense that Blue Rondo a la Turk did not approximate the commercial success achieved by contemporaries such as Spandau Ballet, Duran Duran, or even Modern Romance (to whom I return later).[13] Rather than tapping into a New Romantic style that led to class mobility (extending from diamanté to the "proper" Antony Price suit), the stylistic and musical forms that defined Blue Rondo a la Turk aligned the group with working-class and racialized youths whose distinct cultural expressions undoubtedly contrasted with those dressing the part to gain admission to the millionaires' ball.[14] In the words of Christos Tolera:

> I was wearing a pink zoot suit and talking in a cockney accent—a working class expression of flash. We were about style and we got slagged off in all the middle class press. We were working class blokes walking round in suits, and by that time punk was about middle class blokes going around in torn-up clothes. Bob the Tailor in the East End made our suits. He used to be in the merchant navy and had tattoos, a real cockney bloke. He knew how to cut a suit in the American way and understood our desire for extreme cutting and tailoring, long jackets and really high trousers, without making it look ridiculous. (Beckman 2005, 99)

Robin Katz's write-up on the band in the November 26–December 9, 1981, issue of *Smash Hits* affirms Tolera's assessment: "Blue Rondo A La Turk haven't just returned from a trip to High and Mighty (the shop that caters for the *generously* proportioned man) but are modelling the latest in hip haberdashery. They're known as zoot suits and were originally the kind of gear that your grandad would wear in the 1940s" (Katz 1981, 14). And although the zoot suit, as Kathy Peiss notes above, had indeed been taken up by working-class British youths in the 1940s, the infamous Teddy Boy subculture that would emerge during the succeeding decade similarly incorporated it as part of its devised style.[15] (One might also argue that Teddy Boy style, rooted in a hypercartoonish masculinity, sets the stage for Blue Rondo's secondhand revitalization in a very punk way.) Yet Chris Sullivan's own detailed accounts—from his 1981 article "The Zoot Suit: A Historical Perspective" in the *Face* to a contribution to the men's fashion magazine *Jocks and Nerds* thirty-three years later titled "Zoot Suit" (2014b)—make explicit the stakes of Blue Rondo's fashion and music sensibilities articulated from a British trajectory that nodded to and transformed American and, more to the point here, global US Latino and Latin American cultures.[16]

SOUNDING LATIN

Since the band's initial emergence, several features spotlighting Blue Rondo a la Turk in the British press noted their adopted Latin aesthetic in terms of fashion and music. A more thorough exposé, however, more often than not revealed the amalgamation of diverse influences contouring this vibrant ensemble. Take, for example, the early, one-page feature by Robert Elms in the May 1981 issue of the *Face* familiarizing its readers with these "Young Turks" poised to take the world by storm. The introduction begins:

> Blue Rondo a la Turk is a classic Dave Brubeck number. Blue Rondo a la Turk is also now a group of North London musicians who play a perverse mix of jazz, Latin, African and funk, with a heavy emphasis on '50s mythology and '80s method. Blue Rondo is manic congas, zoot suits, searing sax and beat berets; "Philly Rolf," "Ay Ay Merengue," "Dial D 1113," and "The Method." In their first group photo they are (l to r) Chris Sullivan, Jimmy O'Donnell, Kristos, Chocko Mick, Moses (rear), and Mark. Blue Rondo a la Turk is a name to know; pretty soon they'll be a band to see. Look out for May Day. (Elms 1981b, 7)

Although forenames are misspelled (Kristos rather than Christos) and last names are excluded (such as Mark Riley's), the text by Elms and the accompanying "first group photo" by Graham Smith simultaneously detail the multiethnic and sophisticatedly orchestrated band which the *Face* and other publications like *Record Mirror, Melody Maker, New Musical Express, Smash Hits,* and *Noise!* would go on to promote in cover-page spreads and extensive write-ups. One particular magazine, however, affirmatively sang the praises of Blue Rondo while situating the band in the context of an emergent Latin culture circulating in early 1980s Britain. This publication was *New Sounds New Styles.*

First published as a pilot issue in March 1981 (with issue no. 1 appearing in July later that year), *New Sounds New Styles* arrived on UK newsstands for the express purpose of covering the burgeoning New Romantic scene, focusing in detail on the music, nightclubs, fashion, and people associated with it. The brainchild of Kasper de Graaf, production editor of *Smash Hits, New Sounds New Styles* lasted thirteen issues and included features and information largely absent from the magazines with which it shared occasional resemblance (namely *i-D*, the *Face, Blitz,* and *Smash Hits*).[17] The cover of the August 1981 issue (fig. 5.2)—featuring Andy Polaris, lead singer of the band Animal Nightlife, and Holli Hallett, artist and Chris Sullivan's significant

5.2 *New Sounds New Styles* (August 1981). Photo of Andy Polaris and Holli Hallett by Brian Griffin. Coutesy of Brian Griffin.

other at the time—underscores a "Latin" movement, as the second page of the magazine notes, "stoking up the dance floors of Britain." Presenting Polaris decked out in a stylish beige suit with wide tie and Hallett donning a red and black flamenco dress (no doubt using a Spanish cultural signifier desiring to signify "Latin") with head cocked back and tambourine in hand, above Polaris's soprano sax floats the issue's theme heralded in red lettering: "The Rhythm of the Latin Groove." In sync with spotlighting the new sounds and styles of the moment, this particular issue of the magazine pointedly demonstrates keen familiarity with a transnational Latinidad while magnifying its unmistakably deep connectedness to the New Romantic milieu. Three distinct yet thematically interconnected and respectively clustered articles sustain the issue's Latin theme: Geoff Brown's "Shake to the Rhythm of the Latin Groove," Robert Elms and Laura Abbot's "The Look That Suits," and David Johnson's feature on Blue Rondo titled "I Thought I Was Geronimo." The sequencing of these articles ultimately serves to frame Blue Rondo, who follow on the heels of a brief history of Latin music and an appraisal of the zoot suit's contemporary aesthetic currency.

Brown's feature comprehensively traces the roots of Latin sound as extending from various points on the globe (including Africa and the Caribbean), ultimately reaching into and flourishing from the United States. Citing artists as diverse as Tito Puente, Cal Tjader, Sergio Mendes, El Chicano, Santana, Gilberto Gil, Kid Creole and the Coconuts, Joe Cuba, Ray Barretto, Eddie Palmieri, Willie Colón, and Malo, Brown ultimately centers his investigation on the US, "with its large Latin population," to cast attention on how "the music had influenced pop and rock with ever increasing success through the sixties" even though "jazz had incorporated Latin instrumentation and rhythms since the forties" (Brown 1981, 7).[18] John Storm Roberts, in his book *The Latin Tinge: The Impact of Latin American Music on the United States*, echoes Brown in certain respects yet extends his categorical and genealogical assessment of Latin music: "Over the past century, Latin music has been the greatest outside influence on the popular music styles of the United States, and by a very wide margin indeed. Virtually all of the major popular forms—Tin Pan Alley, stage and film music, jazz, rhythm-and-blues, country music, rock—have been affected throughout their development by the idioms of Brazil, Cuba, or Mexico" (Roberts [1979] 1999, ix). Yet despite this rich confluence of musical genres and styles to exemplify how "the whole rhythmic base of U.S. popular music has become to some extent Latinized" (ix), the "very success of Latin idioms at the mass level," Roberts insists, "guaranteed their downgrading by critics and commentators confused by irrelevant criteria of 'serious' and 'popular' music" (1999, x).

Indeed, as Brown documents the history of Latin music touching British culture, such contact, we're told, has materialized in dubious fashion. He writes, "In Britain, Latin was long regarded as a novelty, an excuse to form a conga line at the end of every drunken revel. Hit records only came in the form of bizarre left-field accidents." Additionally,

> Paraguayan music had an unexpected vogue though Y Los Trios Paraguayos and other Latin groups such as Les Chakachas and Los Muchucambos were moderately popular. The more commercial US hits (e.g., The Champs' "Tequila") reached the Top Five in Britain, but on gimmickry alone. For those were the days when Latin in Britain meant Edmundo Ros on the radio, taking anything from "La Cucaracha" to "The White Ciffs of Dover" and arranging it as a rhumba. The nearest most people came to seeing a Latin band was a two-minute TV scene of Desi Arnaz's orchestra in *I Love Lucy*, or a film clip of Carmen Miranda parading her fruitbasket headpiece. (1981, 9)

Further examples to the ones Brown offers abound, such as Pérez Prado's "Cherry Pink (and Apple Blossom White)," a secondhand English rendition of the French song "Cerisiers Roses et Pommiers Blancs," which reached the number one spot on the UK music chart in 1955.[19] Yet Brown's point about Latin as novelty is amplified by Ed Morales when he writes, "Latin music, like Latin American culture, comes across as exotic to North American and European listeners, with its vaguely 'hot' rhythms and emotional vocalists. While for Latinos our music constitutes an essential part of our identity, it appeals to non-Latinos because of its wild complexity and expressive possibilities" (2003, xi). That Latin music had begun to "filter through into British rock and pop," and not simply stand as some random cultural aberration, counteracted heretofore simplistic engagements and exoticizing tendencies.

The flourishing of this distinct sound—particularly the generation of Latin music within the context of "British rock and pop"—runs parallel with London's changing demographic attributable to the diverse ethnic migrations that the members of the band reflected. And such ethnic migrations were as spliced as Latin music's roots. As Johnson's piece notes, "Blue Rondo represents a pocket delegation from the United Nations: there are two Brazilians, a Barbadian, a Greek, an Irish-Jamaican, a Scot and their Welsh leader" (1981, 13). A few months later, *Smash Hits* similarly noted Blue

Rondo's multicultural composition, identifying the band as "a new seven piece who wish to be known as Britain's tastiest Brazilian nuts. In fact, only two of these snappy dressers are true coffee-flavoured Brazilians, the rest of the band hailing from Barbados, Greece, Wales and England" (Katz 1981, 14).[20] These two Brazilians in Blue Rondo were Geraldo D'Arbilly and Kito Poncioni. Soon after placing an ad in *Melody Maker*—"Brazilian drummer seeks work"—D'Arbilly was understandably invited to join the band, bringing along "his huge kit and a collection of exotic percussion that took half an hour to set up" (Elms 1981a, 11). It was this new drummer who would further accentuate Blue Rondo's Latin sound, aiding in replacing the previous bassist Jimmy, who "wasn't keeping up with the frantic Latinisation of the sound that occurred as soon as Geraldo arrived," with "a friend called Kito who was 'the best Latin bass player in England'" (11). For D'Arbilly, the arrival of Blue Rondo a la Turk helped showcase an emergent Latin American demographic and musical presence in London, exemplified by their debut single's B-side titled "Sarava," a track that would also appear on their first LP, *Chewing the Fat* (1982).[21] As he explains, "Sarava" (Portuguese for "good luck") is the first *baião*—an African-influenced northeastern Brazilian rhythm—"ever recorded in Britain. I am showing my culture to lots of new people, and it makes me feel very proud" (12).[22]

The single's A-side, "Me and Mr. Sanchez," however, was tagged as the track primed to jump-start the band's predicted, hard-earned mainstream success. As Chris Sullivan (2014a) explains, "In December 1981 ['Me and Mr. Sanchez'] became the most played single on radio one along with 'Under Pressure' by David Bowie and Freddie Mercury, which was no mean feat. The release therefore raced up the charts, while we appeared on the covers of a gaggle of national publications such as *Sounds*, NME, *Melody Maker* and *The Face*. Meanwhile the likes of *Paris Match*, *L'Uomo Vogue*, and both the *LA* [*Times*] and *New York Times* gave us expansive spreads that accused us of starting a global zoot suit/vintage clothing trend." But given that an appearance on *Top of the Pops* almost guaranteed chart escalation, Blue Rondo—who had been at number forty with "Me and Mr. Sanchez" for two consecutive weeks—never made it onto the show and instead saw their well-touted single take a downward tumble. Tolera recounts, "We were told that as long as we didn't go down a place the following week, we were guaranteed a spot and realistically that would have guaranteed a top twenty hit. Who knows what would've happened, but after dropping two places, the radio plays stopped as they only played records on the up and we were left to chase our own tails a little and pressured to produce a hit" (C. Sullivan 2014a).[23]

Yet prior to the release of "Me and Mr. Sanchez," a band carefully studying Blue Rondo's sound and image would emerge from the wings, turning out two singles that would race to the top of the charts. This band, Modern Romance (formerly and fittingly known as the Leyton Buzzards), was known for altering its image and musical identity accordingly to topical trends. Their singles, "Everybody Salsa" and "Ay Ay Ay Ay Moosey," both released in 1981 and prior to "Me and Mr. Sanchez," unambiguously usurped Blue Rondo by riding the Latin music bandwagon to, respectively, numbers twelve and ten.[24] Despite the proliferation of British-based Latin music at the moment (one might consider the Latin-funk group Arriva that invited noted singer and songwriter Sade [Adu] to audition for the role of lead singer, or Animal Magnet, with songs like "Sinister Latin" and "Amor," who provided opening act support for Duran Duran), Modern Romance would return the signifier "Latin" to what Geoff Brown above identifies as pure novelty.[25] As Christos Tolera states, "Modern Romance ripped off our style and stole our thunder with a very middle of the road pop single called 'Everybody Salsa,' which drunken people at weddings liked to dance to" (Smith 2011, 279). Modern Romance vocalist Geoff Deane did not dispute the charge of imitation. As he notes in a *Smash Hits* feature: "We veered off into a more disco area and it's come alright in the end. We didn't beat Spandau Ballet but we've thrashed Blue Rondo A La Turk" (Birch 1981, 41). While one could argue that this is simply a case of one British act ripping off another British act ripping off Latin music (which is precisely what Ian Birch does in his article "So This Is Romance?"), I refuse to overlook the secondhand knowledge that contours Blue Rondo's sound and image as opposed to Modern Romance's. That is, the steadfast grasp of the musical and fashion sensibilities by the former sharply distinguishes them from the latter, who regarded their adoption of Latin style as a trend to buck rather than a movement to acknowledge and derive influence.[26] Besides, Blue Rondo's mixed racial and ethnic intragroup intimacy was also inextricably bound up with the band's indelible commitment to historical citation.

As we may point to the contributions of Brazilian musicians and the band's admiration of Latin music to sustain their Latin sound, Blue Rondo's channeling of Mexican American culture and history, as reflected by "Me and Mr. Sanchez," helps amalgamate their sonic and visual aesthetics and thus facilitates a transatlantic touch. Written by Chris Sullivan, Kito Poncioni, and Mark Riley, the song begins with a whistle sounding an ensuing four-minute jubilee complete with frenetic percussion, resounding horns, and pulsating bass. The repeated chorus of "ay ay ay" no doubt traffics in a long-standing Latin music lyrical genealogy—arguably stemming from the classic "Cielito Lindo" (written by Mexican composer Quirino Mendoza y Cortés) to Selena ("Como la Flor"), and encompassing Spaniard-cum-"Latin lover" crooner Julio Iglesias's "Ay Ay Ay" to Modern Romance's Blue Rondo–inspired "Ay Ay Ay Ay Moosey." According to Chris Sullivan (2014b), the title refers to the 1978 novel *Zoot Suit Murders,* written by California writer Thomas Sanchez. As noted earlier, Sanchez's novel was one of the first Chicano-themed novels I read, encouraging my decision to major in English and focus on Chicana/o literature. Like Marc Almond, who drew inspiration from John Rechy, Sullivan and Blue Rondo nod to an American writer whose work initiates not only a focus on Mexican Americans but also a transatlantic and transnational Latinidad.

According to his webpage biography, Thomas Sanchez is "a descendant of Spanish immigrants and Portuguese cattlemen dating back four generations to the California Gold Rush." Additionally, he was "born in 1944 in Oakland, California days after his father was killed at the age of 21 in the Battle of Tarawa during World War II."[27] Yet Sanchez's status as a fifth-generation Californian of European descent who wrote a novel about Mexican Americans similarly influencing both a young Mexican American scholar and a Welsh musician who migrates to London and forms a Latin music–inspired band illustrates a cultural network that this book aims to highlight. Similar to resisting the customary impulse in wanting to make Thomas Sanchez a Chicano writer (like Floyd Salas, whose 1967 novel *Tattoo the Wicked Cross* is considered a classic of Chicano/a literature despite the author's Spanish background yet Colorado- and California-rooted genealogy), I suggest reading Blue Rondo's secondhand engagement with Chicano history and culture as charting a network of influence that defies rigid essentialisms and refuses the too-easy charge of cultural appropriation. In her book *The Making of Latin London: Salsa Music, Place and Identity,* Patria Román-Velázquez argues that the overreliance on "origins excludes those who also contribute to Latin American identities (such as a Scottish musician or English disc jockeys)" (1999, 24). Indeed, such an overreliance will always fall short in capturing the dynamic operations of history in the formation of both identities and musical cultures. As Sullivan maintains in Simon Tebbutt's 1982 *Record Mirror* article "Animal Caracas" on Blue Rondo: "Like Picasso said, the only way to work is to pick from the past, to mould things together to come up with the future. And that's what we're doing basically, picking on already known influences that haven't been used in this country and moulding them into something completely different" (20).

When I listen to the lyrics of "Me and Mr. Sanchez," I imagine either Chris Sullivan or Christos Tolera in conversation with Thomas Sanchez.

Me and Mr. Sanchez
Lounging on our bench
Hours ticking slowly
We haven't time to quench
Me and Mr. Sanchez
Just hunting for a drink
Carnival approaching
They think they're in the pink . . .
Carnival is coming
It's breaking up the schools

Anticipating an upcoming Brazilian Carnival, Sullivan and Tolera, who share vocals on the track, also share a bench with the California writer named in the track's title. Idling and finding themselves in good spirits and presumably good health ("They think they're in the pink"), the duo regards the ensuing festivities as holding potential for "breaking up the schools." In other words, Carnival here is imagined as the event with the temporal and spatial capacity to bring disparate histories and geographically dispersed people together, directly called forth by the whistle commencing the song. Among these people are the zoot suiters at the heart of Mr. Sanchez's novel.

We remember long ago
When folks were really smart
All the guys had wide ties
And dancing was an art
We remember long ago
When jazz was really new
Jiving at the High Hat
That was the thing to do

The promotional video for the song makes this clear, as Sullivan and Tolera take center stage adorned in zoot suits and recalling for me the classic dance scene from Luis Valdez's 1981 film *Zoot Suit*. Alongside the zoot suiters conjured in "Me and Mr. Sanchez" are those New Romantics with whom Blue Rondo are intimately connected.

Me and Mr. Sanchez
We come here every day

Ladies wearing minis
I guess they look OK
Me and Mr. Sanchez
Just taking in the air
Men wearing lipstick
I guess it's only fair

Transporting both "men wearing lipstick" and those (no matter what their gender, if any) wearing zoot suits (not to mention ladies wearing minis) to the site of Carnival, Blue Rondo a la Turk not only offers a way to ascertain the potential for queer touch and secondhand aesthetic alignment but also a transatlantic intimacy they share with "Mr. Sanchez" and the Mexican American zoot suiters in his novel. Arising outside the normative registers of time and space, the band signals an original post-punk intervention that stands as rebellious of the norms circumscribing their temporal moment as well as reflective of the shifting racial and ethnic cultural dynamics that transformed late twentieth-century British life and culture.

ME AND MR. TOLERA

Recounting the moment when Sullivan proposed a band of which he, too, would soon become a member, fellow front man and vocalist Christos Tolera explains the influences behind Blue Rondo's signature sound: "It would be all the things we liked musically and stylistically, and, although the attitude was very much born of the Punk DIY ethic, the music was firmly rooted in the pre-punk era and reflected our love of funk, soul, jazz and Latin. In our minds that afternoon we embraced our own mutant disco ethic" (cited in C. Sullivan 2014a). Tolera's contribution to the band, however, was significant not merely for the cultivation of Blue Rondo's musical identity but for its cultural character. As he explains, "My lack of musical ability was more than made up for by my ability to grow facial hair in the style of Chicano low riders and Hungarian wrestlers. Talk of zoot suits and wearing trousers too high and shoulders too big, made for an all-conquering master plan" (cited in C. Sullivan 2014a).

Just as Tolera mentions his ability to approximate Chicano lowrider style (along with playing a Hungarian wrestler), he was also recruited to play the Kid, a Latino boxer "from the wrong side of the tracks" in a 1982 photo story (or fotonovela) for issue fourteen of the magazine *Flexipop!*

5.3 *Melody Maker* (November 21, 1981). Photo of Christos Tolera by Janette Beckman. Courtesy of Janette Beckman.

Following the story line common in films like Kurt Neumann's *The Ring* (1952), "Kid Christos," written by *Flexipop!* cofounder and former *Record Mirror* writer Barry Cain, follows a young man seeking to escape the barrio by way of a successful boxing career to ensure what promoter Chris Sullivan sees as "a golden future in those powerful fists" (Cain 1982, 21).[28]

Tolera undeniably solidified Blue Rondo's cultivated Latin image with a figure best described as a fusion of secondhand knowledges that fused the Chicano *pachuco* and the classically contoured bohemian. In individual and group photos, he is unfailingly sleek and undeniably good-looking. Boy George confirms this in his autobiography: "Christos Tolera was wet-lipped, dark, and especially handsome, dressed in berets, smocky shirts, and leather jodhpurs. All the queens fancied him, and he was too nice for his own good. I always hoped I could bring him round. He was Greek, after all. [My friend] Linard and I used to jump on top of him and stick our hands down his trousers. He went mad but he still hung around with us" (1995, 127–28).[29] The correlating Latinidad of Blue Rondo's musical inclination and Christos Tolera's visual persona, though, is established on the November 21, 1981, cover of *Melody Maker* (fig. 5.3). On it, we glance Tolera, draped in a pink zoot suit, welcoming the reader to the pages of the newspaper where they may become acquainted with Blue Rondo a la Turk, given how above Tolera appears a headline announcing, "Meet Mr. Sanchez." Intending to introduce the reader to the single "Me and Mr. Sanchez," Tolera clearly stands in for "Mr. Sanchez," given his distinctive zoot-suited Latino look.

Almost thirty-seven years later, I would be fortunate to meet—thanks to Stuart Cosgrove—Christos Tolera. Agreeing to meet with me at Café Italia in the Soho district, Christos arrived by bus and instantly welcomed me to London with warmth and kindness. Sitting at a table outdoors on Frith Street, "Me and Mr. Sanchez" repeatedly played in my head but, at this moment, the song lyric befittingly translated to "Me and Mr. Tolera." As I began asking questions about Blue Rondo, the New Romantic scene, and his work as a painter, I couldn't help but call to mind the fact that I was sitting with a British singer from a Greek background previously in a band that adopted the zoot suit style that my grandparents adopted. And his steadfast sense of style and ability to draw attention, as when a member of Blue Rondo a la Turk, was clearly on display. During our conversation, Christos was repeatedly approached by random bystanders who recognized him, including a fashion photographer who asked if he could take his photo (to which he agreed).

As our meeting came to an end, Christos reached for his tote bag and pulled out a book he brought with him: Harold Hayes's 1982 edited collection *Jungle Fever/Jean-Paul Goude*, including essays and photographs by Goude. Christos flipped through the book until he arrived at the section focused on the French artist's attraction to Puerto Ricans in New York. Pointing to the reprinted first page of an op-ed titled "Spic Chic" written by Izzy Sanabria for the magazine *Latin NY*, Christos noted that the book's spotlight of Latino culture was resonant with Blue Rondo's.[30] At the time, however, I failed to ask him in what way, electing instead to write down the name of the book to remind me to track down a copy. I would later learn that in the op-ed, Sanabria, a Puerto Rican afficionado of Salsa music (to which *Latin NY* was mostly dedicated), interrogates the then-recent "Latin craze" that found outsiders venturing into Latino spaces to cavort with and absorb an attendant spicy way of being. But rather than castigating "outsiders" drawn to the allure of "Spic Chic," Sanabria distinguishes what he considers "Chic" from what he sees as "Spic Raunch," the latter exemplified by the photographs of Jean-Paul Goude (one of which is reproduced alongside Sanabria's editorial) as opposed to the distinctive sounds and styles that espouse a sense of "Latin Elegance."[31] Charging Goude and others with promoting "Spic Raunch," Sanabria nonetheless refuses to claim sole possession of "Spic Chic" or, as might be the case in another context, charge others with cultural appropriation. To be sure, he writes, "Let them all imitate us. It's the biggest compliment we can receive" (Sanabria 1977, 65). While imitation may very well be the sincerest form of flattery, Christos, Sullivan, and the other members of Blue Rondo a la Turk, however, aimed to do more than imitate. Instead, they served up evidence of how the migration of fashion and music, not unlike people, can generate some of the most profound connections, therefore making intimacy more momentous than imitation could ever be.

Six

MEXICAN AMERICANOS

I experienced my first family death on September 10, 1984. My maternal great-grandmother—Eulalia Matta Geck, born in Saragosa, Texas, on April 18, 1893—passed away in Santa Ana, California, due to a head injury incurred by slipping and falling in her bathtub. Kind with a wry sense of humor, I admired Great-Grandma's independence and enjoyed the time we spent together at her unforgettably cozy little house filled with knickknacks and photographs. Affectionately nicknaming me "Chinito," she was always quick to serve up a plentiful sum of hugs, kisses, and delectable treats whenever my sister and I would visit the house she shared with our great-uncle Pete, a veteran who would carefully scrutinize World War II movies aired on television to potentially locate himself in the battle scenes with which he was acutely familiar. Great-Grandma's passing shook the entire family, but I was personally devastated in a way I'll never forget. In this instance, the grief I felt joined forces with an unshakable despair designed by both adolescent alienation and the often forecasted and seemingly inevitable nuclear war prompted by world events of the day.

You save me from the worry and the strife.
Holly Johnson, "Love Train"

Familiar with the fact that music was increasingly central to my well-being and sustenance, and thinking that it might assist me in coping with our shared loss, Aunt Irene (who, as noted in the book's introduction, witnessed my first encounter with Boy George and caringly supplied me with a cassette of Culture Club's *Colour by Numbers*) scooped me up from my mother's house and whisked me away to my newfound place of solace: Music Plus on Bristol Street and Warner Avenue. "Pick any album you want," she told me. To her surprise, my "album" choice was a $3.99 twelve-inch single, namely Frankie Goes to Hollywood's recently US-released "Two Tribes." Having already owned the seven-inch single for "Relax," which—with its thumping bass, deliciously lewd electronics, and sexually suggestively lyrics—filled me with great pleasure, the resonance of "Two Tribes" was admittedly more profound at that moment. For while the Smiths had begun to offer me an assortment of gloom-ridden tracks for emotional consolation, unabashed electronic dance songs always seemed to take special precedence. Frankie's "Two Tribes" stood as exemplary.

The elegiac intro and opening sequence to, respectively, the song and the music video is what first pulled me into the gripping orchestrated dynamism of "Two Tribes." While the song materialized and circulated in the form of numerous versions and remixes, it was the "Carnage Mix" on the twelve-inch single I owned that closely matched the video narrative directed by accomplished musicians (as members of 10cc) Kevin Godley and Lol Creme. Sounding a call for a moment of silence—or rather a commanded stillness for reflection on one's experience of (subsequent) bereavement—the song's prefatory piano and strings overture, punctuated by crashing cymbals, successively incites an emotive response that is equally charged with personal and political reverberations. That is, the somber tenor initiating "Two Tribes," soon interrupted by a funky guitar-and-bass combination jostling with synths and percussion, compels the listener's movement—leaping to one's feet to desirously dance (as was my case) as a way to interrupt the staggering space of mourning for shifting into melancholic action.[1] In no small part, Holly Johnson's vocally declarative and learned tenor, laced with exasperation and ecstasy, draws the listener in, inviting them to absorb the pleasure amid destruction felt by a singer who gives to as much as he takes from the song's impassioned rhythm oscillating between carnage and carnality. On a more personal level, "Two Tribes" functioned as a theme song to which I could simultaneously work through my great-grandmother's death and embrace an awakening sense of self that had much to do with the political-sexual dynamism that Frankie represented.

In 1984 Britain, Frankie Goes to Hollywood arose as a phenomenon with both national and personal reverberations. Writing about the scandal of Frankie's first single, gay music journalist Richard Smith notes, "The ban spread like mould to all BBC radio and television stations. 'Relax' stayed at number one for five weeks. Not since the Sex Pistols' 'God Save the Queen' had a record so divided the nation. It wasn't gay against straight. It was young and sexy and naughty against old and prudish and 'nice.' And it felt great being fifteen and on the winning team" (1995, 183). Frankie made me feel the same way as a thirteen-year-old, given how they, as Smith puts it, "thrilled and helped lonely, little me in equal measure" (183). There was indeed something thrilling about the band's image. Discovering the unabashedly brash and queer front-and-center Frankie members Holly Johnson and Paul Rutherford made them a symbol of futurity that flew in the face of lament, stasis, and—perhaps ironically given the theme of "Two Tribes"—world destruction. Again, I identify with Smith when he writes, "You see somewhere between the pain of The Smiths, the politics of Bronski Beat and Frankie's sheer unadulterated pleasure I found myself. In 1984 neither me nor Frankie knew what was around the corner, that this would be the last gasp. But Frankie were the ones that made the future, my future, look exciting" (184).

Before my initial exposure to queer and Chicana/o (and queer Chicano/a) history and culture during my first year as an undergraduate at the University of California at Berkeley during late 1989, Frankie Goes to Hollywood's sonic and image repertoire and the solo efforts of lead singer Holly Johnson allowed me to make a connection between *queer* and *Chicano*. This chapter, then, illustrates how the conjoining of these supposed "two tribes" were mutually constitutive for a young Chicano gay man in California whose attachment to British popular music was as edifying as it was emboldening. For when it seemed like the chips were down—with either the large-looming Cold War promise of nuclear fallout or the adolescent feelings of stagnation and heartache seeping into the interiority of the psyche—the records on the turntable tendered a dual dose of dogged subsistence and bellicose determination.

WARRIORS OF THE WASTELAND

Frankie Goes to Hollywood's punk and post-punk roots run deep. Formed in Liverpool, the band—consisting of lead singer William "Holly" Johnson, vocalist Paul Rutherford, guitarist Brian Philip "Nasher" Nash, drummer/percussionist Peter "Pedro"/"Ped" Gill, and bassist Mark William James O'Toole—took root in 1980, although various members were engaged in the Liverpool music scene years earlier. In particular, Johnson and Rutherford were actively involved in the Merseyside music scene of the late 1970s that gave rise to notable acts like Echo and the Bunnymen, Orchestral Manoeuvres in the Dark (OMD), Dead or Alive, and the Teardrop Explodes with a now-historic association with the venue Eric's Club.[2] The bassist in the influential punk group Big in Japan (also featuring the soon-to-be Siouxsie and the Banshees and the Creatures drummer Budgie, and noted singer Jayne Casey), Johnson claimed the name "Holly" in honor of the Puerto Rican transgender Andy Warhol superstar Holly Woodlawn. After Big in Japan's demise, Johnson would embark on the first iteration of a solo career and release two singles: "Yankee Rose" (1979) and "Hobo Joe" (1980). Subsequently joining Gill, Nash, and Jed O'Toole (Nash's cousin and Mark O'Toole's brother) as a short-lived outfit named Sons of Egypt, Frankie Goes to Hollywood would arise from that band's ashes to unite Johnson, Gill, Nash, Mark O'Toole, and Paul Rutherford, the former singer of the Liverpool punk group the Spitfire Boys.[3]

With the band's name taken from a newspaper headline announcing Frank Sinatra's move to Los Angeles (the newspaper front page was showcased and spotted by Johnson in Guy Peellaert and Nik Cohn's 1973 book *Rock Dreams*), Frankie went on to record two sessions with legendary BBC Radio 1 DJ John Peel in 1982 and 1983, which included early versions of "Two Tribes," "Krisco Kisses," "The Power of Love," and "The World Is My Oyster," all of which would later appear on their 1984 debut album *Welcome to the Pleasuredome*.[4] The year of its release, I purchased this double LP on cassette at the Orange County Fairgrounds, where, as noted in chapter 2, I worked weekends to help finance new acquisitions for my flourishing music collection. Aside from the music, I was struck by the packaging of the album in a way similar to Bronski Beat's album *The Age of Consent*, also released that year.[5] For even in its cassette version, *Welcome to the Pleasuredome* visually exuded an unabashed homosexuality on a four-panel inlay sleeve that advertised "Jean Genet boxer shorts" (complete with a photo depicting a man's hand reaching inside these boxer shorts, modeled here by Paul Rutherford) and "Andre Gide socks." Frankie's queer sex appeal, evident at the band's commencement, was also a key part of their allure for John Peel. In his chronicle of Peel's profound influence on contemporary British popular music, David Cavanagh notes that upon first experiencing the band on stage—"fronted by a pair of flamboyant and overtly gay singers, Holly Johnson and Paul Rutherford" who "wore skimpy G-strings and bondage gear"—Peel "loved them" (2015, 337–38).

6.1 Frankie Goes to Hollywood (L–R, Nasher Nash, Paul Rutherford, Holly Johnson, Peter Gill, and Mark O'Toole). Photo by John Stoddart. Copyright © John Stoddart.

As much as Johnson's and Rutherford's punk origins indeed matched those of other music artists from working-class Britain during this historical moment, the fact that Frankie would be fronted by these two unapologetically out gay men rendered them singularly exceptional. Danny Jackson, in his book *Frankie Say: The Rise of Frankie Goes to Hollywood*, comments:

> No longer is it a question of working-class lads escaping the treadmill of apprenticeship/trade/retirement, but of getting off the Dole, Britain's unemployment benefit scheme. More than ever before the Stones' lyric seemed pertinent: "what *could* a poor boy do, 'cept to play in a rock and roll band?" It always seems inevitable in retrospect; that Lennon should have met McCartney, Jagger met Richards, Stills met Young. . . . What seems utterly remarkable is that the five members of Frankie Goes to Hollywood should have got together to form a band, for not only are two of the band self-confessedly gay and the other three heterosexual—an unusual combination in itself—but there is also an apparently vast difference in tastes and influences between the two singers, Holly and Paul, and The Lads, the musicians in the group. (1985, 7–8)

Despite the "unusual combination" of band members and their respective differences and influences, the public image cultivated by Frankie, even leading up to their worldwide success, was arguably queer given the group's delightful vaunting of unremorseful sex.[6] Although the band's brilliance and originality has been too frequently attributed to the scheming of producer Trevor Horn and journalist Paul Morley, Frankie's queer appeal to

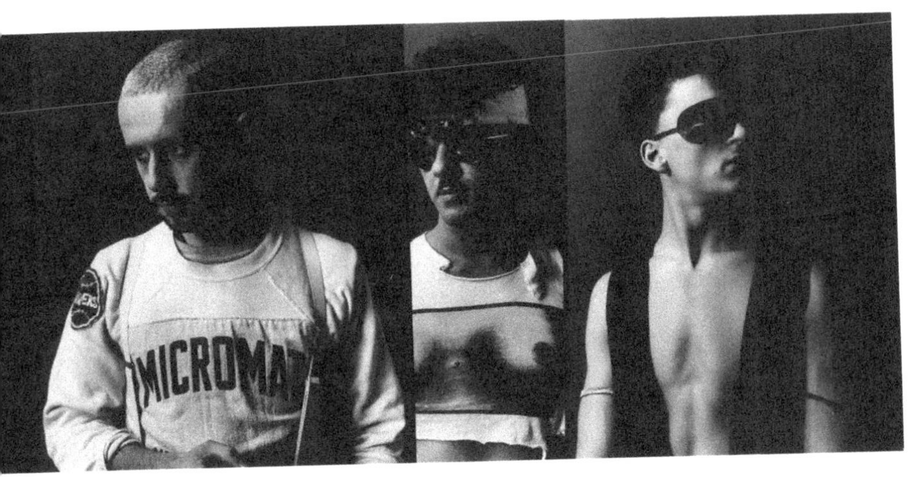

innumerable admirers exceeded the ambitions of these manipulative puppeteers who invested in what they could only perceive as shock-and-awe tactics devised to line their opportunistic pockets.

Along with the ubiquitous Katharine Hamnett–inspired *Frankie Say Relax!* T-shirt becoming a staple of 1980s international fashion trends (one might point to its appearance on a 1997 episode of the American sitcom *Friends* as evidence), Morley's broad marketing campaign included several racy adverts for the group's early record releases.[7] Complete with controversial statements like "All nice boys love sea men" and "Why don't you come . . . ?" and ridiculing their chart competitors with taunting comparisons such as "making Public Image seem like men of good will" and "making Duran Duran lick the shit off their shoes," the photos of Johnson and Rutherford included in these ads, however, index the pre-Morley/Horn makeover moment that for me exemplifies the unabashed queerness that served as a catalyzing force which arguably continued to lie at the heart of Frankie's successive personas (fig. 6.1).[8] The photos depict both Johnson and Rutherford clad in leather/fetish gear. In one, Johnson sports a shaved head and wears black leather gloves and a black side-less muscle shirt. With a cigarette in hand, he sizes up the camera and the viewer of the photograph with a gaze that combines judgment and incitement. In another, Rutherford models a classic white sailor hat that contrasts with his all-black ensemble including, like Johnson, a black side-less muscle shirt and a studded leather wristband. The iconography here matches the band's look discerned from a pre-Horn/Morley appearance in a recorded performance at the Hope and Anchor pub in Coventry and another for the television show *The Tube*, in both of which they play a live, stripped-down (but by no means less funky) version of "Relax."[9] As one YouTube commentator named Chaos Man notes in response to the Hope and Anchor performance: "I'm not a homophobe by any means. I myself am bisexual and mean this as a compliment. This is legit the gayest underground club performance I have ever seen. This looks awesome! We don't see places like this anymore." Such elements embraced by Frankie Goes to Hollywood, particularly by Johnson and Rutherford, were exactly what made them and their music so enticing to many queer listeners and spectators, including those who would initially condemn their appeal but later were willing to acknowledge it.

Take, for example, Boy George. In a letter captioned "George vs Frankie" and published in the May 12, 1984, issue of the British music magazine *Record Mirror*, George addresses not the entire band but Holly Johnson and Paul Rutherford in particular. I quote the letter in its entirety:

> Dear Paul and Holly, when I wrote the song, "Do You Really Want to Hurt Me," people of low intelligence assumed it was a hot tune dedicated to the art of flagellation (whipping) etc., etc. I could have seized the opportunity then to label Culture Club "naughty but nice" and joined the long and boring line of "rock stars" who have sold themselves on pure sexuality for the last 30 years—but people who still consider sex to be risqué are as dull as those who still regard, and use, the guitar as a phallic symbol.
>
> Being "gay" is not exactly a revolution in 1984, neither is sex, rubber or laser beams—they are as much a part of the furniture as your rude (but brilliant) song "Relax." A top selling record, banned or otherwise, brings you into the middle of the road bracket along with "Karma Chameleon" and "White Christmas." (Really Holly, ask your bank manager.)
>
> No one is accusing you of being without talent, but it is obvious to everyone that Paul Morley pulls the strings and Trevor Horn does the cooking. Frankie Goes to Hollywood are a great band with or without the puff pastry, so do you really need to let yourself be manipulated?
>
> Just look at the other three members of Frankie, aside from the two "Fire Queens" up front, and you can see that they have only just discovered *Him* magazine. The video to accompany "Relax," that was branded too rude to be shown, WAS tacky and very insulting to anyone with a brain—a Hilda Ogden-type view of homosexuality.

> You are not educating people, only telling them that being "gay" is like a four-letter word sprayed on a toilet wall—cheap, disgusting and very childish.
>
> If you're so concerned with making people aware of sex why don't you be a little more explicit and intelligent in your interviews? It is not clever to call me an idiot simply because I express a valid opinion. As for Nick Beggs [of Kajagoogoo], why shouldn't he commit himself to religion when you only crawl round the walls of pornography like a little child at school concealing a cigarette from the teacher?
>
> Your video taught me nothing. It just made me proud that I have never used "second-hand information" to further my career; it reminded me not to listen to rumours over garden fences told by frustrated housewives tensed by the tightness of their knicker elastic.
>
> This is Blighty not San Francisco.
>
> BOY GEORGE (1984, 40)

Reflecting the relentless feuding between rival pop stars well-documented in magazines and newspapers throughout the 1980s, the letter reads not only as a rebuttal to Frankie members calling Culture Club's singer an "idiot" but also an attempt to draw a line between Frankie's promotion of homosexuality and Boy George's at the time familiar refusal of it. Thus, whenever the word "gay" is mentioned in the letter, it is contained within quotes, a move that corresponds with Boy George's initial rejection of not only sex but also sexual identity categories. Indeed, when asked at the height of Culture Club's success if he was gay, he famously skirted the question with the oft-quoted declaration that he'd "rather have a cup of tea than sex."[10]

Even if Marc Almond, Boy George, and Pete Burns of Dead or Alive undeniably challenged the hard-and-fast rules of the gender binary in the early 1980s popular music scene, Johnson and Rutherford (and Jimmy Somerville and the other members of Bronski Beat) made no qualms about declaring their homosexual proclivities. Famed music manager and record producer Simon Napier-Bell, known for his work with artists as diverse as the Yardbirds, Marc Bolan, Japan, Wham!, and Candi Staton, writes, "Paul and Holly were not the limp-wristed jolly-boys the British public so loved, like Larry Grayson or Kenneth Williams. They were aggressively queer and out to scare you. They looked 'hard,' had crewcuts and dressed themselves in T-shirts and leather. After years of gay giggling, Britain was now getting outright promiscuous homosexuality" (2002, 296). Napier-Bell continues by quoting Johnson from an interview with *Him Magazine* in which Frankie's lead singer declares, "Although Boy George and Bowie are gorgeous boys if you like that sort of thing, they're working in a grey area, they're playing with androgyny. But we're black and white. There's no pussy-footing with us. We are into PLEASURE and we think that what has been regarded as a sexual perversion should be brought into the open" (Napier-Bell 2002, 296).

In his autobiography *A Bone in My Flute*, a writing endeavor propelled by the belief that he didn't have much time to live given the discovery of his HIV-positive status, Johnson responds to Boy George's letter and his supposed preference for tea over sex:

> We had already been attacked in the press by the cosy, cuddly Boy George, who had not yet come out at that time, and who claimed that our video [for "Relax"] gave gay people a bad name—"Cheap, disgusting and very childish" (*Record Mirror*, 12th May 1984). This "Widow Twanky" act was, of course, pure green-eyed jealousy. He no longer appeared even slightly controversial. His proclaiming that he would rather have a cup of tea than have sex was another way of confirming to the world that his suspect sexuality was something to be ashamed of. (1994, 173)

Johnson's claim that Boy George "no longer appeared even slightly controversial" signals a different kind of inspiration for Culture Club's lead singer—one indeed energized by contempt—that indubitably prompted the letter. Fittingly, immediately following his retort to George, Johnson explains how Frankie Goes to Hollywood's success in inciting fury and appeals for a return to decorum approximated the achievement of their punk forerunners the Sex Pistols:

> It was an exciting moment in time, and just for a moment, I felt all my years of relentless songwriting had at last come to fruition. Frankie Goes to Hollywood was to the Eighties what The Sex Pistols were to the Seventies. The politics that were thrust upon them were wildly different from ours, but the relationships that the two groups had with their particular decades and economic climates were very similar. Frankie Goes to Hollywood might not have been a part of an identifiable movement as The Sex Pistols had been, but the ideas of stylish pleasure and guilt-free sexuality perfectly matched the mood of the time. (1994, 173–74)[11]

This "stylish pleasure and guilt-free sexuality" promoted by Frankie is exactly what shone through for many an awakening young gay man. This was also the case for Boy George, who would eventually come to identify publicly as gay despite early pressures to negate the term at the height of Culture Club's success. Tellingly, George confesses in his autobiography *Take It Like a Man* that Culture Club's single "The War Song," from their third LP, *Waking Up with the House on Fire* (1984), was "influenced by Frankie Goes to Hollywood's 'Two Tribes' even though I would never have admitted it at the time" (Boy George 1995, 249).

FLAME ON BURN DESIRE

Regardless of the timeworn investment in casting shadows over the queer originality and roots of the band for propping up the contended genius of Horn and Morley (exemplified more recently by noted British writer Michael Bracewell, who maintains that "Frankie Goes to Hollywood was the creation of pop journalist Paul Morley" [2012, 383]), others like Paul Flynn get to the heart of what Frankie Goes to Hollywood meant to queer kids coming of age in the Thatcher/Reagan era.[12] In *Good as You: 30 Years of Gay Britain*, Flynn (2017) champions the unharnessed sex expression embodied by Frankie Goes to Hollywood, who provided an essential feeling of uplift for a young gay man who heretofore believed his outsider status was an aberration experienced in isolation.[13] Writing with respect to the popularity of "Relax" and Jimmy Somerville and Bronski Beat's "Smalltown Boy" in 1984 Britain, Flynn maintains:

> If these songs, three listens in and glistening already like national anthems, had occupied my brain space in isolation they might have represented an anchorless life raft. Perhaps if each one of Holly and Jimmy's alumni that kept their sexualities to themselves on *Top of the Pops* and in *Smash Hits* had come to be seen in their honest context rather than in the half-light of a closet door, well, that might have helped. But good pop fortune meant Holly and Jimmy arrived as a twin attack. They opened a conversation others willingly shied away from, delivering the next generation, my generation, the full and complete confidence to be as good as you. (2017, 5)

These songs may have indeed operated for Flynn as "national anthems" (also the title of his chapter), but their transmission across the Atlantic—not to mention other songs in Frankie's and Bronski Beat's repertoire—translated fairly well so as to suitably establish a link between his English teenage self and my Mexican American me. Moreover, "good pop fortune," often materializing unexpectedly on the television screen, in the pages of one's favorite pop music magazine, or on the radio, is more often than not—at least initially—received untainted by the knowledge of who produced the song or executed the photo shoot. Hence beyond the tired proclamation of Morley and Horn making Frankie, I prefer to highlight how Frankie made us: their music and example touching their gay acolytes and serving as the arousing catalyst for generating erotic inducement, self-affirmation, and communal intimacy. This could very well be said to signify, particularly on a queer register, the electrifying dynamics of the power of love.

Even Simon Napier-Bell points out that Frankie's historical and cultural depth was too often ignored in favor of granting credit to Paul Morley and Trevor Horn for making the band. As he writes, "the truth was, the band had not only written ["Relax"] themselves, they'd performed it on television [on *The Tube*] before they even met Morley, which was why Holly Johnson became increasingly agitated about the way Morley spoke of the group as puppets" (2002, 297).[14] Thus, for as much as the band's sonic studio sheen and cleverly executed public image unquestionably profited from Morley's and Horn's prowess, their decidedly queer character rooted in a defiant punk scene and gay subcultural worlds is what defines the profoundness of Frankie Goes to Hollywood for Richard Smith, Paul Flynn, and myself.[15] Recalling Malcom McLaren's weighty if not manipulative hand in ushering the Sex Pistols' rise to infamy-tinged stardom, the Liverpool band's indelible influence on countless youths in Britain and elsewhere, like that of the Pistols, is hardly determined by managerial mastery but instead provoked by a combination of sound and vision engaged by audiences who in turn imbue new meaning in their lives and derive motivation to yield expressions of one's own design. Like Richard Smith who, with the help of "Relax," was made to feel "young and sexy and naughty," the song for Flynn "represented a satisfactory solution for rendering both the loins and emotions of gay men for full public display" (2017, 19). This pop song attributed to Frankie Goes to Hollywood "flung a door wide open, without apology. Watching all of this play out from a south Manchester sofa at the age of 12 could not have been any more scintillating" (19).

"Relax" also had such an effect on me and would come to hold even greater sybaritic splendor once I relocated to the San Francisco Bay Area, as I'll soon detail. But here I want to again declare my adoration for "Two Tribes"—an affection encompassing the numerous existent versions of the song, but the "Carnage Mix," the A-side of the US twelve-inch single, being the one to which I feel a stronger bond. I attribute this reaction to how the mix recalled the promotional video by which I was frightened, fascinated, and stimulated. Along with the ominous and repetitive voice of British actor Richard Allen declaring, "Mine is the last voice that you will ever hear / Don't be alarmed," the song's and video's address to, yet critique of, nuclear war seemed to simultaneously encompass the despair and desire underpinning the Cold War 1980s and my very real fear of nuclear war. In *Bang! A History of Britain in the 1980s*, Graham Stewart writes that "the lyrics of 'Two Tribes' were given visual amplification by an accompanying pop video in which actors playing Reagan and the new Soviet leader, Konstantin Chernenko, slugged it out in a boxing ring, egged on by a crowd which included other world leaders" (2013, 209). In the "fear-driven world of the arms race" (209), as Stewart puts it, "Two Tribes" unquestionably narrated and visualized what the world's end might look like, yet its bleak depiction of war is not exclusively guided by what Freud identifies as the death drive; that is, the impulse toward death and destruction. On the contrary, the antiwar message of the song, further amplified by the B-side cover of Edwin Starr's "War," demonstrates a concurrent embrace of Eros, the psychoanalytic counterpoint of the death drive that entails self-preservation, sex, and creativity.[16]

The multipronged magnitude of "Two Tribes" is keenly described by Holly Johnson in an interview with Max Bell in the August 4, 1984, issue of *No. 1* magazine, explaining, "It's about friction—between you and me, men and women and yes, Russia and America. It's the first nuclear war record that hits the nail on the head. On the other hand, two kids came up to me the other day and asked me to sign a copy. 'That's the best dance record ever made, mate'" (Bell 1984, 28, 30). Indeed, the meaning behind—as well as the desires generated by—Frankie's second single proved just as potent as "Relax" but situated that desirous impulse—be it for sex or to dance or both—within the context of world politics. To be sure, with the combined effort of "Relax" and "Two Tribes," Frankie knew very well how to mix carnage with carnality.

After the band split up in 1987 (their second and final LP, *Liverpool*, was released the year before), the band would reunite in 2004 and tour the following year without the participation of Holly Johnson and Brian Nash. Yet Frankie's demise also gave way to Johnson's solo career beginning with two singles, "Love Train" and "Americanos," both subsequently appearing on his 1989 debut album, *Blast*.[17] Featuring American singer, songwriter, and producer Dan Hartman, *Blast* went to number one in the UK Albums Chart, generating four noteworthy and successful singles. While the first single, "Love Train," filled me with joy at first listen (with the power to continue to do so, if truth be told), the second single, "Americanos," was in particular personally and deeply felt. Released in March 1989, my senior year of high school and a few days after I turned eighteen, "Americanos" went to number four in the UK while reaching number thirty-six on the US Billboard

Dance/Club Play Song Chart. The idea for "Americanos," however, germinated when Johnson was still tied to Frankie, who were preparing to embark on another tour. Longing to move away from the increasingly intolerable rock 'n' roll lifestyle cultivated by his fellow bandmates, Johnson began contemplating a music career in which he alone was in command. Toward the conclusion of *A Bone in My Flute*, Johnson recounts his Christmas trip to and from Pittsburgh, Pennsylvania, the hometown of family members of his long-term partner Wolfgang Kuhle:

> We flew back to England with a few days to go before the Frankie Goes to Hollywood 1987 European tour, which was to be the last. I had already made up my mind that the next musical venture I got involved with would be a solo project, so I would have more control over the finished product. Already the idea for a new song had germinated in my mind after my American Christmas. Americanos! was a word I kept repeating to myself after hearing a news report on Radio Pittsburgh concerning Spanish-speaking immigrants, who were multiplying so fast that Spanish had become the second language of the USA. (1994, 245)

Needing "to get away from the pompous, designer-rock sound that Frankie Goes to Hollywood had just put out, wanting instead to make pop music with a definite dance influence that street people would appreciate" (245), Johnson's 1989 debut solo album clearly represented a marked departure from *Liverpool* and its singles "Rage Hard," "Warriors of the Wasteland," and "Watching the Wildlife." Johnson's desire to make "pop music with a definite dance influence that street people would appreciate" would not, however, sidestep politics. As with the dance-inducing "Two Tribes" and its focus on the arms race, "Americanos" broached the momentous issue of immigration circulating in the US at the time.

On November 6, 1986, then-president Ronald Reagan signed the Immigration Reform and Control Act (IRCA), also known as the Simpson-Mazzoli Act, which sought to curb undocumented migration to the US, particularly from the southern border. Yet this attempt to restrict the traffic flowing across the border by legalizing undocumented workers who had arrived in the US prior to January 1, 1982, and making it illegal to knowingly employ undocumented individuals was hardly a success. As historian Ana Raquel Minian notes, "Reagan's claim that future generations would be thankful for [the IRCA] proved incorrect. Scholars, Mexican American activists, and U.S. politicians from both the left and the right of the political spectrum soon declared the law a failure" (2018, 183). After all, as Minian rightly points out, "By not acknowledging that for migrant communities going to *El Norte* had become a part of life, policy makers failed to address the true roots of migration and proposed only fruitless solutions" (184). For me, Johnson's statement regarding Spanish becoming "the second language of the USA" illustrates how Mexican and Latin American migration was indeed contributing to a shifting demographic but which was already an integral part of the country's history, a fact that was not going to disappear either by assimilation or the refusal of admission.

The song and the video for "Americanos" reveals Johnson's astute awareness of media representation and historical phenomena pertaining to Mexicans and Mexican Americans. Consider the following refrain:

> Americanos
> Blue Jeans and Chinos
> Coke, Pepsi and Oreos
> Americanos
> Low riding Chicanos
> In the land of the free
> You can be what you want to be

Juxtaposing US mass cultural products (Coke, Pepsi, Oreos) with cultural practices (lowriding) by Chicanos whose presence more often than not stands as—drawing from the title of Minian's introduction—"from neither here nor there," Johnson connects contemporary discourses of immigration with the long-standing history of Mexican American communities in the US. Furthermore, Johnson applies his knowledge acquired from the news report on Radio Pittsburgh about the rising number of "Spanish-speaking immigrants" to those common, if not contradictorily espoused, assumptions pertaining to the US's embrace of immigrants. That is, the US's status as "the land of the free" where "you can be what you want to be" is never unilaterally applicable to all immigrants, particularly those whose racial and class standing renders them difficult, if not impossible, to integrate into middle-class white America. By keenly taking on mass-mediated representations that more often than not exclude Mexicans and Mexican Americans, Johnson conveys in his own words the racialized and contradictory history of the United States, a history that at once upholds the promise of hope for those existing in its margins while remaining hopelessly mired in a nostalgic past.

The video for "Americanos," directed by Eric Watson and which suitably features Christos Tolera from Blue Rondo a la Turk, crystallizes these politics.[18] Contrasting two American families, the Rockwells and the Gomezes,

6.2 Screenshot from "Americanos" video directed by Eric Watson.

the video—drawing inspiration from John Waters's 1988 film *Hairspray*—depicts the latter family as the live-in help for the former family.[19] Johnson appears in the video as the television host for *The Solid Gold Lottery Show*. Glued to their television sets (the Gomezes viewing from the kitchen while the Rockwells watch from the living room), both families sit in anticipation of their lottery ticket numbers matching those flashed on the screen. We soon discover that the Gomez family hold multiple tickets, each with winning numbers, thus granting them the prizes of an extravagant house, a yacht, and a car. The screen is soon split by a white dividing line. Above the line is the Rockwell family, who look down upon the Gomez family below (fig. 6.2). Another number is drawn, however, and the Rockwells this time possess the winning numbers, for which they may claim the prize of a year's supply of dog food.

As the video comes to a close, we witness the Rockwell family entering the kitchen to congratulate the Gomez family on their success, with the Gomez family patriarch quickly introducing his son to the Rockwell daughter. The camera quickly cuts to a shot of the Gomez son paired with the Rockwell daughter, both adorned in wedding wear. After the young man tosses a handful of money in the air (with the Rockwell son perplexedly looking out a window at his sister now coupled up with the Americano who presumably once waited on his family), the video comes to a close as Johnson sings:

> Americanos
> Movies and heroes
> In the land of the free
> You can be what you want to be

One might read the video for and lyrics to "Americanos" as an uncritical adoption of "the American dream." However, the title of the song, and the neologism "Americanos," refuses the easy assimilation of this impoverished aspiration by keenly blurring the line between "Americans" and "Mexicanos." Indeed, Johnson is well aware that Mexicans and Mexican Americans more often than not don't qualify as Americans given their historically maligned racial and class identities. Music critic Chris Heath concurs in a review of *Blast* when he writes that "Americanos" is an "'80s update of David Bowie's 'Young Americans' in both its content and its spirit, where he acknowledges the superficiality of the American dream but isn't narrow-minded enough to simply condemn it" (1989, 80).[20]

In "Americanos," then, the history of Mexican "Americanos" becomes inextricably connected to the white normative Norman Rockwell–like family, as their labor and mere existence prop up what gets to count as "American." In my mind, "Americanos" sharply contrasts with Genesis's blood-curdling 1983 hit single, "Illegal Alien." As cultural studies scholar Leah Perry argues, the song "'Illegal Alien' is not an enlightened attempt to expose the struggles of the undocumented to a popular audience; rather, Genesis capitalized (pun intended) on stereotypes of Mexicans and thus perpetuated the problem of racism and exploitation that underscores undocumented immigration" (2016, 59). While still operating within the realm of representation with which Perry takes issue, Johnson's "Americanos," in marked contrast, aims to represent Mexicans and Mexican Americans in the United States in a context that upends the dominant narrative of citizenship by awarding dog food to those historically granted the top frame.

When I relocated to Berkeley in June 1989, I would always carry around in my backpack the cassette versions of *Welcome to the Pleasuredome* and *Blast* (along with other tapes acquired at Rasputin Music and other record shops on or near Telegraph Avenue by artists discussed in this book).

While I'd often play the tapes in their entirety on my Sony Walkman, the three songs that formed an essential trifecta were "Relax," "Two Tribes," and "Americanos." Indeed, these songs served as a soundscape that captured the world I was then inhabiting. Not only was I becoming more adamant about my identity as a Chicano (for which I thank Holly Johnson's "Americanos" for intimately incorporating it into my lexicon prior to my membership in the organization Movimiento Estudiantil Chicano de Aztlán or MEChA), but "Two Tribes" had renewed meaning as the Cold War came to an end, HIV/AIDS impacted our burgeoning desires, and the Gulf War commenced.[21] At Berkeley I recall the fear of being drafted, and thus the fear of war I held years earlier continued. Therefore, "Two Tribes" was again important for assuaging this fear while "Relax" returned with a vengeance at the start of my sexual awakening where my peers and I attempted to love ourselves and others in the face of an epidemic.[22] Early on at Berkeley, my friend Armando would take me to my first Castro Street Fair, telling me that our trip on the BART train to San Francisco was to study in a quiet café in the city when in fact we ended up backpack-clad in a bar packed with leather-clad men. It was in this bar that I first saw the uncensored version of the video for "Relax" directed by Bernard Rose. Feeling a bit like Holly Johnson in my proper attire at a seedy bar, I was excited to witness the correlation between the song, my placement in a bar that looked a lot like the one in the video, and the reemergence of a song, a band, and a singer who touched me in more than one way.[23]

Fatefully, it would turn out to be, to put a spin on Boy George's critique of the video, San Francisco and not Blighty where the video enabled this touch by bringing the song back into my life just like its extraordinary return to the number two spot—right behind "Two Tribes" comfortably ensconced in the number one position—in the July 1984 British pop charts.[24] Boy George's parting epistolary jab at Johnson and Rutherford comes in the form of a catty reminder of where Frankie is from and where they should linger: "This is Blighty not San Francisco." Yet when I finally saw the "uncensored" version of "Relax" (after years of sole familiarity with "The Laser Version" or the "Live Version" on MTV and various music video programs), Blighty and San Francisco were intimately entwined. And while four hundred miles away from Santa Ana was at the time, to quote from the title track of Frankie's first album, "a long way from home," I was advantageously equipped with a familiar but newly revitalized soundscape that suitably welcomed me to a newly unearthed pleasuredome.

TO RICKY WITH LOVE

During a summer 2015 trip to London with a dear friend and colleague, I was lucky to see Holly Johnson live at Shepherd's Bush Empire. Every song performed—from each of Frankie's singles to his hits, as well tracks from his recently released album *Europa*—was flawless.[25] But when he introduced "Americanos," the evening became even more special. Before launching into the song, Johnson began with a story about the history of racism in the US directed against Chicanos, this being one of the factors that inspired him to write the song. Needless to say, I was overjoyed to hear one of my all-time favorite artists revealing his knowledge of Mexican American history to an audience of mostly British fans but also to two people who, a much longer way from home as it were, felt seen. In the audience with Melli, a Puerto Rican woman from Chicago, we both sensed a connection to Johnson as he had seemingly reached out to both of us—as two Latina/o Americanos—whose love for him in the Frankie years and into the present had an added touch of transatlantic fellowship.

Not unlike Suzan Colón who, as mentioned in book's introduction, traveled to London to secure an interview with a member of the band Japan, I reached out to Holly via Facebook Messenger through his page, which I suspected he himself oversaw. Traveling once again to London, but this time for an academic conference, I thought I might be lucky to meet Holly to ask him a few questions. It was my great fortune that he indeed managed his page and kindly agreed to connect. Taking a taxi to Chelsea, I arrived early (almost an hour early) at the restaurant he suggested. When he arrived in a shiny black taxi, we quickly identified one another, hugged, and made our way in. As it was crowded and somewhat pricy, he politely asked if I would mind walking to another spot down the street. Without much thought I replied, "Not at all!" We soon found ourselves in a greasy spoon whose English breakfast was more to both our liking.[26] During breakfast I told Holly about how he and Frankie were important to me as a teenager. I recounted the stories of Irene and the twelve-inch single of "Two Tribes," and my repeated plays of *Blast* on my Walkman while walking the streets of Berkeley and San Francisco. I also told him about the singular significance of "Americanos" for me, and how I interpreted the song lyrics. Our conversation lasted close to two hours, and we shared stories that seemed to highlight the similarities between growing up in Liverpool and in Santa Ana. Before we left the restaurant, I asked Holly to sign my CD single of

6.3 Compact disc single for Holly Johnson's "Americanos" with inscription.

"Americanos." Not wanting to read the inscription, I placed it in my backpack and off we went for a stroll down the King's Road. He took me to a shoe shop where he introduced me to a longtime friend and then to the historic Worlds End, formerly Seditionaries and Sex.[27]

I promised myself I would not read what Holly wrote on the CD until I had boarded the plane at Heathrow that would take me from London to Los Angeles. Once seated (and somewhat ready for the eleven-hour flight), I took the CD out of my daily planner. In blue marker, it read, "To Ricky with love and respect for getting the meaning of this song. Love, Holly" (fig. 6.3). I immediately shed what felt like a flood of tears as memories of my first encounter with Frankie Goes to Hollywood's and Holly Johnson's music returned to me, bringing with them reminders of both the hurdles I endured because of my class, race, sexuality, and ethnicity, and the perseverance congealed with no small help from a soundtrack of songs that struck many a personal chord. Johnson's touching inscription on the CD single cover was now even more intimately linked to "Americanos," a praise song for Mexican Americans, that is more than an uncritical affirmation of the colorblind American dream but an homage to those systematically consigned to historical absence. The memory of time spent with Holly, and the lasting significance of his music, can't help but signify a bridge that reaches across the Atlantic Ocean, queers and Chicanos, death and desire, dancing and politics, Holly and me.

Seven

LATIN/O AMERICAN PARTY

The first time I heard a Pet Shop Boys song was on an AM radio station broadcasting from Tijuana, Mexico, called the Mighty 690. I don't recall how I first learned about the station, but its overall style was quite eclectic and therefore, in my opinion, more interesting than the station to which I otherwise listened: 106.7 KROQ-FM. While the Mighty 690 had a less pretentious vibe and, as a result, an unsophisticated reputation (I distinctly recall some peers hurling insults at those who admitted to liking the station), its unconventional programming, although at times overlapping with KROQ's "alternative sound," felt largely unfettered by what was deemed an appropriate alternativeness to uphold an emphatically cool public image. For while Duran Duran's "The Reflex" was seemingly inescapable during the summer of 1984 given its heavy rotation on KROQ, the Birmingham band's track "Secret Oktober"—the B-side to their single released the previous year, "Union of the Snake"—consistently found itself at number one on the Mighty 690's evening playback of the top five most requested songs of the day. And although KROQ indeed played Pet Shop Boys' first single, "West End Girls," when it was first released in 1984, its more frequent (to my mind at least) airtime on the Mighty 690 holds for me greater association with not only the Tijuana-based radio station but an even deeper connection to the twelve-inch, almost eight-minute-long Bobby "O"

¿Cuanto tiempo tengo que esperar?
Pet Shop Boys, "Discoteca"

(Bobby Orlando)–produced version of the song, complete with cowbell, that played unedited on the AM dial.

Pet Shop Boys (fig. 7.1), the duo made up of Neil Tennant and Chris Lowe, is one of the most successful synth-pop acts to emerge from the 1980s. Including them in a book about post-punk cultures might elicit skepticism if not provoke outright disdain. There are sound reasons why, however, they help close this book on music artists whose beginnings owe much, if not everything, to Britain's prototypical punk scene. Principally inspired by electronic music geniuses and genres ranging from Kraftwerk and Giorgio Moroder to Hi-NRG and Chicago house, the band's unabashed adoption of pop music seemingly positions them light-years away from punk and most of its sonic descendants. Yet at the start of the band's career, Tennant interpreted the Pet Shop Boys ethos as running parallel to punk's DIY standard although in their case replacing the three-chord foundation for starting a band with synthesizers.[1] In an early, uncredited, and brief Pet Shop Boys feature in the May 12, 1984, issue of *Record Mirror*, Tennant and Lowe's recently "waxed" debut single "West End Girls" is announced as "a slice of Hi-NRG with hip hop elements and *very* English sounding vocals produced by legendary NY ultradisco knob-twiddler Bobby 'O' [Orlando] (the Boys' big hero, responsible for Divine's saucy output)." Tennant, though, raises the punk stakes and intimates a DIY ethos fueling the Bobby "O" version of the track. As he asserts, "It was great, 'cos he turns down production offers all the time—Dead or Alive wanted to work with him. Both our approaches are very punk—electro enables you to do that" (3).[2]

It is not my intention to vigorously corroborate the punk roots of Pet Shop Boys as a means to justify their classification as post-punk. I am, however, invested in expanding the analytic frame through which to consider the multiple points of musical contact that simultaneously underscore the band's myriad influences and in turn animate their musical versatility. Thus, along with Tennant's early reference to Pet Shop Boys' approach as "very punk," is the acutely accurate description of the Bobby "O" version of "West End Girls" as "a slice of Hi-NRG with hip hop elements and *very* English sounding vocals" that represents only one nodal point at which these particular genres converge. As precursors to, intimates with, and successors of Tennant and Lowe's debut single, one may well point to the Clash's and Blondie's citation of and engagement with the nascent New York hip-hop scene, collaborating with and playing alongside, respectively, Grandmaster Flash and the Furious Five and Fab 5 Freddy;[3] Arthur Baker and John "Jellybean" Benitez's

7.1 Chris Lowe and Neil Tennant of British pop duo Pet Shop Boys on the streets of Soho in London, England, on December 7, 1985. Photo by John Stoddart/Popperfoto via Getty Images.

work with New Order on the track "Confusion";[4] Malcolm McLaren and the World's Famous Supreme Team teaming up for the classic hip-hop track "Buffalo Gals"; as Time Zone, John Lydon and Afrika Bambaataa's emphatically apocalyptic "World Destruction"; the innovative partnership between Mick Jones and Don Letts as Big Audio Dynamite; Siouxsie and the Banshees' 1988 single "Peek-a-Boo" (described by *Melody Maker* journalist Paul Mathur as "thirties hip hop" [1988, 29]);[5] and, under the aegis of Scritti Politti, Green Gartside's partnership with Mos Def and Meshell Ndegeocello on 1999's *Anomie and Bonhomie*. Like the faulty argument I take issue with in chapter 3 that perceives goth music as untouched by Black and other non-Anglo musical traditions, the intimacy between punk, post-punk, and hip-hop is extensive and unmistakable. Moreover, on a personal level, the mixing of all these ostensibly distinct genres and traditions reflects their inevitable touch in my own collection of records, compact discs, and digital library tracks.

The history of Pet Shop Boys, stemming from a punk/post-punk context and entwined into a hip-hop one, demonstrates a similar ability to promiscuously brush up against and sensually draw inspiration from a wide range of prototypical and contemporaneous musical figures and cultural traditions.[6] David Stubbs notes this particular trajectory by comparing and contrasting them to their renowned Manchester-based contemporaries: "Whereas The Smiths, somewhat worryingly, hankered for the restoration of guitar-driven whiteness to post-punk and a cessation of its dialogue with funk, soul, reggae and disco, the Pet Shop Boys felt quite the opposite" (2018, 215). Affirming while building on this argument, I maintain that the duo's patent British character (signaled above, for example, in reference to their "*very* English sounding vocals") on which many music critics have repeatedly commented is thrown off course—or queered, as I see it—when the Boys specifically begin to flirt with, then to outright court, the sounds and styles of Latin musical genres, including those stemming from the early hip-hop scene.[7] Undoubtedly, the point at which to conspicuously register their long-term queer relationship with Latinidad begins with their 1988 single "Domino Dancing." According to the group's early manager, Tom Watkins, Tennant compared "Domino Dancing" to Soft Cell's "Numbers," albeit updated in purview of the AIDS pandemic, given its status as "an ode to endless cruising" but which found "all the lovers . . . falling down" (Watkins 2016, 267–68).[8]

QUEER DAMAGE

In a 2012 feature in *Vanity Fair*, music journalist Mark Spitz informs Pet Shop Boys lead singer Tennant—in the event he was unaware or forgot—that the duo "have a tremendous gay following" and that perhaps "this might have ultimately damaged the run of hit singles they had in America." Tennant does not dispute either of these points, responding instead in the affirmative regarding diminishing chart success: "Something happened to us in America. The theory is it was the video for 'Domino Dancing.' I never really believed it. America is quite homophobic, but it's also totally gay. It's really weird. America is traditionally a country of extremes living side by side" (Spitz 2012). Although Spitz does not mention the persistent rumors of Tennant and Lowe being gay prior to Tennant's coming out in 1994 in an interview with *Attitude* magazine (Burston 1994), knowledge of the Boys' homosexual identities was quite the open secret early on, at times through roundabout suggestiveness and other times through virulent homophobia.[9] As an example of the former, consider the 1987 interview with pioneering gay music journalist Kris Kirk in which discussion arises regarding Tennant's speculative adoption of a female persona in "Rent" (with Kirk recalling as a precedent Marc Almond's single "A Woman's Story," a cover of Cher's version of the song, which "didn't exactly get saturation airplay" [1999, 189]). Of the latter, one might consider the Pogues' lead singer Shane MacGowan contemptuously categorizing Tennant and Lowe as "two queens and a drum machine" and "faggots with synths" in light of the duo beating out "Fairytale of New York" (infamously known for containing the word "faggot" in the lyrics) with their cover of "Always on My Mind" for the coveted number one British Christmas single in 1987.[10]

The claim that the homoeroticism ignited by two bare-chested Puerto Rican men wrestling on a beach in the exceptionally exotic "Domino Dancing" video "damaged the run" of Pet Shop Boys' American hit singles has received a great deal of critical attention. In his 1989 *Rolling Stone* feature "Beyond the Big Hair" about the art of the music video, Jim Farber writes that "Pet Shop Boys' 'Domino Dancing' addressed sex education from a different angle. Eric Watson's lushly romantic work was probably the most homoerotic pop video ever made, featuring two finely chiseled boys who 'wrestle' as crashing ocean waves embrace them (in slo-mo, no less)" (1989, 235). Farber reprovingly continues, "The video exemplified the mainstream exploitation of gay sex in the Eighties, most evident in Calvin Klein ads and feature films like *Top Gun*. Unfortunately, 'Domino Dancing' was every bit as dishonest, titillating the straight world with images it could never acknowledge, then doubling the repression by keeping openly gay expression closeted" (235).

Literary critic Ian Balfour's reading of the video, however, offers a more compelling assessment.[11] Balfour asks his reader to

> consider the video of "Domino Dancing," where we watch the machinations of a young woman and two young men, both of whom apparently rival for her affections, as they jockey for position. Yet the heterosexual model, so to speak, is undermined when we often are treated to seeing the two strapping young men stripped to the waist. The video closes with a scene, repeatedly cut and replayed, of the two men seemingly "fighting" with each other over the young woman—but in doing so they are pictured clutching each other as they fall to the sandy beach and the surf, caught in each other's arms, a little like Burt Lancaster and Deborah Kerr in the famous beach scene in *From Here to Eternity*. (2002, 363)

Balfour rightly maintains that all of this does not exactly "add up to a simple statement about sexuality nor a statement that sexuality is simple" (364), even if, I must note, the viewer catches a reflection of these two strapping Puerto Ricans on Chris Lowe's sunglasses. This is indeed what makes queer (despite Balfour's use of "queen" in his article) a useful framework through which to grapple with the politics of intimacy, sexual or otherwise, emerging in proximity to the song. Thus, when I maintain that there's something queer about the connection between the Pet Shop Boys' embrace of Latinidad, my reference to queer nods to Eve Kosofsky Sedgwick's invaluable definition of the term as signaling an "open mesh of possibilities, gaps, overlaps, dissonances and resonances, lapses and excesses of meaning when the constituent elements of anyone's gender, of anyone's sexuality aren't made (or *can't be* made) to signify monolithically" (1993, 8).

Yet another allegation regarding the group's diminishing chart success in both the UK and the US concerning "Domino Dancing" and made two years after the appearance of the *Vanity Fair* interview is the one on which I cast a more luminous spotlight. In 2014, the LGBT media network Logo listed on its website what they considered Pet Shop Boys' "top ten songs." Despite making number three on Logo's list, "Domino Dancing" is described as "their final top 40 hit" that "was one of their most maligned singles, presenting an entirely different freestyle sound that freaked people out" (Snicks 2014). Pet Shop Boys' aspiration to embrace a sound that reso-

7.2 Sleeve for Pet Shop Boys' "Domino Dancing" (1988). Design by Farrow/PSB. Photo by Peter Andreas.

nated with Exposé's, a sound one might possibly hear at a "Latin/o American Party," as signaled by the words on a van parked at a Miami beach and spotted by Tennant and Lowe who would in turn pose for a photo in front of the van for the image appearing on the front sleeve of the seven-inch and twelve-inch singles for "Domino Dancing" (fig. 7.2), motivated the duo to work with noted Cuban American freestyle producer Lewis Martineé. This, I maintain, arguably conveys a deeper queer resonance given the sonic propensity to "freak people out" rather than the hazy film footage of tumbling boys on a Puerto Rican beach. Refocusing attention on South Beach in Miami, Florida, where the song came into being and away from the lush Caribbean island populated by "really pretty young people" where the video was shot stands for me as the most significant of the group's cross-Atlantic cavorting with Latinidad.[12] Building on the astute readings of "Domino Dancing" by Balfour and other popular music scholars like Stan Hawkins, my queer reexamination of the song stems from the historical trajectory of freestyle and the band's ensuing involvement with Latin American and Latino music and artists. Queer here not only encompasses that which merely represents same-sex desire as ascertained in the promotional video but an analytic through which to comprehend the (for some) questionable and unlikely linkages cultivated across ethnic, gendered, and transatlantic divides.

FREESTYLING PET SOUNDS

In his entry "Freestyle" for David Toop's edited book *Modulations: A History of Electronic Music,* Peter Shapiro argues that "in the hands of producers like the Latin Rascals, Chris Barbosa, Carlos Berrios, and Andy 'Panda' Tripoli, the video-game bleeps, synth stabs, and Roland TR-808 clavés became an android *descarga* called Freestyle that was emblematic of New York culture clash" (2000, 104). Fittingly, Shapiro argues that "Freestyle's ground zero . . . was Shannon's 'Let the Music Play,'" the 1983 song he describes as a "cross between Gary Numan and Tito Puente" (105), which Tennant and Lowe also credit as one of their major influences in 1986 while appearing on *The Latin Connection,* a short-lived American television music program known for featuring freestyle acts.[13] Although the term *Latin* is not always appended to *freestyle* (and when it is, it often provokes ire among many fans and practitioners due to the fact that Latinas/os are hardly the sole listeners of and practitioners of freestyle), there's no debate that freestyle emerges from particular US Latina/o geographies and nods to stylistic elements discernably derived from Latin American and Latino musical contexts.

In *Oye Como Va! Hybridity and Identity in Latino Popular Music,* Deborah Pacini Hernandez echoes Shapiro in her assessment that freestyle "began as a local New York phenomenon" but further notes its burgeoning popularity in "neighborhood clubs catering to young Spanish Caribbean Latino audiences and on local radio stations, although its popularity later spread to other cities with large Latino populations, especially Miami and metropolitan Los Angeles" (2010, 63). From working with Bobby "O" to a few years later with the Latin Rascals (the duo of consisting of DJs, producers, and remixers Tony Moran and Albert Cabrera, who remixed the "Versión Latina" of Pet Shop Boys' second single "Opportunities (Let's Make Lots of Money)," Latin-tinged dance music swayed Tennant and Lowe so fervently that they flew to Miami to work with Martineé, one of the most recognizable and respected freestyle producers, to attain his signature sound. This move would do more than mark a fleeting cultural impact on the British duo but would initiate a long-term engagement with a capacious Latin sound that too often disappears from historical assessments of the duo's catalog. As performance studies scholar Alexandra T. Vazquez declares in her luminous article on freestyle, "The ghosted 'Latin' enables a sense of influence and belonging that empiricism can't contain" (2010, 111).

No doubt, Tennant and Lowe's ambition to capture the freestyle sound they so admired as orchestrated by Martineé—a distinguishable and delicious tonality so successfully translated that one can't help but conceive the perfect mix where Exposé's "Point of No Return" seamlessly flows into Pet Shop Boys' "Domino Dancing"—was skeptically received by some who regarded the merging of white British pop and Latin dance music a dubious endeavor at best. Portentous assessments like music critic Chuck Eddy's, which identify the Latino sound adopted by Pet Shop Boys and berate its incorporation by the duo in scoffing at their appeal to "authenticity," invariably result in a dismissal of a "Latino sound" reduceable to a potpourri of frivolity emanating everywhere and anywhere south of the US-Mexico border: "The booklet inside the Pet Shop Boys' *Introspective* claims they aimed for 'authentic Latin sound' on 'Domino Dancing,' their current single. (Lewis Martinée [*sic*] nicks some maraca/piano jump from one of his Miami-disco Exposé productions, and midway through it combusts like Mexican Independence Day fireworks; the words could conceivably celebrate revolution in Central America.) That this Anglotwerp duo would want 'authentic' anything stumps me—I always figured inauthenticity (i.e., rejection of soul/folk sincerity for show-tune irony) was their *point*" (Eddy 2016, 133).[14] This glib and self-satisfied appraisal depends on isolating any kind of serious transatlantic exchange. Indeed, the admittedly questionable claim to an "authentic Latin sound" is not so much a challenge to essentialism for Eddy as it is motivated by smug skepticism of one wishing to understand and embrace those very distinct traditions by which one is influenced. This is clear when he surmises about Pet Shop Boys' sound (save "West End Girls"—"'cause (just like 'All the Young Dudes') the first two lines suggest young people should blow their brains out"): "British whiteboys singing like British whiteboys beat British whiteboys singing like black men"; and "next to Exposé's nubiles, [Tennant's] sickly, burned out. He whines about betrayal, then betrays us" (Eddy 2016, 133–34). The greatest betrayal in such an appraisal, however, lies in the critic's inability to discern what a Latino cultural influence looks and sounds like.

Eddy's judgment additionally recalls how Latina/o participation in historical accounts of hip-hop are habitually overlooked, dismissed, or forgotten by those committed to policing the authenticity of musical genres all the while calling out others' implausible claims to them, a move obviously evident in his assessment of the Pet Shop Boys' track. Sociologist Raquel Z. Rivera (2003), in her book *New York Ricans from the Hip Hop Zone,* notes that before its recognition as Latin freestyle, this emergent form of electronic dance music with a discernable Latino musical influence was called Latin hip-hop (a point not lost on Pet Shop Boys, as I'll soon clarify).[15] With its subsequent merging with rap (which was qualified as freestyle if the lyrics of a rap song were improvised), hip-hop and freestyle eventually became understood as two distinct genres despite their historical overlap and mutual influence. The major characteristic difference between hip-hop and freestyle, I would argue, is the latter's eventual dismissal as a vacuous form of dance music, particularly given its consistent and indisputable linkage to disco. As Vazquez points out, freestyle is more often than not "relegated to that seemingly less hard-core and less politicized milieu called 'dance music'; its makers are available and then forgettable" (2010, 109). Additionally, the gender politics circumscribing generalized assessments of freestyle promoted the fissure between it and hip-hop. In her research on the centrality of women's voices in freestyle (which interestingly teases out the influence of performers like Liza Minnelli, Judy Garland, Barbra Streisand, and Donna Summer on singers such as Lisa Lisa, Judy Torres, and Lisette Melendez), Vazquez argues that even "freestyle's most foundational voices" are "perceived as frivolous, inconsequential bumps in the masculinist lineage that has been perpetuated by much music scholarship, especially the progressive line that jumps from disco to hip-hop" (113). Pet Shop Boys operates alongside these foundational voices (even collaborating with Minnelli), undermining or incorporating others in the genealogy of freestyle defiant of a masculinist lineage. Consider how Tennant's thin, nasal vocals signal an intimate affinity with the nearly helium-induced femme vocals characteristic of freestyle's lineup of women singers (think also of Cynthia, the Cover Girls, Company B, and Debbie Deb). Discounting Tennant and Lowe's desire to achieve an authentic Latin sound, from the trajectories of both Eddy's assessment and a heteronormative genealogy of hip-hop, evinces a refusal to consider the interlocking and generative queer connections of distinctive popular musical practices.[16]

THE GRAIN OF THE VOICE IN FASHION

Key for the context at hand, Tennant and Lowe offer some explanatory reflections on the origins of "Domino Dancing" in the liner notes to the 2001 CD rerelease of 1988's *Introspective*. According to Tennant, "When we had been in Antigua, playing dominoes, our friend Pete [Andreas, Lowe's former roommate who passed away in 1994] would do a dance when he won and Chris said to him, 'stop doing your domino dance,' and I wrote in my notebook: 'watch them all fall down, domino dancing.'" He continues, "We wrote 'Domino Dancing' in the studio in Wandsworth . . . but we could never think of a chorus for it. We thought it was a bit like 'La Isla Bonita' by Madonna." Lowe adds, "Only in that it's Latin. I love this song." Their exchange continues:

> TENNANT: We wanted something Latino because we used to go to America and hear all these Latin hip hop records and like them.
>
> LOWE: We liked all these great Latin hip hop records made by this bloke in Miami, Lewis Martineé.
>
> TENNANT: He was having all these hits with Exposé. We were so excited by "Domino Dancing" that we flew immediately to Miami and made the record with him. We stayed in the Hilton on South Beach, which smelled of hamburgers. There was this van there on the beach—Latin American Party—and as soon as we saw that, we thought that would be the cover of the record. Pete took a Polaroid, and that's the photo we used on the sleeve. All the musicians on it are Cuban. There's tons of people playing on it.

Along with Nestor Gomez, a guitarist known for his work with the Miami Sound Machine, and a host of brass musicians, a Miami-based and Martineé-produced freestyle group called the Voice in Fashion contributed the backing vocals on "Domino Dancing." The group was formed in 1985 by Salvador Hanono and Ony Rodríguez. Hanono's brother David would join the group then later replace Rodríguez, who parted ways to pursue other projects. Their first major dance hit, "Only in the Night," which reached the number two spot on Billboard's Dance Chart in 1987, was produced and mixed by Martineé.

Astutely assessing Ian Balfour's queer reading of the music video for "Domino Dancing," Stan Hawkins further suggests another way of understanding the politics of the song in general: "While queer readings can include a wide range of responses outside the essentialist categorization of identity, they should not necessarily be positioned as alternative or wishful misreadings" (2002, 136). Hawkins drives his point home when he asserts, "the mobile trajectories of queering operate in destabilizing further what is already an uncertain domain. And, in terms of musical expression, it is the Pet Shop Boys' disco riffs, with superimposed simple tunes on synthesizers that help capture the romantic frankness and exuberance of the expression in 'Domino Dancing'" (136). He further maintains, "Constructed around the lyrics *All day, all day, watch them all fall down, Domino Dancing*, the chorus section consists of a descending broken minor seventh chord, symbolic of the 'falling down' reference in the lyrics. Interest also centres on a Latin-style chordal riff in the piano part, as well as a typical 1970s disco two-bar riff that is an embellishment of the first three notes of the chorus" (136).

To be sure, the frank romanticism and expressive exuberance of the song, especially in its multilayered capacity to queer gender codes in its distinct fusion of disco and Latin style, is accentuated when we spotlight its lyrical focus on a deep-seated love—sometimes unrequited, in other times reciprocated—as expressed from the narrative protagonist/singer to the desired object of address, a focus largely evident in the extensive archive of freestyle tunes. Exposé's "Point of No Return" not only fits this categorization but, as indicated earlier, also tonally resonates with "Domino Dancing" given its "Latin-style chordal riff in the piano part, as well as a typical 1970s disco two-bar riff," which "forms one of the various layers of the mix" (Hawkins 2002, 136).[17] If the goal was to achieve the Latin authenticity on "Domino Dancing" that was made possible by Martineé's handiwork on "Point of No Return," the result undeniably proves successful not only given the sonic resonance between both tracks but also given the producer's facilitation (vis-à-vis Martineé's Latin touch) of an intimate bond between them.

When beginning research for this chapter, I turned to YouTube to track down live or televised performances of "Domino Dancing."[18] Perhaps the most striking of my discoveries were the Boys' performances of the song on two British television programs: *Top of the Pops* and *Wogan* (hosted by Irish radio and television broadcaster Terry Wogan). I was indeed delighted to witness the numerous Latino musicians accompanying Tennant and Lowe on stage (even if they were lip synching) wearing T-shirts paying homage to Chris Lowe, whose Issey Miyake–sunglassed visage from the "Suburbia" single cover and the "Paninaro" video adorned their chests. But what especially gave me pause was the realization that the backing singers of "all day, all day / Domino dancing" were not women but men, more specifically the Miami-based Freestyle duo the Voice in Fashion. Rather than recruiting women vocalists who were so pivotal to generating the love songs that are part and parcel of the freestyle classics catalog (recall it was the music of Exposé that served as motivation for Pet Shop Boys to work with Martineé in the first place), "Domino Dancing" instead incorporates two male singers—Ony Rodríguez and Salvador Honono—whose voices defy easy gender identification.

In *Performing Rites*, Simon Frith maintains that "voices can be used, like any other instrument, to make a noise of the right sort at the right time." He continues, "Both of these terms (right sort, right time) are apparent in the most instrumental use of the voice, as 'back up.' Here the singers' sound is more important than their words, which are either nonsensical or become so through repetition; and repetition is itself the key to how such voices work, as percussive instruments, marking out the regular time around which the lead singer can be quite irregular in matters of pitch and timing" (1996, 187). Additionally, Frith makes an observation that is significant for the present context: "Even in this case, though, the voices can't be purely sound effects; at the very least they also indicate gender and therefore gender relations" (187). While Frith comments on what he reads as "the butch male choral support for Neil Tennant on the Pet Shop Boys' 'Go West,'" we can also see how this operates with respect to the gender-ambiguous (or a freestyle feminine?) choral support from the Voice in Fashion. In other words, the "gender relations" here are contoured by a knowledge of Latinidad that fails to achieve the kind of cultural authenticity to which a critic like Eddy assumes Tennant and Lowe aspire and instead intimately links up to a cultural form whose inability to approximate legitimate masculinity (they are, in his words, "Anglotwerps" who are "sickly, burned out") is precisely what guarantees its Latin freestyle success.

Twenty-eight years later, the "romantic frankness" Pet Shop Boys displayed toward Latin freestyle was returned by the Voice in Fashion when in 2012 they covered "Domino Dancing." The liner notes to *The Moment of Truth Re-Loaded*, a double CD on which their version of "Domino Dancing" appears (not to mention a cover of David Bowie's "The Man Who Sold the World"), mention that they "were invited to tour Europe [with Tennant and Lowe,] however other obligations did not permit the tour."

Their version, which would become a popular Latin freestyle track of their own, illustrates the inextricable bond between both acts that, through the interweaving of distinct voices, including Tennant's, animates the initial and enduring give-and-take significance of "Domino Dancing." Not unlike "the grain of the voice" that Roland Barthes attributes to "the materiality of the body" (1977, 182), the grain of the Voice in Fashion is about the embodiment of a distinct Latina/o cultural history that brushes up against a distinct British musical style resulting in a touch that is mutually enabled as it is reciprocally felt.

By focusing on the musical texture of "Domino Dancing," I have tried to move beyond the commonly held belief that the video for the first single from *Introspective* was the primary culprit for short-circuiting the band's major commercial success in the United States and in Britain. Recall, with the help of Tennant's words, how this assumption was made about the band's fall from chart-topping superiority in Britain in the aforementioned *Introspective* liner notes: "I remember driving back from my house in Rye and listening on the radio when ["Domino Dancing"] entered the charts at number nine and I thought, 'That's that, then—it's all over.' I knew then that our imperial phase of number one hits was over." In response to Tennant, Lowe maintains that "the English don't generally like Latin-tinged music, anyway." As evidence of this alleged British dislike of "Latin-tinged music," we might recall Blue Rondo a la Turk's inability to achieve the success many thought they would. Ironically, in his *Smash Hits* review of Blue Rondo a la Turk's single "The Heavens Are Crying," then-journalist and future Pet Shop Boy Tennant writes, "If Blue Rondo have missed the (banana) boat—and one suspects that they have—they could always get a job writing background music for American cops-and-robbers TV programmes or KP cinema adverts. This Latino disco sounds like they've already started to. Peanuts!" (1982, 28).[19] Not quite the same "Latino disco," Tennant would, however, eventually find one to his liking (and Lowe's, who declares, "When you look back, the chart positions are irrelevant. I love this track so I couldn't care less"). Perhaps more important than confirming or denying the claim that "Domino Dancing" and its noted freestyle influence spelled the demise of the band's "imperial" success, I find it more compelling to historicize the song's backbeat in order to simultaneously explore its intertextual significance, including the duo's queering of commercial interests and external artistic expectations, subsequently leading to further engagement with Latin/o American artists and musical traditions in their extensive catalog.

IT COULD HAPPEN HERE

In a conversation between Tennant and noted Mexican American/German American artist and singer Joey Arias (notably known for appearing alongside Klaus Nomi as accompaniment for David Bowie's December 15, 1979, *Saturday Night Live* performance of "The Man Who Sold the World," "TVC 15," and "Boys Keep Swinging"), Tennant expresses excitement about the band traveling to New York City to promote their then-recently released album *Nightlife* (1999). He also confesses his love for the group of Latinos who helped make the video of "Domino Dancing" possible:

> TENNANT: We can't wait to be in New York City.
>
> ARIAS: Oh, there's so much going on; it's all different but great! I went to a Latin club the other night, and I couldn't believe the energy—oh, it was incredible. Those Puerto Ricans are crazy!
>
> TENNANT: Yes, we love Puerto Ricans!
>
> ARIAS: I'm sure you do! [both crack up]
>
> TENNANT: In a platonic way, of course. [laughs] (Arias 2002, 94)

One way to read this exchange is through the dulled lenses of fetishism or cultural appropriation. Doing so, however, flattens out the rich history of transatlantic cultural exchange underpinning the group's collaborative histories. Indeed, Tennant's love—platonic or not—of Puerto Ricans in particular and Latinos in general is a fitting way to capture Pet Shop Boys' enduring engagement with Latino music and music artists well beyond "Domino Dancing." Take, for example, 1996's *Bilingual*. According to Tennant in issue 16 of *Literally*, the official magazine of the Pet Shop Boys Club, the album track and third single released from it, "Single-Bilingual," was originally titled "Latino."[20] Also on the LP are songs with an unmistakable Latin sound, most notably "Discoteca," "Metamorphosis," "Se A Vida É (That's the Way Life Is)," and "Before."

Extending beyond their Miami-based partnership with Martineé and the Voice in Fashion, Tennant and Lowe would go on to work with another Latino group, although this time in California. This group, Prayers—"an electronic-goth music duo from San Diego, California, comprising vocalist Rafael Reyes and DJ Dave Parley" (Anguiano 2018, 177)—would first cover Pet Shop Boys' "West End Girls" in 2015. José G. Anguiano explains:

> "West End Girls" by Prayers is a cover of the original 1984 song by the Pet Shop Boys. The original song is a 1980s British synthpop classic that features lead singer Neil Tennant melodically flowing through a tale of social class pressures exemplified in the divide between west and east London. In the Prayers version the soft melodic chorus and flow are hijacked-at-gunpoint by a faster, industrial-sounding melody backed by a hard-hitting drumbeat provided by Travis Barker of Blink 182 fame; the song's lyrics are screamed and howled by Reyes. Visually, the Prayers video transports us from London streets in the original video to noir scenes in the barrios of San Diego (The West End Town of Prayers's vision). (2018, 187)

The following year, Pet Shop Boys would recruit Prayers to star in the video directed by Gavin Filipiak for their single "Twenty-something" from the 2016 LP *Super*.[21] An unmistakably "Latin-tinged" track that, according to Chris Lowe, was influenced by reggaeton (which he describes as "a music genre with roots in Latin and Caribbean music [that] blends musical influences of Jamaican dancehall and Trinidadian soca with those of Puerto Rico such as salsa"), the narrative behind the video for "Twenty-something" takes place in the San Diego context Anguiano describes in Prayers' video for "West End Girls." (Newsroom 2016). Although the lyrics of the song were inspired by the changing face of London's Soho neighborhood and its appeal to the twenty-somethings aspiring to upward social mobility at a precarious temporal moment, the message conveyed in the lyrics is translated to video where we witness a twenty-something Chicano postincarceration trying unsuccessfully to secure employment but resorting to drug dealing to support his family. Similar to how Pet Shop Boys previously featured a working-class neighborhood in the Southern California Latina/o-majority city of Duarte in the video for their 1986 single "Suburbia," their recent return to US West Coast terrain continues to endear me to them, not unlike how I felt when I first encountered them.[22]

Admittedly, when I first imagined this project, I tried to resist the urge to take on a personal narrative and keep the focus as impartial as possible. Yet to make sense of each of the artists I've discussed, and the queerness of Latin freestyle in a Pet Shop Boys context no less, requires it. In fact, making sense of the touch between freestyle and Neil Tennant and Chris Lowe extends back to 1988, my senior year in high school. When I first heard "Domino Dancing," I immediately connected it to Exposé and other groups whose music typified the freestyle sound popular with many of my peers. And myself. The hesitation in admitting that I liked freestyle manifested in the mid- and late 1980s, when growing up in the predominantly working-class Mexican American community in Santa Ana, California, meant that lines had to be clearly drawn between musical tastes. These musical tastes more often than not reflected one's cultural (or subcultural) alliance—metal head, party crew affiliate, or "new waver." While I fell on the side of new waver—if not always based on fashion sense then certainly on my musical attachments—I had a secret obsession with freestyle and other dance music genres adopted by the party crew set. When my friends who also listened to Depeche Mode, the Smiths, Siouxsie and the Banshees, or Pet Shop Boys came over, I would hide certain tapes and records so as not to be ridiculed for liking music embraced by the kids with whom we did not associate.[23] As a seventeen-year-old, I unconsciously knew that Neil Tennant and Chris Lowe were also inspired by a Latin-tinged dance beat originating in New York, extending over into Miami, and reaching west to a working-class Chicano/a Southern California. This beat, first heard on the radio, also traveled from my stereo and into my heart: that always unequivocal location of love, unrequited or—when luck is on one's side—mutually returned.

Conclusion

DEDICATED TO THE ONE I LOVE

> This is the dawning of a new era.
>
> **The Specials, "(Dawning of a) New Era"**

Although the idea for this book took flight while I was living in Chicago and teaching at the University of Illinois, Urbana-Champaign, my move back to Southern California for a position at the University of California, Riverside, provided the necessary impetus to complete it. This isn't to say that the book couldn't have been written in the Midwest (which I had fallen in love with after living there twelve years; and no, I didn't mind the winter weather). The return to the geographical region that I always called home, however, prompted the recollection of memories about my teenage years, which in turn made clear how important a space Southern California was—and continues to be—for the enduring traffic between British post-punk music and US Latinidad.

In the summer of 2017, the moment at which I began to thoroughly conceptualize this project, I attended two concerts at the two venues that in my teen years enabled and bolstered my love of the music on which I've written in the preceding pages: the Pacific Amphitheater (where I first saw Culture Club) and the Orange County Fairgrounds (where I stacked crates to earn money for purchasing pricey imported British records, cassettes, and magazines). The latter being the location where I would memorably purchase the seven-inch single of Adam Ant's "Vive le Rock" I mention in chapter 2 and the cassette version of Frankie Goes to Hollywood's *Welcome to the Pleasuredome* referenced in chapter 6, the former was the venue where my father, who worked as a security guard, would sneak in me, my sister, and one or two of our friends for lawn seating for shows whose tickets did not sell out. Yet unlike these concerts in the mid-1980s by Culture Club, Adam Ant, Eurythmics, Simple Minds, Squeeze, and Public Image Limited, these two recent shows featured two headlining Los Angeles–based tribute bands: Strangelove (paying homage to Depeche Mode) and Sweet and Tender Hooligans (in honor of the Smiths). Experiencing these two bands performing—and belonging to the enraptured audiences they commanded—left me both stunned and elated. I was not only stunned by the fact that they possessed the ability to generate a level of excitement on par with the bands to which they respectively paid tribute but elated by the fact that the respective lead singers of Strangelove and Sweet and Tender Hooligans, Freddie Morales (referred to often as "Devotional Dave"; fig. C.1) and José Maldonado (also known as the "Mexican Morrissey"), were Latino. This two-pronged affective response also fittingly captures my successive encounter with the band the Curse—a tribute to the Cure and fronted by singer and guitarist Brian Soto—at the Concert Lounge in downtown Riverside (fig. C.2).[1]

Shane Homan, in his introduction to *Access All Eras: Tribute Bands and Global Pop Culture,* identifies two arguments by which to understand the tribute band. The first regards it as a "new era of musical Fordism, part of an assembly line of unreflective, model-kit acts that flatten pop and rock history to a series of shiny surfaces" (Homan 2006, 14). The other argument, alternatively, regards the tribute band as offering "a practical means for audiences and musicians to begin thinking about not only how particular stars and songs are reproduced, but how they are constantly re-engaged and re-interpreted" (14). Fully understanding the former argument in light of the incessant attempts to revisit "The 80s," efforts intent on promoting hollowed-out nostalgia and stirred by excruciating bids for resuscitating the era's most frivolous elements for Generation X market appeal, I prefer, however, to read Strangelove and Sweet and Tender Hooligans in the context of the latter. Thus, while one (like myself) may recall with fondness Dave Gahan's opening vocals for "Black Celebration" at Depeche Mode's performance at the Irvine Meadows Amphitheatre on July 14, 1986, as Freddie Morales vocalizes Strangelove's cover version of the song over thirty years later at the Pacific Amphitheatre, Morales's rendering nonetheless offers something new to his audience.

C.1 Freddie Morales fronting Strangelove, 2017. Photo by Mary Jane Valdez.

C.2 Flyer for the Curse at the Concert Lounge, Riverside, California, 2018.

While their version without a doubt aims to faithfully pay homage to the original, Strangelove's "re-engagement" with and "re-interpretation" of Depeche Mode's "Black Celebration" without question requires an originality that is theirs alone—given, of course, the impossibility of performing the original—that manifests by way of approximate intimacy. As much as Morales's distinctively emotive dancing may evoke the moves of Dave Gahan, Morales's gestures, to extrapolate from queer theorist Juana María Rodríguez's "Gesture in Mambo Time," "function to assign new meanings to established signifiers" (2014, 132). Thus, as one may see Gahan's movement in Morales, Morales's gestures consistently exceed attachment to a resolutely British signifier given their corporeal and verbal resignification vis-à-vis Morales's discernable Latinidad. (In the case of Sweet and Tender Hooligans, this, for example, manifests in José Maldonado's Spanish-language rendition of "There Is a Light That Never Goes Out.") Morales's performance further indexes the impassioned desire shared between the scores of multigenerational Latina/o/x fans in the audience for British bands like Depeche Mode. Observing (while swaying to) Morales and the members of Strangelove who owned the stage with refined assuredness, I was under no illusion that they were Depeche Mode. Looking around the venue, it was clear that others in the audience were not either, based alone on the incandescently knowing smiles I spied. This, however, held no consequence in sustaining our collective joy; for Strangelove's ability to touch Depeche Mode meant that we, too, could touch the "Boys from Basildon" by way of a Southern California tribute band with whose singer we could additionally identify.[2]

At this Strangelove performance, as was the case for the Sweet and Tender Hooligans and the Curse shows I attended, the Latino body—Morales's, Maldonado's, and Soto's, respectively—operated as the mediating force between the British singers they were channeling (Dave Gahan, Morrissey, and Robert Smith) and the adoring audience members. Indeed, these singers represent a recent iteration of the multidirectional touch—an emblematic "kiss across the ocean"—as described in the previous chapters. In this instance, though, touching is mediated by the tribute band, which in turn establishes an intimacy between not only the singers of the tribute band and the original band to which it is dedicated, but also between the fans of both tribute and original bands.[3] The audience therefore is capable of touching Depeche Mode, the Smiths/Morrissey, and the Cure through Strangelove, the Sweet and Tender Hooligans, and the Curse, particularly during the live performance, a moment for one to witness audience members reaching out and touching the tribute band singers to in turn activate a multilayered hapticity operating across time and space. Through our devotion to both the original band and the tribute band, the promise for those who have dedicatedly listened and relistened—like the young me did as noted at the start of this book, and as the middle-aged me does now at the end of it—we often find ourselves reliving (or rather not forgetting, as implored by the Smiths in "Rubber Ring") those songs that made us cry and the songs that saved our lives, continuously inspiring us to persist in often hostile climates.[4] Here, the tribute band mediates a transatlantic touch, generating a bond simultaneously remote and familiar, which is necessarily infused with the stuff that history and memory are made of.

....

And let's not forget the original crop of post-punk bands and singers still active and touring. One such band is the Specials. Principally associated with the 2-Tone movement, the Specials, according to Dave Thompson (2017), appealed "to a new generation whose own social prospects were as appalling as the original Rude Boys [in Jamaica]" and "offered them an escape route" (12).[5] And "just as punk had grabbed centre stage following the [Sex] Pistols' now-legendary appearance on Today in December 1976," argues Mick O'Shea, "the dawning of the Eighties heralded the 2-Tone explosion" (2018, 4). Equally influenced by the sounds of ska, punk, reggae, and soul, all of which circulated and comingled in 1970s and '80s Britain, the emergence of 2-Tone bands like the Specials, the Beat, the Selecter, and the Bodysnatchers would reflect the increasingly multiracial makeup of the working-class population while commenting on the pervasiveness of racism, fascism, and economic despair, of which the band members were acutely aware.

Writing about the significant albeit short-lived Rock against Racism movement in the face of nostalgically deadly British nationalism, Paul Gilroy, in his essay "Rebel Souls: Dance-Floor Justice and the Temporary Undoing of Britain's Babylon," notes that although it "did not endure . . . it led, along a twisted path, to the [Toxteth] riots of 1981 and to 'Ghost Town,' Jerry Dammers' lucid, luminous projection and exposition of the country's crisis which occupied the number one spot on the singles chart while Britain's cities burned between April and July" (2015, 25).[6] Rightly crediting founding member Dammers, who wrote the song, "Ghost Town" was indeed, to paraphrase Gilroy, the Specials' "luminous projection and exposition" of the racial and economic crises of the moment.[7] And not only would "Ghost Town" become the band's most widely recognized song, but its political commentary would reverberate across the Atlantic, reaching listeners in Southern California by way of KROQ's radio waves and dubbed cassettes and borrowed vinyl played on home and car stereos, catalyzing attentive listeners in the service of social change.

This fact was even more clear to me when, in 2019, Los Angeles City Councilwoman Monica Rodríguez declared May 29 the Specials Day. When introducing the resolution to honor the band at a council meeting, Rodríguez—a Latina politician known for her unflinching advocacy for immigrants and undocumented residents and workers' rights—cited the band's long-standing Southern California fanbase, maintaining that "the Specials' legacy is emblematic of the strength derived from our diversity here in Los Angeles. Their music is an example that embracing our differences and uniqueness makes us more powerful" (Vozick-Levinson 2019). I was therefore elated that I could see the Specials at the House of Blues in Anaheim a few days after Rodríguez bestowed the honor upon the band. When I entered the venue with my friend Dionne, a group of young Latinos near the merchandise booth caught my attention. Adopting a look that assembled knit polos, plaid trousers, black Oxford Doc Martens, and, for one young man, a Harrington jacket and a Blue Beat hat, they instantly reminded me of the Mod kids from my high school days whose smart style I admired. What stopped me in my tracks, however, was the large banner that they unfolded to collectively hold for a group photo. This banner—a DIY creation made of "cloth from a local vendor at the Anaheim swap meet, number 2 pencils, Sharpie and other black markers, and heart"—declared "ANAHEIM AGAINST RACISM."[8] Not only did I do a double take, but I had to get as close as possible to guarantee I was reading the banner correctly. Seeing these stylish young men unabashedly making their presence known at the concert, all the while announcing without apology their political convictions, unleashed a flood of emotions in me. I immediately approached them to express my deep admiration, telling them how they were the group I was looking for when in my teens I began attending shows at which I was often rendered an outcast.

I discovered that this group of young Latinos from Anaheim, the neighboring city of my hometown of Santa Ana, made up the collective Ghostown, named after but modifying the spelling of the Specials song "Ghost Town" (fig. C.3). Originating as a group of selectors (whose role is akin to a DJ's but more nuanced, given the nonstop, back-to-back musical canvasing for which a selector is known), Ghostown's political convictions were heightened—as members José "Che" Bracamontes and Cristian Nuñez explained to me—by their participation in protesting a Nazi rally held at Pearson Park in Anaheim, the event for which the "ANAHEIM AGAINST RACISM" banner was created (fig. C.4). It was clear that the Specials had not only inspired these Latino rude boys' deep love of ska, reggae, soul, rocksteady, and dub, but that their respect for and love of Black music from both the UK and the US also motivated their antiracism activism. I learned that night at the House of Blues that Ghostown was as dedicated to the Specials as they were to translating the Coventry band's class and race politics rooted in Cold War Britain for an increasingly anti-immigrant and white supremacist twenty-first-century US nationalist culture.[9] Performing at community happenings and fundraising events in predominantly working-class neighborhoods in Orange County and Los Angeles, Ghostown conjures and embraces a sonic spirt of the past and recasts it, on their own terms, for political consciousness and collective solidarity. In this vein, we might call to mind the line "Government leaving the youth on the shelf" from "Ghost Town" and translate its trenchant appraisal, alongside Ghostown, for ascertaining the US government's neglectful detainment of migrant youths on the US-Mexico border.[10]

C.3 Ghostown, "Anaheim against Racism." Courtesy of Che Bracamontes.

C.4 Ghostown, "Rude Boys/Ska es Vida." Courtesy of Che Bracamontes.

As 2-Tone and ska in 1970s and '80s Britain signal a merging of black and white, in terms of articulating both a monochromatic style and solidarity across racial difference, we might also highlight their deep connection to Latinidad. As one might note the contributions of Cuba-born and Jamaica-raised trombonist Emmanuel "Rico" Rodriguez on songs by the Specials, Bad Manners, and Madness or the formation of the transnational Latin ska movement since the mid-1980s, the link between politics and pleasure at the heart of Ghostown not only exemplifies another instance of transatlantic intimacy but also animates the enduring impact of British post-punk music on a younger generation of Latinas/os/x in Southern California. In the February 9, 1980, issue of *New Musical Express*, Paul Rambali's article on the Specials' tour of the United States, "The Promised Land Calling," expresses doubt that many American youths are truly capable of being swayed by the political messages tendered by an emergent and imperative 2-Tone band from Britain. Decades later, the inspired example of Ghostown emphatically quells this doubt.

....

Strangelove, Sweet and Tender Hooligans, the Curse, and Ghostown have helped me understand the past, present, and future registers on which touch operates. Whether geographical (not merely with regard to how Britain touches the United States but how Anaheim touches Santa Ana) or cross-generational (how the music artists who came to my emotional rescue as a teenager continue to do that years later for others), these serve as illustrations of the intimacy with which this book has been concerned. Initially, I imagined *A Kiss across the Ocean* as written for music fans of my generation who grew up listening to the same music and now regularly attend Totally 80s Live concerts (headlined by Boy George and Adam Ant) at the Honda Center in Anaheim and frequent spots like Totally 80s Bar and Grille in Fullerton. And perhaps on occasion, I thought, some stray scholar of popular culture and music studies might find interest in what it has to say.

Yet thanks to the tribute bands and the Anaheim selectors, each of whom have revitalized my appreciation of the music discussed in the preceding pages, I have discovered that this book also has in mind a younger generation—with whom I have found an unexpected kinship—that also embraces British post-punk cultures and, like the aforementioned tribute bands, refuses to "flatten pop and rock history to a series of shiny surfaces" (Homan 2006, 14). After all, the aptitude for traversing temporal and spatial divides, especially when sharing a profound love for the music and the people across the ocean to which we are mutually dedicated, is made possible by a fortuitous touch—be it in the form of a kiss, a cinematic citation, a fashion-based adaptation, a conversation over breakfast, a queer musical collaboration, or a newly established friendship—that emotively, and unforgettably, speaks of intimacy.

Notes

A KISS ACROSS THE OCEAN: AN INTRODUCTION

1. In his illuminating book I *Wonder U: How Prince Went Beyond Race and Back*, Adilifu Nama maintains that "during the early 1980s racially integrated bands, such as The Specials and Culture Club, also contributed to creating deeper fissures in the structured absence of blackness at MTV and helped undermine MTV's strident Jim Crow programming. The optics of racially integrated bands playing British new wave pop songs on the emergent music channel helped to destabilize the erroneous notion and prevailing racial politics of the American music industry that black artists play only R&B music" (2020, 48). Indeed, the "Karma Chameleon" video exemplifies Nama's argument.

2. I would like to make a point here, before proceeding, for those given pause by the fact that I start this book with Culture Club. A few years back on my Facebook page, I mentioned Culture Club's August 17, 1985, show at the Pacific Amphitheater in Costa Mesa, California, as the first concert I ever attended. I was quickly met with derision from some "friends" and colleagues who thought it fun to berate a silly 1980s pop band, perhaps because Culture Club didn't match the stature of a respectable act noted for their tacit seriousness, critically acclaimed musicianship, and assured heteronormativity. I could make the argument that it was Culture Club that led me to artists like Roxy Music, David Bowie, Siouxsie and the Banshees, and so on—which, in a way, I do—but I also refuse to deny that I continue to value my Culture Club albums, and I will not pretend they are no longer in my collection, nor deny that I ever owned them to boast in elitist fashion a collection devoid of bands and singers that test one's bogus sophistication in musical taste.

3. Here I am drawing on Welsh literary critic and cultural studies scholar Raymond Williams's notions of culture as "ordinary" and "a whole way of life" (see Williams ([1958] 1983, [1958] 1989). I also nod here to the excellent Cherry Red Records compilation CD *Shake the Foundations: Militant Funk and the Post-Punk Dancefloor 1978–1984* (2021).

4. Important to note is that this second British Invasion, like the one preceding it, was in no way uniform or static, as the artists constituting such invasions were diverse and hailed from disparate locations in the UK. For more on this point, see Jack Hamilton's (2016) important book, *Just around Midnight: Rock and Roll and the Racial Imagination*. *Creem* magazine, under the auspices of its special series *Creem* Close-Up, would publish in June 1984 an edition titled *The British Invasion, 1964–1984*, that connected these British invasions regularly rendered as temporally distinct.

5. It was Scritti Politti, with their song "Jacques Derrida" from the album *Songs to Remember* (1982), that inspired my interest in literary theory and my sitting in on Derrida's lectures while I was an intercampus exchange student in 1995 at the University of California, Irvine. Relatedly, Mark Fisher notes in *Ghosts of My Life: Writings on Depression, Hauntology and Lost Futures* that his introduction to the French philosopher "came in the pages of the *New Musical Express* in the 1980s, where Derrida's name would be mentioned by the most exciting writers" (2014, 17).

6. In a feature titled "The Americanization of John Lydon: A Progress Report," published three years earlier in the noted British music-fashion magazine the *Face*, Lydon notes the "awfulness" of London that prompted his relocation to the US (Salewicz 1981a). The feature concludes by informing the reader that "a camper van was being inspected prior to a projected drive to Mexico—John is very fond of Mexican beer" (49). Worth noting is Lydon's observation of the Sex Pistols' show in San Antonio, Texas: "There was a lot of Mexicans in the audience. They looked like wild Indians to me. This very large Mexican contingency decided that they liked us, so that shut the cowboys up and the bottles stopped being slung" (Lydon 1994, 243). This show is the basis of Jim Mendiola's film *Pretty Vacant* (1996). For an insightful reading of Mendiola's film, see Habell-Pallán (2005).

7. I admittedly find these revisionist histories reductive and much too quick to erase the contradictions and complexities of music genealogies. In the rush to decolonize punk, for example, history is rewritten in an ironically sanitized and politically expedient fashion.

8. *Latinidad* is a term that enables comparative or parallel consideration of distinct Latin American–origin groups in the United States. Coined by sociologist Felix M. Padilla (1985) for examining the cohabitation of Mexicans and Puerto Ricans in Chicago, Latinidad is often contested by those who, on the one hand, hold fast to nation-based attachments to culture and ethnicity and, on the other hand, those who prefer to dismiss its quotidian realities and political potentiality, often imposing Latin American cultural phenomena on racialized, working-class US communities. For two brilliant and queer exceptions to these exhausted takes, see Juana María Rodríguez (2003) and Ramón H. Rivera-Servera (2012). Furthermore, throughout this book I oscillate between,

and at times simultaneously reference (*Latina/o/x*), *Latino*, *Latina*, and *Latinx*, the last term of which registers a refusal of the male/female gender binary. Unlike recent books that adopt *Latinx* (or *Chicanx*) in indiscriminate fashion, my continued use of the first two terms is motivated by an attentiveness to historical context (and thus working against the anachronistic tendencies of those mainly aspiring to convenience) and an insistence on reading *Latinx* as a queer signifier with its distinct temporal resonances. See my essay "X Marks the Spot" (Rodríguez 2017) for a more detailed discussion.

9. Pierre Bourdieu's (1979) *Distinction: A Social Critique of the Judgement of Taste* guides my thinking here. An exemplar of these tedious articles is Chuck Klosterman's "Viva Morrissey!" in the August 2002 issue of *Spin*. Also, while this project might very well index an intimacy between two continents, my use of *intimacy*, as will soon be made clear, is distinct from how Lisa Lowe (2015) adopts it in her book *The Intimacy of Four Continents*.

10. In *Multidirectional Memory: Remembering the Holocaust in the Age of Decolonization*, Michael Rothberg's use of "multidirectional" helps ascertain that which is "subject to ongoing negotiation, cross-referencing, and borrowing; as productive and not privative" (2009, 3). Aiming to illuminate how inspiration often operates on a two-way street with intimacy mutually felt, this project adopts the multidirectional to offer a layered historical account of the cultural politics of influence.

11. Inspiration here derives from José Esteban Muñoz's (1996) classic essay, "Ephemera as Evidence: Introductory Notes to Queer Acts."

12. I am well aware of earlier examples—whether it be Beatlemania in the 1960s or the arrival of cross-Atlantic punk bands like the Sex Pistols and the Clash in the 1970s—signaling a connection between Latinas/os and British music artists. While recognizing the porousness of decades, his book, however, starts with and builds from the 1980s.

13. Consider, for example, Gustavo Arellano's (2002) insightful "Their Charming Man: Dispatches from the Latino-Morrissey Love-In."

14. See Ruiz (2015). Ruiz's work builds on Paul Gilroy's (1993) foundational book, *The Black Atlantic: Modernity and Double Consciousness*, which also influences my project given Gilroy's refusal of a nation-based analytic framework. Peter D. O'Neill and David Lloyd's (2009) edited collection, *The Black and Green Atlantic: Cross-Currents of the African and Irish Diasporas*, has been equally instructive with its transatlantic approach inspired by Gilroy's paradigmatic lead.

15. It is fitting that Doonan titles his essay "Mundo Goes to Hollywood," the afterword for *Axis Mundo: Queer Networks in Chicano L.A.*, the accompanying catalog for the exhibition of the same name that underscores the artistic work and influence of Mundo Meza. Given Meza's love of British popular music, he

was no doubt a fan of Frankie Goes to Hollywood whose singles "Relax" and "Two Tribes" and album *Welcome to the Pleasuredome* commanded a considerable audience, and especially a gay male fan base, in the US. I discuss the group and singer Holly Johnson in chapter 6.

16. See the insightful blog post "Post-Punk Pirates, Princess Diana, and Bow Wow Wow at World's End" (Gorman 2016).

17. The quote from Mulcahy is taken from the blog post "80sonVEVO GAMV Takeover Week 9 w/FEATURED VIDEO Kim Carnes' 'Bette Davis Eyes'" (Golden Age of Music Video 2013). For more on the history of the "Planet Earth" video, see Stephen Davis's (2021) *Please Please Tell Me Now: The Duran Duran Story*. Mulcahy also directed the videos for foundational New Romantic band Spandau Ballet's "Chant No. 1 (I Don't Need This Pressure On)" and "True." Worth noting is the striking similarity between the dancers' movements in "Bette Davis Eyes" and the video for David Bowie's "Ashes to Ashes," directed by Bowie and David Mallet and featuring Steve Strange and others associated with the New Romantic–populated clubs Blitz and Billy's in London. See Boy George's (1995) *Take It Like a Man* for more on Strange and company's enlistment in the video.

18. Bow Wow Wow would, however, play the Ritz later in September 1981. See John Rockwell's (1981) review in the *New York Times* and Paul Gorman's (2020) exhaustive biography *The Life and Times of Malcolm McLaren*.

19. See also Drew Stone's 2017 documentary, *Who the Fuck Is That Guy? The Fabulous Journey of Michael Alago*.

20. Fittingly, all three acts at one point shared the same American label, Sire Records.

21. My thanks to Suzan Colón, who informed me in a personal conversation that "Jackie" was really her and editor David Keeps answering *Star Hits* readers' letters.

22. Benedict Anderson's (1983) notion of "imagined community" is quite fitting here, given the way preinternet print cultures—namely fanzines—assisted in assembling networks of fans organized around particular bands, singers, and musical movements.

23. Taken from a post on Simon Napier-Bell's Facebook page dated March 26, 2018.

24. Some may take issue with my identification of Japan as post-punk, especially since the band early on eschewed punk aesthetics for a glam sound and style. However, their move away from a discernable glam inflection, most commonly marked by *Quiet Life* (1979) and *Gentlemen Take Polaroids* (1980), their third and fourth albums respectively, would subsequently position them alongside musical contemporaries influenced by punk but now, like Japan, gravitating toward a more post-punk electronic sound.

25. Personal communication via Skype with Suzan Colón, August 8, 2017.

26. For two important accounts of Genesis Breyer P-Orridge, see their posthumously published memoir *Nonbinary* (P-Orridge 2021) and Simon Ford's (1999) classic *Wreckers of Civilisation: The Story of Coum Transmissions and Throbbing Gristle.*

27. I wish to note here Greil Marcus's assertion in a 1980 *Rolling Stone* article that "postpunk pop avant-garde" was a term that he had "thought up in California, after listening to the new music coming out of England: some of it willfully obscurantist and contrived, and some of it—most notably the late-1979 debut albums by Essential Logic, the Raincoats (both Rough Trade bands), and the Gang of Four (a leftist group signed to the EMI and Warner Bros. multinationals)—sparked by a tension, humor, and sense of paradox plainly unique in present-day pop music" ([1980] 1993, 108).

28. Nevertheless, Rimmer acknowledges that while his book "is the story of Culture Club . . . it's also the story of pop music since punk" (1985, 5), therefore about, temporally speaking, post-punk. The phrase "like punk never happened" was spoken by Paul Weller, singer for the Jam and later the Style Council, in a *Smash Hits* interview with then-journalist and later Pet Shop Boy Neil Tennant. See Watkins (2016, 212).

29. See Kasper de Graaf and Malcolm Garrett's (1983) *When Cameras Go Crazy: Culture Club.*

30. Bassist John Taylor also makes this point but within the context of Duran Duran's success, in which *Smash Hits*—and not the pretentious weekly music papers like NME—had a hand. See Zoë Dobson's (2019) documentary *Duran Duran: There's Something You Should Know.* Pat Long's book, *The History of the NME: High Times and Low Lives at the World's Most Famous Music Magazine,* further reasons, "Until MTV, radio and press had been the most important way for record companies to break new bands. Now that it was shifting to television, a generation of new British bands appeared without the sanction of NME's writers. The paper was left at a loss as to how to deal with them, but *Smash Hits* thrived" (2012, 144).

31. For an illuminating oral history covering the emergence of Rock against Racism and Red Wedge, see Daniel Rachel's (2016) *Walls Come Tumbling Down: The Music and Politics of Rock against Racism, 2 Tone and Red Wedge 1976–1992.*

32. Here I'm thinking of X's 1983 "I Must Not Think Bad Thoughts" ("Will the last American band to get played on the radio please bring the flag?") and the Dead Milkmen's 1987 "Instant Club Hit (You'll Dance to Anything)" ("You'll dance to anything by any bunch of stupid Europeans / Who come over here with their big hairdos / Intent on taking our money instead of giving your cash / Where it belongs / To a decent American artist like myself").

33. In this vein, I see my book in conversation with Daphne A. Brooks's (2021) stunning *Liner Notes for the Revolution: The Intellectual Life of Black Feminist Sound*, especially the chapter "'If You Should Lose Me': Of Trunks and Record Shops and Black Girl Ephemera."

34. Of course, with the advent of the internet, many previously hard-to-find or out-of-print materials are more readily accessible, whether through official institutional databases or unofficial social media archives (found on Facebook, for example) established by dedicated followers.

35. *You Weren't There: A History of Chicago Punk, 1977–1984* was written and directed by Joe Losurdo and Christina Tillman and released in 2007. Laina Dawes's (2013) book, *What Are You Doing Here? A Black Woman's Life and Liberation in Heavy Metal*, makes clear by title alone the interrogation she's accustomed to receiving at events where she, as a Black woman, purportedly does not belong.

36. On the complexity of attending gigs, I've learned a great deal from Graham Duff's (2019) superb *Foreground Music: A Life in Fifteen Gigs*.

37. Matthew Worley's keen assessment of youth culture operates in a similar fashion. He writes, "Youth culture should not be understood simply as a model of consumption, or a product of media invention, but as a formative and contested experience through which young people discover, comprehend, affirm and express their desires, opinions and disaffections" (Worley 2017, 2–3).

38. For more on Northern Soul, see David Nowell's (2011) *The Story of Northern Soul: A Definitive History of the Dance Scene That Refuses to Die* and Stuart Cosgrove's (2017) *Young Soul Rebels: A Personal History of Northern Soul*.

39. And there are also moments when I'm stopped in my tracks by stumbling upon unsavory depictions of Latinos/as in my favorite music performers' song lyrics or memoirs. This will be clear at various moments in the book. One such example is found in the pages of *True*, the autobiography of Spandau Ballet's bassist Martin Kemp (2000). Writing about the aftermath of the 1992 Los Angeles uprising (rendered by the mainstream media as "riots" inciting looting, arson, and indiscriminate violence) provoked by the Rodney King verdict, Kemp details queuing with his wife, Shirlie Holliman, for a British Airlines flight to London "next to a cheap Mexican flight to Mexico City" (2000, 236). Instructed by her to glance upon the neighboring gate, Kemp expresses disbelief as "every other young Mexican was carrying a TV or a microwave on his shoulders, or pushing them around on trolleys—not in boxes, just wrapped in paper tied with string. . . . It looked as if they had definitely been out shopping for their cousins back home over the last couple of days, or nights" (236).

40. The phrase "possessive investment in whiteness" is George Lipsitz's (2018). See his book *The Possessive Investment in Whiteness: How White People Profit from Identity Politics*. My connection to Blondie may have been an unconscious

awareness of their connection to Latinidad as exemplified by their incorporation of Mexican mariachi in their 1980 hit single, "The Tide Is High." See Josh Kun's (2017) insightful introduction to his edited collection, *The Tide Was Always High: The Music of Latin America in Los Angeles.*

CHAPTER 1: RED OVER WHITE

1. For more on Blade's formative influence on Southern California fans of British post-punk music and *Video One*, see his autobiography, *World in My Eyes* (Blade 2017).

2. Relatedly, Ned Raggett's (2019) "A Long Term Effect: Tim Pope on Four Decades of Work with the Cure" for the *Quietus* is a stellar piece on the history of Pope's video work, particularly with the Cure.

3. Or, as Michael Jaime-Becerra elegantly puts it in his essay "Todo se acaba" about being a young Chicano from El Monte, California, who spends his first paycheck on the *Wild Things* EP by the Creatures, the Banshees side project featuring Siouxsie and Budgie, it was "something only mentioned in fan books or alluded to in interviews" (2019, 111).

4. This icy disaffection keys into Sioux's nickname of the Ice Queen, as declared on the December 3, 1977, cover of *Sounds* and on which she appears wearing the classic Sex shop "tits" T-shirt. This issue of *Sounds* also features Vivien Goldman's (1977) highly regarded and now classic interview "Siouxsie Sioux Who R U?"

5. For another account of Siouxsie and the Banshees' coming-of-age impact, see Sue Webster's *I Was a Teenage Banshee*, in which the author identifies the band as her "teenage obsession that dragged me kicking and screaming throughout my adolescence" (2019, 11).

6. Vivien Goldman's (2019) brilliant *Revenge of the She-Punks: A Feminist Music History from Poly Styrene to Pussy Riot* offers a detailed genealogy of such "really wild women." Goldman's analysis stands in stark contrast to that offered by critic Sean Egan, who is incapable of seeing the sexism behind the "inordinately long time" it took Siouxsie and the Banshees and the Slits "to get a record deal" (2019, 172). Perhaps this is why Egan dismisses the Banshees' *Join Hands* as "unmelodic and tedious" and the Slits' *Cut* as "hardly offer[ing] profound insight" (173).

7. See Caroline Coon (1977), *1988: The New Wave Punk Rock Explosion*, for an account of the 100 Club festival.

8. The quotes from Sioux and Pirroni are taken from the segment "Siouxsie Sioux" from the 2009 BBC documentary *The Queens of British Pop*. For a recorded version of Siouxsie and the Banshees' 100 Club performance, see "Siouxsie & the Banshees—the Lord's Prayer (100 Club Punk Festival 20-09-1976)," posted

by James Haine, YouTube, January 13, 2014, https://www.youtube.com/watch?v=aKzT5hHNa54.

9. Sioux, Severin, and a young Black woman named Simone Thomas, central figures of what journalist Caroline Coon called "the Bromley Contingent" (a name that Sioux and Severin have repeatedly declared their hatred of) appeared alongside the Sex Pistols during their notoriously recognized and now historically significant appearance on *Today*, the television show hosted by journalist Bill Grundy.

10. See, for example, the work of historian Gilbert G. Gonzalez, particularly his monograph *Chicano Education in the Era of Segregation* ([1990] 2013). For an example of how this relates to the status of undocumented students, see the unpublished pathfinding work of anthropologist Jennifer R. Nájera, *Undocumented Education: Intersections of Activism and Education Among Undocumented Students* (Duke University Press, forthcoming).

11. While I have elected to use "Native American," the reference to "Indians" unquestionably derives from the white cinematic and televisual portrayals of indigenous people.

12. "Red over White" is the B-side track to Siouxsie and the Banshees' 1980 single "Israel." While the lyrics do not reference American Indians (and the band's commentary about the track in the booklet included for the 2004 compilation of B-sides titled *Downside Up* indicates no such referential motivation), I adopt the title of the song metaphorically to signal the various cross-cultural identifications and intimate alignments explored in this chapter.

13. I owe this insight to Andy Polaris, lead singer of the band Animal Nightlife, who followed the Banshees as a teenager and made this point in a private conversation about the charge of cultural appropriation.

14. Chapter 3, focused on the Northampton band Bauhaus, engages in a more thorough discussion of goth, particularly around the 1979 single "Bela Lugosi's Dead," their most famous song, considered by many the first goth record and the unofficial goth anthem. Siouxsie has on more than one occasion expressed her regret for wearing the swastika, primarily on an armband. As she explains, "Maybe I had been naïve in thinking people would understand what I was doing with the swastika. I must have been, because we started to get a lot of National Front skinheads turning up to gigs. They used to piss me off so much. I tried everything to stop them coming, drawing attention to them and slagging them off, even stopping a gig and beating the shit out of them a few times. But they just wouldn't fuck off. I was so pissed off that I decided to use another equally strong symbol, the Star of David, which would completely alienate the idiots. When we played this gig in Derby, we tried everything to stop them, but nothing seemed to work. So we went off stage, put the 'Israel' T-shirts on and did 'Drop Dead' with the lights spotlighting them. It was fantastic. The whole audi-

ence felt empowered and turned on them" (Paytress 2003, 104). Despite adopting the Star of David on T-shirts and for their single "Israel" (and featuring "Red over White" on the B-side) as "an atonement" and writing the song "Metal Postcard (Mittageisen)" in the memory of anti-Nazi visual artist John Heartfield, journalists and scholars continued to take note of the too-casual incorporation of Nazi imagery in punk contexts of which Siouxsie was a part. For a discussion on Sioux's range of styles, see Kevin Petty (1995), "The Image of Siouxsie Sioux: Punk and the Politics of Gender"; and Simon Reynolds and Joy Press, *The Sex Revolts: Gender, Rebellion and Rock 'n' Roll,* which notes how Sioux's "career has consisted of an endless succession of costume changes and sexual personae" (1995, 291). Lucy O'Brien's ([1995] 2020) foundational *She Bop* also provides an excellent arch for assessing Siouxsie's initially controversial public image to her sui generis role in the British punk and post-punk scenes.

15. Severin's words are from the liner notes written by Mark Paytress for Polydor's 2006 remastered CD release of *Juju.*

16. The persistence of the Siouxsie clone extends into the recent present, as illustrated in a 2013 episode of the American sketch comedy television series *Portlandia,* where the character Alexandra models herself after Siouxsie, hilariously mispronouncing her name "Suxie Sux."

17. Taken from Manson's interview in *The Queens of British Pop* (Newton 2009).

18. These songs are no doubt nods to Alfred Hitchcock's *Spellbound* (1945) and Gene Fowler Jr.'s *I Was a Teenage Werewolf* (1957).

19. For additional information, see "Kid Congo Powers Oral History" (2005).

20. For an insightful local history of Kid Congo Powers, see Melissa Hidalgo (2021), "Gente from La Puente: Underground Punk Icon Kid Congo Powers Still Rocks."

21. John Wombat's (2018) *The Cramps, Beast and Beyond: A Book about Bryan Gregory* provides an insightful account of Gregory's personal history.

22. Additional Santisi photos of the Disneyland visit can be found in Ray Stevenson's (1986) *Siouxsie and the Banshees: Photo Book,* although they are reproduced in a much smaller scale. I thank Donna Santisi for clarifying that her photos were taken in January 1982.

23. This Santisi quote is taken from an interview with Alice Bag (2016).

24. For an interesting analysis that understands Kid Congo Powers's future embrace of the vampire (and thus tallying another example of what she calls the "Chicano Dracula" figure) see Paloma Martinez-Cruz (2020), "Chicano Dracula: The Passions and Predations of Bela Lugosi, Gomez Addams, and Kid Congo Powers." Martinez-Cruz's argument about Kid Congo Powers-as-vampire superbly assists in refusing his categorization as some standard-issue goth.

25. In the case of the former, see Alice Bag's (2011) excellent autobiography *Violence Girl: East L.A. Rage to Hollywood Stage, a Chicana Punk Story*; Jayna Brown (2011), "'Brown Girl in the Ring': Poly Styrene, Anabella Lwin, and the Politics of Anger"; Michelle Cruz Gonzales (2016), *The Spit Boy Rule: Tales of a Xicana in a Female Punk Band*; Colin Gunckel (2017), "'People Think We're Weird 'Cause We're Queer': Art Meets Punk in Los Angeles"; and Celeste Bell and Zoë Howe (2019), *Dayglo! The Poly Styrene Story*.

26. My thanks to Professor Pete Sigal of Duke University for accompanying me to the show.

27. For the most astute appraisal of Davis's work to date, see José Esteban Muñoz (1999), *Disidentifications: Queers of Color and the Politics of Performance*.

28. Sioux is also seen partaking in LA nightlife in *Reynaldo Rivera: Provisional Notes for a Disappeared City* (Rivera 2020).

29. Perhaps due to the limited life span of blog posts allowed on her page, this post is no longer viewable as of late 2020. I was, however, fortunate to capture a screen shot of the post for historical preservation.

30. One might also include Dave Navarro, the Mexican American guitarist who, while a member of Jane's Addiction, toured with the Banshees during the inaugural Lollapalooza music festival and claims to have made out with Severin and slept with Sioux. Severin, however, denies this claim in Paytress's biography.

31. Michael Jaime-Becerra alerted me to the fact that after this appearance, the Creatures performed in Tijuana, Mexico, one night later at the club Iguanas. In Matthew T. Hall's (2016) article for the *San Diego Union-Tribune* about the historic club, a patron describes it as "the greatest, most dangerous venue that ever existed."

32. For an excellent history of Rodney Bingenheimer's English Disco, which, along with his show on LA's noted radio station KROQ-FM, facilitated the American entryway for numerous British punk and post-punk acts, see George Hickenlooper's (2003) documentary *Mayor of the Sunset Strip*.

33. "Shoegaze" without a doubt counts as a post-punk subgenre, particularly for its derived stimulus from bands like Siouxsie and the Banshees and the Cure. As Simon Scott, drummer of the foremost shoegaze band, Slowdive (named after the song of the same name by Siouxsie and the Banshees), notes, "I always thought Robert Smith, when he was in Siouxsie and the Banshees playing guitar, was the coolest as he just stood there and let the music flood out. That anti-showmanship was perfect so I never really understood why people began to use 'shoegaze' as a negative term" (Gourlay 2009).

34. "Shizu Saldamando, Survive, 2012," Self Help Graphics and Art website, accessed January 19, 2022, https://www.selfhelpgraphics.com/large-format-prints/shizu-saldamando-survive-2012.

35. All quotes are taken from Dione Newton's 2017 BBC documentary *The Queens of British Pop.* This claim to difference evokes Siouxsie's refusal of the goth tag. Bearing in mind the band's preference for identifying *Juju* as "psychological horror" rather than goth/goff, we may also note Siouxsie's multifaceted view of death that negates a normative, Western logic. Consider the Banshees' track "El Dia de los Muertos," the B-side to the 1988 single "The Last Beat of My Heart." Sung partially in Spanish, the song is another case in point (along with "Manchild") of Siouxsie's familiarity with Latin American history and culture. Inspired by an exhibition she saw of the work of Mexican lithographer José Guadalupe Posada at the Serpentine Gallery in London, Siouxsie explains that the exhibition got her "thinking about All Souls Day and how Halloween is traditionally associated with blackness and witches. In Mexico, they paint their skulls in bright colours, and the whole thing is a real irreverent celebration of death" (Paytress 2003, 173).

CHAPTER 2: TOUCHING PRINCE CHARMING

1. I wish to confess here that my admiration for Adam Ant indeed follows his "imperial phase" (as Pet Shop Boy Neil Tennant would put it) of stardom; that is, succeeding the apex of his celebrity—arguably represented by his less successful 1983 album *Strip*—and during his subsequent chart-topping decline. Speaking of Tennant, his admiration of Adam would begin around the same time, as he notes in a 1985 *Smash Hits* interview with Tom Hibbert: "I have a history of liking pop stars when they go down the dumper. I didn't like Adam Ant until he went down the dumper, then I developed a kind of pathetic devotion to him. Gary Numan was never fantastically interesting until *he* went down the dumper, and now I love him to death. I always love them when they go on the slippery slope" (Hibbert 1985, 13).

2. Worth noting as well is that "Vive le Rock" also cites the artist Tom of Finland ("Well I've been where I was going / And it's not Tom of Finland"), whose drawings of hypermasculine men (consistently with enormously exaggerated genitalia) in homoerotic situations are an enduring fixture in gay male culture.

3. See Adam Ant's (2006) autobiography *Stand and Deliver,* which explains in detail his childhood and Paul McCartney giving him an advanced pressing of the Beatles' album *Revolver.*

4. Saloman's formative influence is discussed in Ant's aforementioned autobiography as well as in John Moulson's 2003 documentary *The Madness of Prince Charming.*

5. *Jubilee* was met with fierce criticism upon its release, a significant amount of which might be called homophobic given Jarman's queer identity. As Jarman biographer Tony Peake writes in his "Liner Notes" to the Criterion Collection's

2003 DVD release of the film: "The film opened in February 1978—exactly a year after Jarman had first put pen to paper—to decidedly mixed reviews.... Vivienne Westwood even went so far as to have a T-shirt printed, in which, at some length, she detailed why she despised the film. It was, she said, "the most boring and therefore disgusting film" she had ever seen. She could not "get off watching a gay boy jerk off through the titillation of his masochistic tremblings. You pointed your nose in the right direction then you wanked." For an excellent history of Jordan, see *Defying Gravity: Jordan's Story* (Mooney 2019), by Jordan Mooney with Cathi Unsworth.

6. Fred and Judy Vermorel note that McLaren "had got many of his fashion ideas from Allen Jones' paintings and so Adam was interested in these weird rubber and leather garments. But 'it really used to make me tremble, just to go in there,' he recalls" (Vermorel and Vermorel 1981, 4).

7. Journalist Robert Palmer takes aim at Adam and the Ants and Bow Wow Wow for lifting the Burundi sound, calling them the "pop pirates in search of plunder" (Palmer 1981). Thus, for Palmer, not only did their aesthetic approximate pirating but their mining of tribal sounds did as well. Speaking of pirating, Adam would settle out of court in 2010 when it was revealed by a musicologist that "Prince Charming" was identical to Rolf Harris's 1965 song "War Canoe." I refer my reader to the interview between Harris and BBC Radio host Danny Baker: "Danny Baker and Rolf Harris Discuss Adam Ant's Prince Charming," posted by cthomer5000 on YouTube, May 17, 2020, https://www.youtube.com/watch?v=ot8wc6Soylo.

8. For an account of the pirate image in the genealogy of Westwood's fashion history, see her autobiography, cowritten with Ian Kelly, *Vivienne Westwood* (Westwood and Kelly 2014). While elements of the pirate style indeed made their way into his aesthetic repertoire, Adam notes in his autobiography, "Malcolm tried to get me to model Vivienne's new pirate clothes, but I preferred my own look" (Ant 2006, 146), thus signaling his refusal of McLaren's well-known unscrupulous scheming. Additionally worth noting is Palmer's (1981) assessment of the shared musical and visual characteristics of the Ants and Bow Wow Wow.

9. I follow the lead of Native activists by replacing the *i* with an asterisk, given how, as Brian Cladoosby argues, "Redsk*n is a racial slur, no matter how many weak justifications defenders try and come up with to keep using it" (2014).

10. "Antmusic" and "Ant music," and "Antpeople" and "Ant people," are used interchangeably in Adam merchandise and lyric sheets, explaining why various spellings appear in the body of the text. Fittingly, the myth of the Ant People, who saved the Hopi tribe from destruction vis-à-vis their model survival tactics, is an additional link connecting Adam and Native American cultural history. For more on the myth, see Frank Waters (1977), *Book of the Hopi*.

11. Drawing from American Indian culture, along with a long-standing pillaging of gay culture, was clearly part of McLaren's sustained effort, as famously articulated by Dick Hebdige (1979) in *Subculture: The Meaning of Style*, to form a sense of style through bricolage. Former Ants guitarist Leigh Gorman notes that McLaren's idea for Bow Wow Wow, to which Gorman defected, was to be a gay band with a Native American aesthetic. As he pointedly explains, "Homosexual Apaches is what he wanted us to be" (Jones 2020, 247). For a brilliant analysis of McLaren's and Westwood's appropriation of gay culture for Sex shop fashion, see David Wilkinson's (2015) "Ever Fallen in Love (with Someone You Shouldn't Have?): Punk, Politics, and Same-Sex Passion."

12. The "North American Community Indian Association in New York" mentioned by Maw was most likely the American Indian Community House, founded in New York City in 1969, to which Stonefish and Martin belonged.

13. Carol Spindel's (2002) *Dancing at Halftime: Sports and the Controversy over American Indian Mascots* offers an excellent account of "The Chief" at the University of Illinois, Urbana-Champaign.

14. See Teresa de Lauretis (1976–77), "Cavani's *Night Porter*: A Woman's Film?," for an astute reading and historical contextualization of the 1974 film, which allows for ascertaining how critical condemnation of the film and its director parallels the disapproving appraisals of the song.

15. Dave Barbarossa's (2015) brilliant *Mud Sharks* provides a gripping account of growing up in 1970s Britain amid the rise of racist and fascist sentiment represented by the National Front. Also, for an important distinction between racism and fascism, which, in the formation of Rock against Racism, were often blurred, see Paul Gilroy's (1987) now-classic study *"There Ain't No Black in the Union Jack": The Cultural Politics of Race and Nation.*

16. References to the song in print have more often than not included the hyphen between "Puerto" and "Rican." I therefore refer to the track as "Puerto-Rican."

17. Aside from its listing on numerous bootleg recordings, "Puerto-Rican," to my knowledge, appears only on the 2001 release *Adam and the Ants: Live at the BBC* on the Strange Fruit label.

18. See Allen L. Woll (1980), "Bandits and Lovers: Hispanic Images in American Film," and many of the essays in Chon A. Noriega's (1992) anthology *Chicanos and Film: Representation and Resistance.*

19. This performance is at "Adam Ant—Cannon and Ball Show—Complete Segment," posted by Slapdash Eden on YouTube, original broadcast May 29, 1982, https://www.youtube.com/watch?v=xCtXuVHSZpw.

20. The title of Caroline Sullivan's January 10, 2002, article for the *Guardian*—"'Anyone Over 30 Belongs to Me—Bisexual, Male, Female, Gay, Whatever'"—taken from an interview with Adam, makes this crystal clear.

21. I wish to also note Adam's enduring occasional nod to Latino and Latin American cultural expressions as resources for accentuating his sexualized image. Consider, for example, the song "Spanish Games" from his 1983 LP *Strip*.

22. While I reference this scene from *Less Than Zero* in the introduction, consider another passage fitting for the context at hand: "A dark boy with a thin mustache and an 'Under the Big Black Sun' T-shirt bumps into me and Rip grabs his shoulders and pushes him back into the dancing crowd and shouts 'Fuckin' spic!'" (Ellis 1985, 185).

CHAPTER 3: DARKER ENTRIES

1. Murphy notes: "Look at the cover of 'Bela,' which is a still from pure Gothic cinema, *The Cabinet of Dr. Caligari*. That was the aesthetic we identified with a lot, although it wasn't on an academic level, it was that relativity of the songs and also what we looked like. I looked at stills of *Dr. Caligari*, having never seen the film, and I said, 'That's me, that's what I look like.' After the fact. I looked like this somnambulant character without knowing he existed, so it wasn't a mask or an emulation or anything, that's what we were" (Thompson 2002, 59).

2. For a comprehensive account of "deathrock," see Mikey Bean's (2019) *Phantoms: The Rise of Deathrock from the LA Punk Scene*. More recently, the term *dark wave* has come to stand in for music previously associated with both goth and deathrock. *Emo* is another recent category that approximates goth. For more on emo, see Marissa López's (2012) "Soy Emo, y Qué? Sad Kids, Punkera Dykes, and the Latin@ Public Sphere."

3. For illustration, see Andi Harriman and Marloes Bontje (2014), *Some Wear Leather Some Wear Lace: The Worldwide Compendium of Postpunk and Goth in the 1980s*. Despite the book's purported "worldwide" focus, it nonetheless remains mired in whiteness.

4. Bordal fittingly refers to Bauhaus as "reluctant proto-goths."

5. In Suzan Colón's article "The Gloom Generation," Murphy further explains, "I know that Bauhaus presumably started what the critics coined the 'gothic' genre in 1979 with 'Bela Lugosi's Dead,' but goth was a myth dreamt up by journalists sometime back in the '80s to describe Bauhaus, Joy Division, Iggy's vocal vibe on *The Idiot*, and so on" (1997, 123).

6. "No wave" is in reference to the New York City avant-garde music and art scene spanning the late 1970s and early 1980s. See Marc Masters's (2007) *No Wave*, and Thurston Moore and Byron Coley's (2008) *No Wave. Post-Punk. Underground. New York. 1976–1980* for detailed histories.

7. The comparison to "Freebird" and "Stairway to Heaven" is made on the website Postpunk.com ("40 Years of Bauhaus' Bela Lugosi's Dead" 2019).

8. Paul Sullivan, in *Remixology: Tracing the Dub Diaspora*, argues that "as a genre (or perhaps subgenre, since it developed out of roots reggae), dub was fairly short-lived in Jamaica, peaking in the mid to late 1970s and already winding down in the early 1980s. But its creative strategies and associated rituals—the sound system, the deejay, the remix—have continued far beyond its island of origin" (2014, 11). For insightful explorations of reggae and dub's influence on punk and post-punk musicians, see Dick Hebdige (1987), *Cut 'n' Mix: Culture, Identity and Caribbean Music*; Michael E. Veal (2007), *Dub: Soundscapes and Shattered Songs in Jamaican Reggae*; Christopher Partridge (2010), *Dub in Babylon: Understanding the Evolution and Significance of Dub Reggae in Jamaica and Britain from King Tubby to Post-Punk*; and Eric Doumerc (2018), *Jamaican Music in England: From the 1960s to the 1990s*.

9. For more on Don Letts and his illustrious history in the UK punk scene, see his books *Culture Clash: Dred Meets Punk Rockers* (Letts 2006) and *There and Black Again* (Letts 2021).

10. The next sentence finds Haskins witnessing one of his favorite bands at the time, the Slits, also hanging out at Letts's flat. As Christopher Partridge notes, "Certainly, one of the most significant punk bands to be explicitly influenced by dub, The Slits, trace their interest in the genre to 'Don Letts and his DJing stints at the Roxy'" (2010, 169).

11. Taken from the uncredited liner notes of the 2009 Omnibus Edition of Bauhaus's *Mask*, p. 26.

12. Boy George also fittingly notes that "at the end of punk I became a big Bauhaus fan" (Blade 2021, 486).

13. The most (in)famous is unquestionably Steve Southerland, who spent an amicable couple of days with the band for a feature in the publication *Melody Maker*, which, according to David J, read as "completely opposite to what we thought it would be due to the way he behaved. He was very two-faced. Very snidey" (Shirley 1994, 83). The band subsequently invited Sutherland to engage in a live interview before their October 14, 1982, London gig at the Lyceum (in lieu of the Cult opening) to confront him about the piece. Sutherland was unrelenting, introducing the event as follows: "Good evening ladies and gentlemen. I'm Steve from *Melody Maker* and this is Bauhaus, otherwise known as Ziggy Stardust and the Spiders from Mars" (83). A subsequently released bootleg vinyl picture disc, titled *The Interview Situation*, documents the encounter between Sutherland and the band.

14. In Ian Shirley's *Dark Entries: Bauhaus and Beyond*, Ash explains, "We recorded ['Walk This Way'] and the record company said, 'That sounds just like Tito Puente'—a track by him which Santana had a lot of success with. So Beggars [Banquet] took it to a musicologist who said, 'Yeah, you've got a problem with this.' It was even in the same key!" (1994, 176). Shirley further notes that "Beggars contacted Puente's music publishers and they agreed [to] a 50/50 split with Puente

being credited as co-writer" (176). Daniel Ash acknowledges the important work of the late British conguero Robin Jones, a friend of engineer Pete Barraclough, in an interview included on the US promo CD single for "Walk This Way."

15. These shows were canceled due to the COVID-19 pandemic.

16. See the video "David J and the Bauhaus Logo Controversy," posted by Reviewer, YouTube, May 20, 2015, https://www.youtube.com/watch?v=kCHSr7yLfww.

17. Kevin Haskins, email to author, July 27, 2020.

18. Although his memoir is published under the name "David J. Haskins," I have elected to use "David J" in the text to avoid confusion with his brother Kevin Haskins.

19. Here I cannot help but think of the line "Those Indians wank on his bones" from the Bauhaus track "Antonin Artaud" from 1983's *Burning from the Inside*, a song recalling Artaud's time in Mexico among the Tarahumara Indians, captured in his book *The Peyote Dance* (Artaud 1976).

20. Jaime Hernandez's best biographical portrait of Izzy is unquestionably found in *Flies on the Ceiling* (Hernandez 1997).

21. I cannot help but think here of the Southern California band Blink-182, whose 2016 song "She's Out of Her Mind," originally titled "Orange County Girl," spotlights an "antisocial" young woman who's "got a black shirt, black skirt and Bauhaus stuck in her head." The subject of the song, however, is presumably Orange County white, just as everyone is who stars in the promotional video.

22. Plans were made to see Bauhaus perform in Chicago in July 2020 with my dear friend and colleague, Mirelsie Velázquez. However, as noted above regarding the band's most recent shows, the concert was canceled due to the COVID-19 pandemic.

CHAPTER 4: THE SHINING SINNERS

1. While Soft Cell's first release was the 1980 EP *Mutant Moments*, the 2005 compilation *The Bedsit Tapes* collects some of the duo's earlier tracks—recorded in a Leeds Polytechnic art studio and in their bedrooms—since 1978. For an excellent early history of Soft Cell, see Tebbutt (1984).

2. For an excellent account of Soft Cell's role in the early 1980s queer pop scene, see Hilderbrand (2013), "'Luring Disco Dollies to a Life of Vice': Queer Pop Music's Moment."

3. In *Tainted Life*, Almond (1999b) cites 1977 as the year he and Ball first met. However, in Majewski and Bernstein's *Mad World*, he recounts, "I'd met David Ball in 1978 when I was doing a fine arts course at Leeds Polytechnic" (2014, 213).

In *Electronic Boy*, Dave Ball (2020) also identifies 1977 as the year he began attending Leeds and soon thereafter met Almond. I have therefore decided to stick with 1977 given the preponderance of references to this year as when the two first came into contact. For more on the Leeds post-punk scene, see Gavin Butt's *No Machos or Pop Stars: When the Leeds Art Experiment Went Punk* (2022).

4. For more on the history of the "three-chord thrash of punk," see Matthew Worley's (2017) excellent book *No Future: Punk, Politics and British Youth Culture, 1976–1984*.

5. While Siouxsie Sioux and the Banshees bassist Steve Severin hailed from nearby London suburb Bromley, Throbbing Gristle got their start in Kingston upon Hull whereas Cabaret Voltaire and the Human League both emerged from the historically industrial city of Sheffield, locations that are a significant distance from England's capital.

6. See Simon Frith and Howard Horne's (1987) *Art into Pop* for an extensive discussion on the art school influence on postwar British popular music.

7. Thus, when a critic like Sasha Geffen writes, "Curiously, [Soft Cell's] lead singer, Marc Almond, got involved in the UK's industrial scene after he had already become a popstar" (2020, 122–23), the palpable unfamiliarity with the duo's origins or their long-standing connections to avant-garde artists outside the mainstream shortsightedly casts Soft Cell as a flighty "synthpop" act whose sole impact was "Tainted Love" and a few other tracks meriting mention, given their sexually "shocking" titles. Indeed, in Geffen's book Soft Cell is discussed solely in the chapter "The Fake Makes It Real: Synthpop and MTV" and not once mentioned in the earlier chapter, "Wreckers of Civilization: Post-Punk, Goth, and Industrial."

8. Although I hope to make this clear in this chapter largely dedicated to Almond, I also refer my reader-listener to Dave Ball's solo LP *In Strict Tempo* (1983), which features collaborations with Genesis P. Orridge.

9. David Hepworth (2016) discusses the historical significance of Bowie's performance in "How Performing 'Starman' on *Top of the Pops* Sent Bowie into the Stratosphere."

10. In many ways, Soft Cell paved the way in general for numerous other acts commonly associated with the second British Invasion. As Almond explains regarding their 1983 US tour: "All the reviews on the tour were ecstatic. It was only in America that Soft Cell made complete sense. Our dark themes and Goth references were understood, yet at the same time our sound was recognized as warmer and fuller than many of our synthesizer contemporaries who had started to break in America—owing to the success of 'Tainted Love.' This was what they labelled 'the Brit Invasion.' Soft Cell paved the way for so many bands to break America in the early eighties, but that also bred jealousies. Gary Kemp of Spandau Ballet laughed and sneered at us, comparing us to the grocer's shop, while they were the chain store. I replied that it was the grocer's shops that

sold the fresher specialist goods, while the chain stores had the mass-produced rubbish" (1999b, 235). See also Robert Palmer's (1982) *New York Times* article, "Britain's New Pop—Synthetic Bands," which spotlights Soft Cell, along with Orchestral Maneuvers in the Dark (OMD), the Human League, and Depeche Mode who, we are told, "have not yet had a significant impact here" (D19).

11. Worth noting is Almond's additional citation of Jean Genet's *Our Lady of the Flowers*, given how Rechy, Genet, and Almond arguably align to form a genealogy of gay male sexual outlaw writing. Jeremy Reed (1999) has picked up on the linkage between Almond and Genet, discussing both in his intriguing book *Angels, Divas and Blacklisted Heroes*. Reed has written extensively about Almond as a biographer (*Marc Almond: The Last Star* [1995]), essayist (in Jamie McLeod's book of photographs titled *Marc Almond: Adored and Explored* [2001]), and poet (*Pop Stars* [1994] and *Piccadilly Bongo* [2010]). *Piccadilly Bongo* suitably includes a CD of "Soho Songs"—"Eros and Eye," "Fun City," "Brewer Street Blues," "Seedy Films," "Sleaze," "Twilights and Lowlifes," and "Soho So Long"—by Almond. For another gay male genealogy encompassing Almond, one might consider by title alone the National Lesbian and Gay Survey's (1993) *Proust, Cole Porter, Michelangelo, Marc Almond and Me: Writings by Gay Men on Their Lives and Lifestyles* (1993).

12. Almond's poetry and spoken-word collections—*The Angel of Death in the Adonis Lounge* (1988), *Beautiful Twisted Night* (1999a), and *The End of New York* (2001)—also contain the lyrics to recorded songs.

13. Although the exclusive focus of this chapter is Soft Cell's and Almond's solo work, additional projects of which Almond and Ball were a part, such as Marc and the Mambas with their two LPs, *Untitled* (1982) and *Torment and Toreros* (1983), also bear the stamp of Rechy's influence.

14. Almond was not the first to draw lyrical inspiration from Rechy's novel. In the Doors' famous 1971 track "L.A. Woman," singer Jim Morrison repeatedly recites the words "City of Night." Almond's "City of Nights" appears as the B-side to his 1990 CD single "Waifs and Strays" and on his later compilations, *Treasure Box* (1995) and *Trials of Eyeliner* (2016).

15. See Leon Hunt's (1998) *British Low Culture: From Safari Suits to Sexploitation*. David Stubbs offers a brilliant and apt assessment of the LP: "Soft Cell . . . brought a beautiful scum to the surface of pop's liquid caldron. On the likes of *Non-Stop Erotic Cabaret*, Almond sang of the tacky, drab, gaudy, thrilling, dangerous, full of uppers and downers of pop and club life in the early 1980s, a scary act of 'escapism' indeed, one that could bring either ecstasy or the agony of a split lip" (2018, 211).

16. This falls in line with Chad Heap's (2009) brilliant historical account of New York and Chicago sexual underworlds in *Slumming: Sexual and Racial Encounters in American Nightlife, 1885–1940*.

17. See *Sounds* (November 8, 1986) and *Gay Times* (April 1999). Despite an earlier hesitancy to come out, Almond's appearance in various publications showcases his unabashed honesty about his sexuality and his embrace of sexual subcultures. See, for example, the cover and the inside feature on Almond in the spring 1996 issue of the British fetish magazine *Skin Two*.

18. For more on La Escuelita and its closing in 2016, see Michael Musto's (2016) "RIP Latin LGBT Dance Club Escuelita." Musto's writing in general, particularly his 1984 book *Downtown*, offers an illuminating view of Manhattan on the verge of gentrification.

19. See Georgia Jeffries's "The Low Riders of Whittier Boulevard" and Gene Lees's "Tony Bill: Maverick Producer" in the February 1979 issue of *American Film* for ascertaining the circulation of the Latino gangster in late 1970s Hollywood film.

20. That is, earlier pieces are sometimes reprinted in subsequent publications of Almond's writing.

CHAPTER 5: ZOOT SUITS AND SECONDHAND KNOWLEDGE

1. See my book *Next of Kin: The Family in Chicano/a Cultural Politics* (Rodríguez 2009), which brings together British cultural studies with Chicana/o cultural studies.

2. For an informative study of the value of the "secondhand," which in media contexts is typically cast as inaccurate or flawed, see Mark Coddington (2019), *Aggregating the News: Secondhand Knowledge and the Erosion of Journalistic Authority*.

3. Aside from the early 1980s magazines like the *Face*, *New Sounds New Styles*, and *iD*, which charted the emergence of the New Romantic scene, the following books are also important for detailing its historical and cultural contexts: Ian Birch etal. (1982), *The Book with No Name*; Dave Rimmer (2003), *New Romantics: The Look*; Graham Smith (2011), *We Can Be Heroes: London Clubland, 1976–1984*; and Dylan Jones (2020), *Sweet Dreams: The Story of the New Romantics*. See also the "key-player" memoirs by Boy George (1995), *Take It Like a Man*; Steve Strange (2002), *Blitzed*; and Gary Kemp (2009), *I Know This Much*. Claire Lawrie's 2018 documentary *Beyond "There's Always a Black Issue Dear"* brilliantly challenges the assumption of an all-white New Romantic scene, particularly from the perspective of Andy Polaris.

4. The news report can be viewed on YouTube: Robin Denselow, "New Romantics 1981: Crucial TV Report That Meant Lift-Off," *Newsnight*, BBC, posted on YouTube by Shapersofthe80s, January 4, 2017, https://youtu.be/7CApOAaxUuc.

5. Frank Mort's excellent *Cultures of Consumption: Masculinities and Social Space in Late Twentieth-Century Britain* observes that "punk has been celebrated as the authentic reference point, against which later developments have been found to be wanting" (1996, 28). Mort importantly contests this common supposition, insisting that cultural forms of seemingly distinct temporal moments must be understood as "part of a much longer-term history" (28).

6. While most participants in the scene indeed make reference to "New Romantics," they also note that this was not a term they themselves coined or, at the time, adopted. See, for example, Boy George in Ian Denyer's 2016 documentary *Boy George's 1970s: Save Me from Suburbia.*

7. In Denyer's abovementioned documentary, George additionally maintains that "punk had been a beautiful distraction, but we were moving on." George also recalls being violently attacked at a Gang of Four gig, a moment when he recognized a splintering of the punk scene, with some audiences aggressively triggered by those like himself who dressed flamboyantly.

8. Significant to note is the transatlantic adoption of the New Romantic style by Prince, which, according to Professor Alexandra Vazquez of New York University, was first embraced by one of his noted collaborators and friends: singer and percussionist Sheila E.

9. With detailed honesty, Steve Strange discusses in his autobiography his struggle with claiming a specific sexual identity: "I didn't know what gay was, let alone bisexual. In some ways it just confused me even more. I wanted to be with women and I also wanted to be with men. What did that make me?" (2002, 29).

10. Philip Sallon, the iconic queer Bromley Contingent member and punk and New Romantic icon, notes in *Boy George's 1970s* that upon entering the doors of Louise's he immediately found himself gazing upon a group of women in suits (Denyer 2016).

11. Evidence of Black youths in Britain wearing zoot suits may be found in a photograph of three Jamaican immigrants—"John Hazel, a boxer; Harold Wilmot; and John Richards, a carpenter"—"arriving at Tilbury aboard the Empire Windrush, 22 June 1948" in Paul Gilroy's (2011, 71) *Black Britain: A Photographic History*. The photo is reproduced on the cover of Chicano historian Luis Alvarez's (2008) book, *The Power of the Zoot: Youth Culture and Resistance during World War II.*

12. Anthony Macias (2008) also notes how while the zoot suit traversed ethnic divides, the Mexican American *pachuco* subculture (particularly with regard to music and language) had a reverberating effect on youths from varying cultural backgrounds.

13. One can also witness the adoption of the zoot suit by other bands at the moment, including but not limited to Swans Way. And while Adam Ant wears a zoot suit in the music video for "Puss 'N Boots" (1983), he has insistently distanced him-

self and the Ants from the New Romantic scene. See Decca Aitkenhead (2012), "Adam Ant: 'To Be a Pop Star You Need Sex, Subversion, Style and Humour.'"

14. In this vein, consider Andy Beckett, who observes in his 2015 book *Promised You a Miracle: Why 1980–82 Made Modern Britain* how the shift from punk to pop (in which his trajectory aligns post-punk squarely with the former rather than the latter) leads to a consumerist individualism of which pop stars "dressing posh" is emblematic. Dominic Sandbrook makes a similar point in *Who Dares Wins: Britain, 1979–1982* when he notes that Martyn Ware and the other members of Heaven 17 "did not look like radicals" in their suits but rather "yuppies" (2019, 299). Sandbrook's surface-level assessment, unfortunately, prevents him from considering the band's biting critiques of Reagan and Thatcher in a song like 1981's "(We Don't Need This) Fascist Groove Thang." The alignment of "new romanticism" and Reagan/Thatcher is, however, as common as it is superficial. Consider most recently historian Kevin Mattson, whose argument profits from oversimplification when he writes, "New romanticism was more than a trend, though, because it offered an implicit conservatism that went along with Thatcherite (and now Reaganite) politics. These bands and their fashion sensibilities replaced the anger of punk—heard in the curdling cry of Johnny Rotten—with a despairing quietude" (2020, 53).

15. See Chris Steele-Perkins and Richard Smith (2002), *The Teds*; and Michael Macilwee (2015), *The Teddy Boy Wars: The Youth Cult That Shocked Britain* for two distinct accounts of British Teddy Boy subcultures.

16. I would be remiss not to acknowledge the charge of cultural appropriation directed at British youths who wore zoot suits. Consider, then, the segment on jazz and Sade in the BBC documentary *I Love 1984* (Smith 2001) in which Johnny Marr, former guitarist for the Smiths, comments on the zoot suit's popularity in Britain: "Well people shouldn't be really walking around in zoot suits anyway, should they? It's not right. And it also costs money, y'know, so it wasn't working-class so we didn't really think it was that cool. It cost money to wear that sort of stuff. Even the second-hand gear. Y'know, a tie would cost you 4 quid. At least." I am assuming that Marr is referring to Blue Rondo given that the Smiths' live debut was supporting them at the Ritz in Manchester. Perhaps as a rejoinder to Marr's point, we might consider the Smiths' lead singer Morrissey's (2019) reflection on Blue Rondo's aesthetic: "They were one of the very few groups that the Smiths supported, but there was a skepticism about them being just 'club models' . . . who asked and got. This was said also about very early Roxy Music . . . who appeared to be quite affluent before they'd even had a hit. With Blue Rondo, again, you suspected that they were given all of their fantastic suits for free whilst the rest of us had to dream of being able to buy SOMETHING that didn't look TOO abysmal."

17. For more on *New Sounds New Styles*, see "New Sounds New Styles Magazine," Mag@Zone, n.d., https://michaelmouse1967.wixsite.com/mag-a-zone

/new-styles-new-sounds. De Graaf, along with Malcolm Garrett, is the coauthor of the notable 1983 book on Culture Club, *When Cameras Go Crazy*.

18. I have taken the liberty of using a capital "L" for "Latin" although Brown uses the lowercase "l."

19. British trumpeter Eddie Calvert would achieve equal success with his version of the song the very same year. For a dazzling reading of Pérez Prado's version in relation to Cuban music, see Alexandra T. Vazquez's (2013) chapter "Itinerant Outbursts: The Grunt of Dámaso Pérez Prado" in *Listening in Detail: Performances of Cuban Music*.

20. Yet as they reflected the changing face of London in terms of ethnic, racial, and national-origin composition as much as signaling the various musical styles influencing the band's sound, Blue Rondo was recurrently cast as an anomaly in the press. Consider, for example, a feature in the October 14–27, 1982, issue of *Noise!* magazine, which begins, "Imagine a hot night in Havana, zoot suits, long cool drinks and short, hot romances. You're in a club; a customer kicks up a fuss while the band kick up a row. Hey, what's this? Those meaty, percussive rhythms must be Latin which makes the musicians . . . Welsh?" (Prince 1982, 10).

21. Angelo Martins Junior points out that Brazilians began to migrate in significant numbers to the United Kingdom due to social, political, and economic factors in the 1980s. See his important book *Moving Difference: Brazilians in London* (Martins Junior 2020). While the debate as to whether Brazilians count as Latino continues in some quarters, it is evident that they qualify as such, particularly in a queer British context, as evidenced in the November 2001 issue of the London-based *Gay Times* with its cover story "Latino Lovers: Latin America and Homosexuality" and an accompanying feature by Antonio Pasolini titled "The Boys from Brazil."

22. The December 1981 issue of the *Face* in which D'Arbilly's quote appears mistakenly uses the word "barrios" instead of "baião." I thank Christos Tolera for alerting me to this translation error. For a brief assessment of the *baião* in the United States, particularly with regard to singer-composer Luis Gonzaga, see John Storm Roberts ([1979] 1999). Worth noting is the spectacular history of musician, writer, and activist Caetano Veloso, which illustrates a dynamic mutual influence between British and Brazilian music. As he notes in his book *Tropical Truth: A Story of Music and Revolution in Brazil*, "Many people ask me to what extent British music influenced me during those London years. The fact is that the most profound influence of British pop had occurred before I even dreamt of going to London: it was the Beatles pre-*tropicalismo*. The many pop and rock shows I heard in England would serve more to demystify the 'First World' productions on the one hand, and on the other acquaint me with their genuine technical advances" (Veloso 2002, 281).

23. While Blue Rondo's single "Klactoveesedstein" would find the band in heavy circulation on club turntables, posters, and even in a promotional music video

frequently broadcast on television, a significant supply of copies was unavailable to the general public due to distribution problems as they were, as Tolera explains, "stuck in a bloody warehouse" (C. Sullivan 2014a). Yet "Klactoveesedstein" would make an impact whose history illustrates its overall matchless significance: "Still the record was the biggest club record that year and was in the top 100—up to 50, down to 70, up to 62, down to 80, and so on for six months, selling like 100,000 copies" (C. Sullivan 2014a). Former Blue Rondo members Mark Riley and Danny White's future band, Matt Bianco, would follow in their former band's footsteps by adopting a Latin sensibility in music and fashion style. Kito played with Matt Bianco on their 1984 debut album, *Whose Side Are You On*?

24. Release and chart information may be found at http://www.officialcharts.com.

25. Some members of Arriva believed that Sade's vocals were not compelling enough. The band eventually gave in and invited her to come on board. The band, however, split, morphing into a group named Pride. When Pride disbanded, Sade the band formed and was composed of members from the two previous bands. Sade (both the singer and the band) played Chris Sullivan's Wag Club and, with help from promotion by the *Face*, soon became global sensations. See Graham Smith (2011, 294), *We Could Be Heroes*. Also fitting for the context at hand is Sade's track "Sally" from the 1984 album *Diamond Life*, which references "Dave," "once seventeen," who wore a "zoot suit and shiny shoes."

26. David Grant, member of the Black British soul/funk band Linx, comments in the *Face*, "I mean, the Leyton Buzzards changing their name to Modern Romance, and then doing something that a lot of people thought was a Latin record. But I'm sure even the guys in the band knew that 'Everybody Salsa' has as much to do with Latin music as I have to do with the Nazi party, which isn't very much, I can assure you" (Salewicz 1981b, 39). Grant also notes how style at this moment tended to eclipse the music one would produce: "'Actually I used to be really into zoot suits,' he concludes, irritated, 'and then all this started happening. You feel you're aligning yourself so closely with a movement that people whether they hear your music or not will start thinking of you as part of that movement'" (39). The same issue of the *Face*—fittingly featuring Blue Rondo on the cover—includes a feature on Modern Romance that relates how greatly despised "Everybody Salsa" was, including by Elvis Costello and Soft Cell.

27. This excerpt from Thomas Sanchez's biography is taken from his author website, accessed January 19, 2022, https://www.thomas-sanchez.com/en/biography/bio_index.html.

28. The photo story is reproduced in *Flexipop! The Book*, edited by Barry Cain and Neil Matthews (2015). Cain offers the following insights regarding *Flexipop!*: "*Smash Hits*, and later *No. 1*, were published by big companies where everyone was on wages with built-in pension plans. But we, that's Tim Lott [*Flexipop!*'s other cofounder and editor] and my not so good self, were flying

by the seat of our pants. This was punk publishing in its truest sense. By the time we hit issue No. 4, an Adam Ant special, we were selling six figures. Not bad for a backstreet office set up" (Cain and Matthews 2015, 2).

29. In the liner notes to the CD rerelease of *Chewing the Fat*, Boy George declares, "Christos was the Justin Bieber of the Zoot Suit and Blue Rondo were a delicious Latin myth" (cited in C. Sullivan 2014a).

30. Sanabria was also the editor and publisher of *Latin NY* magazine. I thank him for providing me with a complete version of "Spic Chic" as only the first page is published in Hayes's book.

31. Here I'm reminded of queer theorist Deborah R. Vargas's (2014) embrace of "*lo sucio*" and how Sanabria's "Spic Chic" approximates *lo sucio*—a working-class embrace of denigrated aesthetics—in contrast to "Spic Raunch," the sought-after object of white upper-class desire acquired on a slumming expedition.

CHAPTER 6: MEXICAN AMERICANOS

1. This formulation is inspired by Douglas Crimp's (1989) classic essay "Mourning and Militancy," which draws motivation from Freud's ([1917] 1953) "Mourning and Melancholia."

2. See the essays published in the booklet included in the compilation CD *Revolutionary Spirit: Sound of Liverpool 1976–1988* (Connor 2018). For more on Eric's, see Nick Crossley (2015), *Networks of Sound, Style and Subversion: The Punk and Post-Punk Worlds of Manchester, London, Liverpool and Sheffield, 1975–80*.

3. Although Nash would come to replace Jed O'Toole in the Frankie lineup, he would subsequently return to play with the band on the occasion of touring. In his essay for *Revolutionary Spirit: Sound of Liverpool 1976–1988*, Liverpool-based DJ Bernie Connor writes how "punk exploded in Liverpool" in spite of lacking media attention: "It escaped the pages of the tabloids and into the psyche of the oddball kids who didn't fit in their own neighbourhood. When they got to Matthew Street, they found that there were oddballs all over the city, waiting for their clarion call to come join the freakers' ball. Big in Japan's only real competition was Spitfire Boys, all the glory and the indie explosion was to come later, in a deluge that's been going on for years" (2018, 2).

4. David Bowie, inspired by the recently published *Rock Dreams*, commissioned Belgian artist Peellaert to produce the cover art of his 1974 album *Diamond Dogs*. In *A Bone in My Flute*, Holly Johnson writes of his "David Bowie obsession," which "reached fever pitch" (1994, 34). Signaling the particular impact of *The Rise and Fall of Ziggy Stardust and the Spiders from Mars* (1972), he notes, "This record had a huge effect on kids of my generation, not just the homosexual ones. Bisexuality became a fashionable pose, along with the idea

of androgyny in fashion. Small pockets of girls and boys (especially of the apprentice hairdresser variety) all over the country, started to experiment with their appearance as a direct result of the current fashions in Pop music. Bowie, Roxy Music, Alice Cooper et al." (1994, 34).

5. The inner sleeve of *The Age of Consent* includes a list of European countries and their respective minimal legal age at which one is allowed to enter into "homosexual relationships between men."

6. In *Sing Out! Gays and Lesbians in the Music World*, Boze Hadleigh writes that Frankie's "Relax" was "dubbed 'the first song ever addressed to an anus'" (1997, 199). While Hadleigh does not cite where this dubbing originated and how reading the song lyrics might allow one to come to such an interpretation, he does rightly note that "the song stayed on the UK charts longer than any since the '60s, and in the US—where its video was tamely reshot—it activated Congressional wives who tried to censor rock lyrics ('Relax . . . when you want to come') and to lump homosexuality with drugs, prostitution, rape and bestiality" (199).

7. Aside from the "Relax"-themed slogans, others included, upon the release of "Two Tribes," "Frankie Say War! Hide Yourself" and "Frankie Say Armed the Unemployed," which, according to Dean Anthony, at the time "were to adorn every teenager's T-shirt" (1984, 54). In a personal communication, Johnson informed me that he was asked permission to showcase the Frankie shirt on *Friends*. He consented by fax.

8. Such provocation also entailed statements made by Frankie members who claimed that unlike the mock seediness of Soft Cell, Frankie were truly engaged in the sexual underworlds that Almond and Ball merely wrote and sang about.

9. The video is accessible: "Frankie Goes to Hollywood—Relax—Hope and Anchor," posted by PlanetFrankieHD on YouTube, February 9, 2009, https://www.youtube.com/watch?v=LcR2p2zzL-U. Bruno Hizer's (1984) *Give It Loads! The Story of Frankie Goes to Hollywood* also contains images of the band depicted in this fashion and which sharply contrast with later promotional photos.

10. Boy George would later go on to admit that despite his comment about preferring tea over sex, he was, at the time of this declaration, having a great amount of sex. In addition, "Do You Really Want to Hurt Me?" was written for Culture Club drummer Jon Moss, with whom he was engaged in a complicated affair. See "Flashback: October 1982" (2007) and Boy George's *Take It Like a Man* (1995) and *Straight* (2005).

11. Simon Reynolds's book, *Rip It Up and Start Again: Postpunk 1978–1984*, ends with Frankie Goes to Hollywood and the argument that "on one level, Frankie can be seen as punk's last blast. But on another deeper, structural level, Frankie were a taste of pop things to come—the return of the boy band" (2005, 388).

This may be true on one level, but on another level, Frankie's queer sexual politics were hardly adopted by any other "boy band." Moreover, while Reynolds believes that the Frankie/Sex Pistols comparison doesn't hold given the latter's subsequent influence on "thousands of American bands," their common managerial media manipulation (by McLaren for the Pistols and Morley and Horn for Frankie) deserves meaningful consideration.

12. Bracewell's essay originally appeared in 2007, illustrating how the Morley/Horn "invention" of Frankie Goes to Hollywood not only seeps into the twenty-first century but also propels a narrative of consumerist-artistic ambition that, perhaps unwittingly, further deeds credit to an exploitative art market–like music industry.

13. The term "sex expression" is borrowed from feminist literary critic Dale Bauer (2009), who uses it to describe an emergent discourse of desire in late nineteenth- and early twentieth-century American women's writing that refused the subordination of sexual need to sentimental forms of communication.

14. Even "Two Tribes" had a life before Horn and Morley. One need only see the backside of the sleeve for the UK seven-inch single, which reads: "planned in Liverpool, 1982–83; built in London, March 1984." The question that begs asking is, wasn't the song already "built" in the band's 1982 Peel Session?

15. And Chicano gay writer Gil Cuadros (1994), author of *City of God*, who died of AIDS-related complications in 1996 at the age of thirty-four. Cuadros was memorialized by his visual artist friend Laura Aguilar in a retrospective of her work that included an altar for Cuadros, complete with a *Frankie Say Relax Don't Do It!* badge. *Laura Aguilar: Show and Tell* ran from September 16, 2007, to February 10, 2018, at the Vincent Price Art Museum at East Los Angeles College. Aguilar died of complications from diabetes on April 25, 2018.

16. This insight is Sigmund Freud's ([1920] 1953) in *Beyond the Pleasure Principle*.

17. I would certainly be remiss if I did not mention that Paul Rutherford also released a solo album, *Oh World*, in 1989. In an interview, Johnson expresses that he felt "vindicated" the week *Blast* went to number one in the British Albums Chart. Such a response was due to the stressful two-year legal battle Johnson had fought and won against ZTT Records owners Trevor Horn and Jill Sinclair. See Thomas H. Green (2014), "TheartsdeskQ&A" and William Shaw (1988), "Holly Johnson: Frankie Say See You in Court!"

18. Eric Watson was a noted photographer who worked for *Smash Hits* but would go on to direct a number of videos. He is perhaps most recognized for his association with Pet Shop Boys as a photographer and video director. Watson died of a heart attack in 2012 at the age of fifty-six.

19. Johnson notes the John Waters influence in the liner notes to the 2010 Cherry Red Records CD rerelease of *Blast*.

20. In his review of *Blast* for New Music Express, David Quantick signals the "acid irony of 'Americanos' (a severe sibling to West Side Story's 'America'— 'Life is all right in America/If you're all white in America')." See his "Master Blaster" (Quantick 1989).

21. In the way that "Americanos" anticipated my embrace of "Chicano," the music video and single cover art for "So in Love" by Orchestral Manoeuvres in the Dark first acquainted me with the Mexican holiday Day of the Dead (Día de los Muertos).

22. This formulation is a variation on Douglas Crimp's (1987) "How to Have Promiscuity in an Epidemic." My ability to queerly conjoin "Relax" and "Two Tribes" sharply contrasts with Jon Savage's simplistic accusation that "Frankie Goes to Hollywood exploited the gay image of lead singers Paul Rutherford and Holly Johnson—for 'Relax'—and then dropped it like a hot potato as soon as another marketing device—this time, nuclear war—became available for 'Two Tribes'" (1990, 169).

23. I was immediately struck by how familiar the video felt in comparison with Frankie's appearance in Brian De Palma's 1984 film *Body Double*. The original version of "Relax," however, greatly differs from the film-within-a-film sequence in *Body Double* where the band appears on a heterosexually delineated porn set.

24. See Bruno Hizer (1984), *Give It Loads! The Story of Frankie Goes to Hollywood* for more on this achievement and its media blowback.

25. In a touching essay titled "Like a Pfuckking Taart!," an elegant rebuttal to Brexit, the UK's withdrawal from the European Union, Johnson (2019) provides a litany of cultural influences that reminds me of the personal narrative which begins this book. The essay ends with the line, "Do not forget, Europa, we love you" (65), which I also read as a nod to his 2014 album *Europa*.

26. In *Good as You*, Paul Flynn (2017) shares that his meeting with Johnson also occurred over a traditional English breakfast.

27. While mentioned a number of times throughout this book, for a detailed account of Worlds End, Seditionaries, and Sex, see Mal-One and the Punk Collective (2020), *Worlds End/Sex Pistols, McLaren and Westwood: A Chronology 1971–1978*.

CHAPTER 7: LATIN/O AMERICAN PARTY

1. This, of course, is a riff on Tony Moon's classic "Three Chords (Now Form a Band)" diagram published in the fanzine *Sideburns* (and not *Sniffin' Glue*, as is usually presumed) in 1976. See Worley (2017) for more on the diagram and its history.

2. Both Lowe and Tennant were huge fans of Orlando, whose work with Divine and the Flirts made the duo desire this noted producer's touch. Tennant met

Orlando while on assignment to interview Sting and review the Police's New York City concert for *Smash Hits*. See the chapter "The Bobby O Story" in Michael Cowton's (1991) *Pet Shop Boys: Introspection* and Saint Etienne member Bob Stanley's (2015) chapter "*We Were Never Being Boring*: Pet Shop Boys and New Order" from his book, *Yeah! Yeah! Yeah! The Story of Pop Music from Bill Haley to Beyoncé*. Stanley interestingly notes, "Though the sound he spawned was almost entirely confined to gay clubs, Bobby O was a straight Puerto Rican, and obsessed with boxing. His aim was to make the beats sound as tough and pummeling as punches—[Divine's] 'Native Love' and 'Shoot Your Shot' shared the synthesized bass pulse of 'Blue Monday' and (by now five years old) 'I Feel Love'" (457).

3. See Jeff Chang's (2005) *Can't Stop Won't Stop: A History of the Hip-Hop Generation*, which explains how white American punk fans of the Clash pelted Flash and the Furious Five with beer cups and spit given their perceived incompatibility with the headlining act. Chang perceptively notes that "in 1981, the American punks clearly wanted the riot [in reference to the Clash's "White Riot"] to remain exclusively their own" (155). Don Letts's (2000) documentary, *The Clash: Westway to the World*, also notes the influence of the New York hip-hop scene on "The Only Band That Matters," influencing in particular songs like "The Magnificent Seven."

4. Tim Lawrence's (2016) *Life and Death on the New York Dance Floor, 1980–1983* provides a breathtaking historical account of the early 1980s New York music scene, including New Order's connection to Baker and the nightlife of the moment.

5. For more on these connections, see Paul Gorman (2020), *The Life and Times of Malcolm McLaren*, especially 483–87.

6. The enduring Pet Shop Boys nod to hip-hop is clearly evident, as seen in the video featuring a break dancing African American b-boy that accompanies the group's performance of "New York City Boy" for their 2016–19 Super tour and British rapper Example's featured appearance on the track "Thursday" from 2013's *Electric* LP.

7. On the cusp of their 2013 LP *Electric*'s release, the *Daily Mail* featured a story on Pet Shop Boys, who are identified as "thoroughly British observers of life." See "If I Could, I'd Be a Recluse" (2013).

8. This isn't the first time a Pet Shop Boys track is compared to "Numbers." In an interview with Kris Kirk, Tennant notes music journalist Jon Savage's assessment of "Rent" alongside Soft Cell's infamous track: "Jon Savage said to me 'Oh no, it's going to be your "Numbers,"' which was the single that caused so much trouble for Soft Cell—but I don't see it. Really it's just a love song about the relationship between two young people with the refrain 'I love you, you pay my rent'" (Kirk 1999, 188). Furthermore, as previously mentioned, "Domino Dancing" is frequently read as a song about AIDS, the falling dominos signaling

the horrific number of people succumbing to the pandemic during the moment of the song's initial release and circulation. Two years later, however, Pet Shop Boys would address AIDS more explicitly in "Being Boring," the second single from their fourth LP, *Behaviour* (1990). Perhaps one of their most lauded tracks, "Being Boring" was also covered by Bauhaus bassist David J for *Very Introspective, Actually: A Tribute to the Pet Shop Boys* (2001).

9. The idea of "the open secret" is famously D. A. Miller's (1988). See his book, *The Novel and the Police*, especially the chapter "Secret Subjects, Open Secrets" on Dickens's *David Copperfield*.

10. While Lowe has never publicly laid claim to a particular sexual identity, the duo has not shied away from acknowledging their indebtedness to queer culture. One of my favorite examples of this point is the Pet Shop Boys' 2000 cover of Modern Rocketry's disco classic "Homosexuality."

11. In Chris Heath's *Pet Shop Boys versus America*, we are told that Tennant is given a copy of Balfour's essay "Revolutions per Minute or the Pet Shop Boys Forever." While we're not told what Tennant thinks of the essay, Heath asserts, "Amid the heady intellectualism there are some quite awful puns" (1993, 173).

12. In Philip Hoare and Chris Heath's *Pet Shop Boys: Catalogue*, we discover: "'We wanted somewhere full of really pretty young people so I suggested Puerto Rico,' said Eric Watson [the video's director]. 'I had this bee in my bonnet about women being objects, so I did this thing about this girl older than the boys having them both on. It was a bit like those magazine photo stories, but more stylish. It was the video that everyone liked. Neil and Chris pop up every so often—they were basically sunbathing and every so often they'd turn up, say "this is good fun" and about an hour later they'd go away again'" (2006, 101).

13. Worth noting is Shannon's well-known role as the queen of Hi-NRG, Hi-NRG being a genre of uptempo disco which Tennant and Lowe adopted on tracks like "One More Chance," originally produced and remixed by Bobby "O."

14. Eddy's piece was originally published in the December 13, 1988, issue of the *Village Voice*.

15. In the August 1, 1987, issue of *New Music Express*, Richard Grabel reports on the emergence of "Latin hip-hop"—including artists associated with freestyle like Lisa Lisa and Cult Jam, Sa-Fire, and Noel—in his article "Planet Hispanic."

16. Fittingly, recent hip-hop artist Cardi B (neé Belcalis Marlenis Almázar), who is of Dominican and Trinidadian parentage, has cited Pet Shop Boys as a significant influence, writing in a tweet posted on March 21, 2021: "Pet Shop Boys are a really underrated group. I love them!! My mom always used to listen to them." This, however, was the second time she declared her love of the Boys on Twitter.

17. For a brief history of Exposé and the popularity of "Point of No Return," see Scott Mehno (1987), "Miami Thrice: Exposé Ride the Miami Wave." Although

Exposé's history is often rooted in Miami, group member Jeanette Jurado, in the trio's second iteration after two original members departed in 1986, is from Pico Rivera, California. Jurado played Rosie Hamilton—from Rosie and the Originals, best known for their 1960 classic "Angel Baby"—in Gregory Nava's 1995 film *Mi Familia*.

18. The chapter initially began as a talk presented at Pet Shop Boys: Symposium in Edinburgh, Scotland. For information on the symposium, see Luke Turner's (2016) article in the *Guardian*, "Party Conference: Why the Pet Shop Boys Are Worthy of Academic Consideration."

19. Tennant was notoriously known for his sarcastic reviews of records and live shows, including an early performance by Culture Club that led to Boy George and company threatening to "slap him down." See Boy George (1995, 182).

20. The magazine format of *Literally* ran for forty-two issues from 1989 to 2016. Thereafter it became an annual publication in hardback form, oftentimes including a CD of Pet Shop Boys music.

21. Discussing their decision to title the LP *Super*, Tennant and Lowe note that "super" is an "international word. It's a Latin word, in fact." See the uncredited interview with Tennant and Lowe by the *Yorkshire Evening Post* (Newsroom 2016).

22. In the 2021 issue of Pet Shop Boys' annual publication *Annually*, Neil Tennant writes the following in a diary entry dated September 9, 1986: "The idea for the 'Suburbia' video is that it will be filmed in an American suburb and a British suburb. We want an American suburb because the idea of the song has come from Penelope Spheeris's film *Suburbia*—that's also where the dogs in the lyrics have come from. At first Eric Watson comes up with a location which we think is too middle-class—it turns out our idea of suburbia is sort of a working-class Latino suburb. Which is in the video. Eric finally finds the right place, Duarte, and we do the shoot there. And it's a great day—a really fun day" (Tennant 2021, 47–48).

23. And even this grouping of bands was often not looked upon favorably, with Siouxsie and the Banshees perceived as more dark and "unpopular" than Depeche Mode or Pet Shop Boys. Imagine my surprise, then, when reading Michael Cowton's *Pet Shop Boys: Introspective*, to discover that Siouxsie and the Banshees attempted to gate-crash a record company party celebrating Tennant and Lowe receiving the British Record Industry's (BPI) Best Single Award (from Boy George no less at the awards ceremony) in 1987 (Cowton 1991, 70). Although Tennant attempted to escort them in, the bouncer, under instruction from the record company, denied entry to those without an invitation. In December 2019, a photo went viral featuring Sioux and Tennant enjoying a bottle of wine at the London café-restaurant the Delaunay.

CONCLUSION: DEDICATED TO THE ONE I LOVE

1. Soto, Maldonado, and Morales are indeed aware of one another, with Soto expressing deep admiration of both Maldonado and Morales for their performative artistry. I am thankful to Brian Soto for taking time to answer my questions about his participation in the Curse and Substance and Technique, two bands that pay tribute to New Order and Joy Division.

2. I associate the "Boys from Basildon" descriptor with Los Angeles–based British DJ Richard Blade. Blade's memoir, *World in My Eyes*, offers a detailed account of Depeche Mode's impact on Southern California fans: "Southern California quickly became [Depeche Mode's] biggest fan base and they would usually wrap up their North American tour in LA with multiple sold out shows, including the summer of 1986 with two concerts at Irvine Meadows Amphitheatre followed by a sold out show at the Fabulous Forum, playing to a total of more than 50,000 fans in three nights. It was that success that set the scene for their next tour, *Music for the Masses*, and their most memorable gig ever [at the Rose Bowl in Pasadena]" (2017, 354).

3. Melissa Mora Hidalgo (2016) offers an excellent overview of Morrissey and the Smiths tribute bands in her chapter "When Your Gift Unfurls: Paying Tribute to Morrissey and The Smiths" from *Mozlandia: Morrissey Fans in the Borderlands*.

4. This is not unlike the aim of Andy Bennett and Paul Hodkinson's *Ageing and Youth Cultures: Music, Style, and Identity*, which is to demarcate a "'post-youth' cultural territory that is expanding rapidly to encompass a range of lifestyle and aesthetic sensibilities through which ageing individuals retain tangible cultural connections to tastes and affiliations acquired during their teens and early twenties" (2012, 6).

5. The designation *rude boy* derives from an Afro-Caribbean youth subculture whose members were known for their stylized fashion and embrace of ska and rocksteady. Those associated with the 2-Tone scene in Britain would in turn embrace the categories *rude boy* and *rude girl* (along with *rudy*—as indexed in the Specials' "A Message to You Rudy," a cover of Dandy Livingstone's track "Rudy a Message to You"). See, for example, Miles (1981), *The 2-Tone Book for Rude Boys*.

6. For an excellent book on the Toxteth Riots, see Diane Frost and Richard Phillips (2011), *Liverpool '81: Remembering the Riots*.

7. See Guy Shankland's (2020) interview with Jerry Dammers, "Tension and Turmoil" for a brilliant historical account of the song on its fortieth anniversary.

8. The materials used to make up the banner were kindly itemized by Che Bracamontes in a personal communication.

9. In *Hit Factories: A Journey through the Industrial Cities of British Pop,* Karl Whitney crucially notes how "Coventry's use of cheap immigrant labour drawn from around the world created the multicultural context from which The Specials emerged. Their musical influences were drawn from the mix of cultures that industry drew to the city" (2019, 269).

10. Neil Tennant emphasizes the profound impact of "Ghost Town," calling it one of two songs (the other being Elvis Costello's "Shipbuilding") that truly succeeds in combining politics with pop music. See Jude Rogers (2013), "The Pet Shop Boys on Texting Cameron and Russian Homophobia."

References

"Adam Ant on Fame, Depression and Infamy." 2011. BBC *News*, February 23. https://www.bbc.com/news/entertainment-arts-12546301.

"Adam's Antics." 1982. *News of Adam: Adam Ant's Own Monthly Fanmag*, no. 2, 7–12.

Aitkenhead, Decca. 2012. "Adam Ant: 'To Be a Pop Star You Need Sex, Subversion, Style and Humour.'" *Guardian*, February 19. https://www.theguardian.com/music/2012/feb/19/adam-ant-sex-style-humour.

Alago, Michael. 2020. *I Am Michael Alago: Breathing Music, Signing Metallica, Beating Death*. With Laura Davis-Channin. Lanham, MD: Backbeat.

Albertine, Viv. 2014. *Clothes, Clothes, Clothes. Music, Music, Music. Boys, Boys, Boys: A Memoir*. London: Thomas Dunne.

Almond, Marc. 1988. *The Angel of Death in the Adonis Lounge*. London: Gay Men's Press.

Almond, Marc. 1999a. *Beautiful Twisted Night*. London: Ellipsis.

Almond, Marc. 1999b. *Tainted Life: The Autobiography*. London: Sidgwick and Jackson.

Almond, Marc. 2001. *The End of New York*. London: Ellipsis.

Almond, Marc. 2004. *In Search of the Pleasure Palace: Disreputable Travels*. London: Sidgwick and Jackson.

Alvarado, Leticia. 2017. "Malflora Aberrant Femininities." In *Axis Mundo: Queer Networks in Chicano L.A.*, edited by C. Ondine Chavoya and David Evans Frantz, 95–109. Munich: DelMonico Press/Prestel.

Alvarez, Luis. 2008. *The Power of the Zoot: Youth Culture and Resistance during World War II*. Berkeley: University of California Press.

Anderson, Benedict. 1983. *Imagined Communities: Reflections on the Origin and Spread of Nationalism*. New York: Verso.

Anguiano, José G. 2018. "Voicing the Occult in Chicana/o Culture and Hybridity: Prayers and the Cholo-Goth Aesthetic." In *Race and Cultural Practice in Popular Culture*, edited by Domino Renee Perez and Rachel

González-Martin, 175–94. New Brunswick, NJ: Rutgers University Press.

Ant, Adam. 2006. *Stand and Deliver: The Autobiography*. London: Sidgwick and Jackson.

Ant, Adam. 2016. "The Story of the Album." *Kings of the Wild Frontier*, by Adam and the Ants. CBS/Sony Music. Liner notes.

Anthony, Dean. 1984. *Frankie Goes to Hollywood*. London: Colour Library.

Aparicio, Frances R., and Cándida F. Jáquez, ed. 2003. *Musical Migrations: Transnationalism and Cultural Hybridity in Latin/o America*, vol. 1. New York: Palgrave Macmillan.

Arellano, Gustavo. 2002. "Their Charming Man: Dispatches from the Latino-Morrissey Love-In." *OC Weekly*, September 12. https://www.ocweekly.com/their-charming-man-6426051/.

Arias, Joey. 2002. *The Art of Conversation*. Berlin: Maas Media.

Artaud, Antonin. 1976. *The Peyote Dance*. Translated by Helen Weaver. New York: Farrar, Straus and Giroux.

Bag, Alice. 2011. *Violence Girl: East L.A. Rage to Hollywood Stage, a Chicana Punk Story*. Port Townsend, WA: Feral House.

Bag, Alice. 2016. "Donna Santisi." *Alice Bag*, November 25. https://alicebag.com/women-in-la-punk/donna-santisi.

Balfour, Ian. 1991. "Revolutions per Minute or the Pet Shop Boys Forever." *surfaces* 1 (1): 5–21.

Balfour, Ian. 2002. "Queen Theory: Notes on the Pet Shop Boys." In *Rock over the Edge: Transformations in Popular Music Culture*, edited by Roger Beebe, Denise Fulbrook, and Ben Saunders, 357–70. Durham, NC: Duke University Press.

Ball, Dave. 2020. *Electronic Boy: My Life In and Out of Soft Cell*. London: Omnibus Press.

Barbarossa, Dave. 2015. *Mud Sharks*. Nottinghamshire, UK: New Haven.

Barthes, Roland. 1977. "The Grain of the Voice." In *Image-Music-Text*, translated by Stephen Heath, 179–89. New York: Hill and Wang.

Bauer, Dale. 2009. *Sex Expression and American Women Writers, 1860–1940*. Chapel Hill: University of North Carolina Press.

Bean, Mikey. 2019. *Phantoms: The Rise of Deathrock from the LA Punk Scene*. Morrisville, NC: Lulu.

Beckett, Andy. 2015. *Promised You a Miracle: Why 1980–82 Made Modern Britain*. London: Penguin.

Beckman, Janette. 2005. *Made in the UK: The Music of Attitude, 1977–1983*. New York: powerHouse Classics.

Bell, Celeste, and Zoë Howe. 2019. *Dayglo! The Poly Styrene Story*. London: Omnibus Press.

Bell, Max. 1984. "Chain Reaction." *No. 1*, August 4, 28–30.

Bennett, Andy, and Paul Hodkinson, eds. 2012. *Ageing and Youth Cultures: Music, Style, and Identity*. London: Bloomsbury.

Berlant, Lauren. 1998. "Intimacy: A Special Issue." *Critical Inquiry* 24 (winter): 281–88.

Birch, Ian. 1981. "So This Is Romance?" *Smash Hits*, November 26, 40–41.

Birch, Ian, Richard Strange, Jon Savage, and Paul Tickell. 1982. *The Book with No Name*. London: Omnibus.

Blade, Richard. 2017. *World in My Eyes: The Autobiography*. Pensacola, FL: Indigo River.

Blade, Richard. 2021. *The Lockdown Interviews*. Los Angeles: BladeRocker Books.

Bordal, Christian. 2018. "Bauhaus: Godfathers of Goth Regroup." *Day to Day*, National Public Radio, March 4. https://www.npr.org/templates/story/story.php?storyId=87888546.

Bourdieu, Pierre. (1979) 1984. *Distinction: A Social Critique of the Judgement of Taste*. Translated by Richard Nice. Cambridge, MA: Harvard University Press.

Boy George. 1984. "George vs Frankie." *Record Mirror*, May 12, 40.

Boy George. 1995. *Take It Like a Man: The Autobiography of Boy George*. With Spencer Bright. New York: HarperCollins.

Boy George. 2005. *Straight*. With Paul Gorman. London: Century.

Bracewell, Michael. 2012. *The Space Between: Selected Writings on Art*. Edited by Doro Globus. London: Ridinghouse.

Breward, Christopher. 2016. *The Suit: Form, Function, and Style*. London: Reaktion.

Brooks, Daphne A. 2021. *Liner Notes for the Revolution: The Intellectual Life of Black Feminist Sound*. Cambridge, MA: Harvard University Press.

Brown, Geoff. 1981. "Shake to the Rhythm of the Latin Groove." *New Sounds New Styles*, August, 7–9.

Brown, Jayna. 2011. "'Brown Girl in the Ring': Poly Styrene, Anabella Lwin, and the Politics of Anger." *Journal of Popular Music Studies* 23 (4): 455–78.

Brown, Jayna, Patrick Deer, and Tavia Nyong'o. 2013. "Punk and Its Afterlives." *Social Text* 31 (3): 1–11.

Bryan-Wilson, Julia. 2008. Review of "Phantom Sightings: Art after the Chicano Movement." *Artforum* (summer): 432–34.

Burston, Paul. 1994. "Honestly." *Attitude*, August, 62–69.

Butler, Judith. 1991. "Imitation and Gender Insubordination." In *Inside/Out: Lesbian Theories, Gay Theories*, edited by Diana Fuss, 13–31. New York: Routledge.

Butt, Gavin. 2016. "Being in a Band: Art-School Experiment and the Post-Punk Commons." In *Post-Punk Then and Now*, edited by Gavin Butt, Kodwu Eshun, and Mark Fisher, 57–83. London: Repeater.

Butt, Gavin. 2022. *No Machos or Pop Stars: When the Leeds Art Experiment Went Punk*. Durham, NC: Duke University Press.

Cain, Barry. 1982. "Kid Christos." *Flexipop!*, no. 14, 20–23.

Cain, Barry, and Neil Matthews, eds. 2015. *Flexipop! The Book*. London: Colourgold.

Campt, Tina. 2017. *Listening to Images*. Durham, NC: Duke University Press.

Cann, Kevin. 2010. *Any Day Now: David Bowie: The London Years, 1947–1974*. London: Adelita.

Capote, Truman. (1975) 2012. "Nocturnal Things, or How Siamese Twins Have Sex." In *Music for Chameleons*, 234–53. New York: Vintage.

Cavanagh, David. 2015. *Good Night and Good Riddance: How Thirty-Five Years of John Peel Helped to Shape Modern Life*. London: Faber and Faber.

Chambers, Iain. 1994. *Migrancy, Culture, Identity*. New York: Routledge.

Chang, Jeff. 2005. *Can't Stop Won't Stop: A History of the Hip-Hop Generation*. New York: St. Martin's Press.

Chavoya, C. Ondine, and David Evans Frantz, eds. 2017. *Axis Mundo: Queer Networks in Chicano L.A.* Munich: DelMonico Press/Prestel.

Chibnall, Steve. 1985. "Whistle and Zoot: The Changing Meaning of a Suit of Clothes." *History Workshop Journal* 20 (1): 56–81.

Cladoosby, Brian. 2014. "Would You Call Me a Redsk*n to My Face?" *Huffpost*, January 23. https://www.huffpost.com/entry/redskins-name-change_b_4181199.

Clifford, James. 1997. *Routes: Travel and Translation in the Late Twentieth Century*. Cambridge, MA: Harvard University Press.

Coddington, Mark. 2019. *Aggregating the News: Secondhand Knowledge and the Erosion of Journalistic Authority*. New York: Columbia University Press.

Colegrave, Stephen, and Chris Sullivan. 2001. *Punk: A Life Apart*. London: Cassell.

Colón, Suzan. 1984. "A Meeting of the Minds (Part II), or MADE IN USA Crosses the Second Plateau." *Japan: Made in the USA*, 6–7. Self-published.

Colón, Suzan. 1985. "The Fetish." *Star Hits*, September, 45.

Colón, Suzan. 1997. "The Gloom Generation." *Details*, July, 122–29.

Connor, Bernie. 2018. "Revolutionary Spirit: The Sound of Liverpool 1976–1988." Liner notes for *Revolutionary Spirit: The Sound of Liverpool 1976–1988*. Cherry Red Records.

Coon, Caroline. 1977. *1988: The New Wave Punk Rock Explosion*. London: Hawthorn.

Cosgrove, Stuart. 1988. "The Zoot Suit and Style Warfare." In *Zoot Suits and Second-Hand Dresses: An Anthology of Fashion and Music*, edited by Angela McRobbie, 3–22. Boston: Unwin Hyman.

Cosgrove, Stuart. 2016. *Young Soul Rebels: A Personal History of Northern Soul*. Edinburgh: Polygon.

Covarrubias, Teresa. 2016. "Starry Nights in East LA," with Tom DeSavia. In *Under the Big Black Sun: A Personal History of L.A. Punk*, edited by John Doe, 111–21. Boston: Da Capo.

Cowton, Michael. 1991. *Pet Shop Boys: Introspective*. London: Sidgwick and Jackson.

Crimp, Douglas. 1987. "How to Have Promiscuity in an Epidemic." *October* 43 (winter): 237–71.

Crimp, Douglas. 1989. "Mourning and Militancy." *October* 51 (winter): 3–18.

Crossley, Nick. 2015. *Networks of Sound, Style and Subversion: The Punk and Post-Punk Worlds of Manchester, London, Liverpool and Sheffield, 1975–80*. Manchester: University of Manchester Press.

Cuadros, Gil. 1994. *City of God*. San Francisco: City Lights.

Davis, Stephen. 2021. *Please Please Tell Me Now: The Duran Duran Story*. New York: Hachette.

Dawes, Laina. 2013. *What Are You Doing Here? A Black Woman's Life and Liberation in Heavy Metal*. New York: Bazillion Points.

de Graaf, Kasper, and Malcolm Garrett. 1983. *When Cameras Go Crazy: Culture Club*. New York: St. Martin's Press.

Delany, Samuel R. 1999. *Times Square Red, Times Square Blue*. New York: New York University Press.

de Lauretis, Teresa. 1976–77. "Cavani's *Night Porter*: A Woman's Film?" *Film Quarterly* 30 (20): 35–38.

Deloria, Philip J. 1999. *Playing Indian*. New Haven, CT: Yale University Press.

Denselow, Robin. 1989. *When the Music's Over: The Story of Political Pop*. London: Faber and Faber.

Díaz, Junot. 2007a. *The Brief Wondrous Life of Oscar Wao*. New York: Riverhead.

Díaz, Junot. 2007b. "Wildwood: Teen-age Dominican Runaway." *New Yorker*, June 11, 74–87.

Dinshaw, Carolyn. 1999. *Getting Medieval: Sexualities and Communities, Pre- and Postmodern*. Durham, NC: Duke University Press.

Doonan, Simon. 2009. *Beautiful People: My Family and Other Glamorous Varmints*. New York: Simon and Schuster.

Doonan, Simon. 2017. "Afterword: Mundo Goes to Hollywood." In *Axis Mundo: Queer Networks in Chicano L.A.*, edited by C. Ondine Chavoya and David Evans Frantz, 366–69. Munich: DelMonico Press/Prestel.

Doumerc, Eric. *Jamaican Music in England: From the 1960s to the 1990s*. Stourbridge, UK: APS.

Drayton, Tony, ed. 2018. *Ripped and Torn: The Loudest Punk Fanzine in the U.K.* London: Ecstatic Peace Library.

Duff, Graham. 2019. *Foreground Music: A Life in Fifteen Gigs*. London: Strange Attractor Press.

Duka, John. 1981. "Notes on Fashion." *New York Times*, August 18, B12.

Eddy, Chuck. 2016. *Terminated for Reasons of Taste: Other Ways to Hear Essential or Inessential Music*. Durham, NC: Duke University Press.

Edgar, Robert, Fraser Mann, and Helen Pleasance, eds. 2019. *Music, Memory, and Memoir*. London: Bloomsbury.

Egan, Sean. 2019. *New Waves, Old Hands, and Unknown Pleasures: The Music of 1979*. Lanham, MD: Backbeat.

Ellen, Mark. 1981. "Optimism! . . . and Lots of Dreams." *Smash Hits*, June 25, 38–40.

Ellis, Bret Easton. 1985. *Less Than Zero*. New York: Simon and Schuster.

Elms, Robert. 1981a. "Rise of the Young Turk." *The Face*, December, 8–12.

Elms, Robert. 1981b. "Young Turks." *The Face*, May, 7.

Eng, Viviane. 2021. "The Pen Ten: An Interview with Carribean Fragoza." *Pen America*, March 25. https://pen.org/the-pen-ten-carribean-fragoza/.

Farber, Jim. 1989. "Beyond the Big Hair." *Rolling Stone*, December 14, 235–36.

Fiol-Matta, Licia. 2017. *The Great Woman Singer: Gender and Voice in Puerto Rican Music*. Durham, NC: Duke University Press.

Fisher, Mark. 2014. *Ghosts of My Life: Writings on Depression, Hauntology and Lost Futures*. Winchester, UK: Zero.

"Flashback: October 1982." *Guardian*, October 14, 2007. https://www.theguardian.com/music/2007/oct/14/9.

Flynn, Paul. 2017. *Good as You: From Prejudice to Pride: 30 Years of Gay Britain*. London: Penguin.

Ford, Simon. 1999. *Wreckers of Civilisation: The Story of Coum Transmissions and Throbbing Gristle*. London: Black Dog.

"40 Years of Bauhaus' Bela Lugosi's Dead." 2019. Post-Punk.com, August 6. https://post-punk.com/40-years-of-bauhaus-bela-lugosis-dead/.

Fragoza, Carribean. 2021. *Eat the Mouth That Feeds You*. San Francisco: City Lights.

Freud, Sigmund. (1917) 1953. "Mourning and Melancholia." In *The Standard Edition of the Complete Psychological Works of Sigmund Freud*, vol. 14, translated and edited by James Strachey, 243–58. London: Hogarth.

Freud, Sigmund. (1920) 1953. *Beyond the Pleasure Principle*. In *The Standard Edition of the Complete Psychological Works of Sigmund Freud*, vol. 18, translated and edited by James Strachey. London: Hogarth Press.

Frith, Simon. 1996. *Performing Rites: On the Value of Popular Music*. Cambridge, MA: Harvard University Press.

Frith, Simon, and Howard Horne. 1987. *Art into Pop*. London: Methuen.

Frost, Diane, and Richard Phillips, eds. 2011. *Liverpool '81: Remembering the Riots*. Liverpool: Liverpool University Press.

Gartside, Green. 2016. "'The Weakest Link in Every Chain, I Always Want to Find It': Green Gartside in Conversation with Kodwo Eshun." In *Post-Punk Then and Now*, edited by Gavin Butt, Kodwu Eshun, and Mark Fisher, 166–96. London: Repeater.

Gay, Roxane. 2014. "The Trouble with Prince Charming, or He Who Trespassed against Us." In *Bad Feminist: Essays*, 192–204. New York: Harper Perennial.

Geffen, Sasha. 2020. *Glitter Up the Dark: How Pop Music Broke the Binary*. Austin: University of Texas Press.

Gilroy, Paul. 1987. *"There Ain't No Black in the Union Jack": The Politics of Race and Nation*. London: Routledge.

Gilroy, Paul. 1993. *The Black Atlantic: Modernity and Double Consciousness.* Cambridge, MA: Harvard University Press.

Gilroy, Paul. 2011. *Black Britain: A Photographic History*. London: SAQI/Getty Images.

Gilroy, Paul. 2015. "Rebel Souls: Dance-Floor Justice and the Temporary Undoing of Britain's Babylon." In *Rock against Racism*, edited by Syd Shelton, 23–26. London: Autograph ABP.

Golden Age of Music Video. 2013. "80sonVEVO GAMV Takeover Week 9 w/ FEATURED VIDEO Kim Carnes' 'Bette Davis Eyes.'" March 20. http://goldenageofmusicvideo.com/80sonvevo-gamv-takeover-week-9-w-featured-video-kim-carnes-bette-davis-eyes/.

Goldman, Vivien. 1977. "Siouxsie Sioux Who R U?" *Sounds*, December 3, 26–27.

Goldman, Vivien. 2019. *Revenge of the She-Punks: A Feminist Music History from Poly Styrene to Pussy Riot*. Austin: University of Texas Press.

Gonzales, Michelle Cruz. 2016. *The Spit Boy Rule: Tales of a Xicana in a Female Punk Band*. Oakland, CA: PM Press.

Gonzalez, Gilbert G. (1990) 2013. *Chicano Education in the Era of Segregation.* Denton, TX: University of North Texas Press.

Goodlad, Lauren M. E., and Michael Bibby, eds. 2007. *Goth: Undead Subculture*. Durham, NC: Duke University Press.

Gorman, Paul. 2016. "Post-Punk Pirates, Princess Diana, and Bow Wow Wow at World's End." Flashbak, July 16. https://flashbak.com/post-punk-pirates-princess-diana-and-bow-wow-wow-at-worlds-end-361085/.

Gorman, Paul. 2017. *The Story of* The Face*: The Magazine That Changed Culture.* New York: Thames and Hudson.

Gorman, Paul. 2020. *The Life and Times of Malcolm McLaren*. London: Constable.

Goude, Jean-Paul. 1983. *Jungle Fever*. Edited by Harold Hayes. New York: Xavier Moreau.

"Gospel Groove." 1983. *Record Mirror*, July 23, 14.

Gourlay, Dom. 2009. "Shoegaze Week: DiS Talks to Simon Scott about His Time in Slowdive." *Drowned in Sound*, April 23. https://drownedinsound.com/in_depth/4136609-shoegaze-week-dis-talks-to-simon-scott-about-his-time-in-slowdive.

Grabel, Richard. 1987. "Planet Hispanic." *New Musical Express*, August 1, 42–43.

Green, Thomas H. 2014. "TheartsdeskQ&A: Musician Holly Johnson." Theartsdesk.com, October 4. https://www.theartsdesk.com/new-music/theartsdesk-qa-musician-holly-johnson.

Groom, Nick. 2018. *The Vampire: A New History*. New Haven, CT: Yale University Press.

Guerrero, Desirée. 2018. "Mexican-American Morrissey Fans Abound." *Chill*, August 6. https://www.chill.us/entertainment/2018/8/06/mexican-american-morrissey-fans-abound.

Gunckel, Colin. 2017. "'People Think We're Weird 'Cause We're Queer': Art Meets Punk in Los Angeles." In *Axis Mundo: Queer Networks in Chicano L.A.*, edited by C. Ondine Chavoya and David Evans Frantz, 266–87. Munich: DelMonico Press/Prestel.

Gurba, Myriam. 2007. "White Girl." In *Dahlia Season: Stories and a Novella.* San Francisco: Manic D Press.

Guzmán, Manuel. 1997. "'Pa' La Escuelita con Mucho Cuida'o y por la Orillita': A Journey through the Contested Terrains of the Nation and Sexual Orientation." In *Puerto Rican Jam: Essays on Culture and Politics*, edited by Frances Negrón-Muntaner and Ramón Grosfoguel, 209–28. Minneapolis: University of Minnesota Press.

Habell-Pallán, Michelle. 2005. *Loca Motion: The Travels of Chicana and Latina Popular Culture*. New York: New York University Press.

Haddon, Mimi. 2020. *What Is Post-Punk? Genre and Identity in Avant-Garde Popular Music, 1977–82*. Ann Arbor: University of Michigan Press.

Hadleigh, Boze. 1997. *Sing Out! Gays and Lesbians in the Music World*. New York: Barricade.

Hall, Matthew T. 2016. "Short-Lived Iguanas Nightclub Left a Mark." *San Diego Union-Tribune*, September 2. https://www.sandiegouniontribune.com/sdut-short-lived-iguanas-nightclub-left-a-mark-2011may18-htmlstory.html.

Hall, Stuart. (1973) 2019. "Encoding and Decoding in the Television Discourse." In *Essential Essays*, vol. 1: *Foundations of Cultural Studies*, 257–76. Durham, NC: Duke University Press.

Hall, Stuart. (2007) 2019. "Richard Hoggart, *The Uses of Literacy*, and the Cultural Turn." In *Essential Essays*, vol. 1: *Foundations of Cultural Studies*, 35–46. Durham, NC: Duke University Press.

Hamilton, Jack. 2016. *Just around Midnight: Rock and Roll and the Racial Imagination*. Cambridge, MA: Harvard University Press.

Harper, Benjamin. 2009. "Siouxsie Sioux: Black Eyeliner and Dark Dreams." In *My Diva: 65 Gay Men on the Women Who Inspire Them*, edited by Michael Montlack, 229–33. Madison, WI: Terrace.

Harriman, Andi, and Marloes Bontje. 2014. *Some Wear Leather Some Wear Lace: The Worldwide Compendium of Postpunk and Goth in the 1980s*. Chicago: Intellect.

Haskins, David J. 2014. *Who Killed Mister Moonlight? Bauhaus, Black Magick, and Benediction*. London: Jawbone.

Haskins, Kevin. 2018. *Bauhaus Undead*. Los Angeles: Cleopatra.

Haslam, Dave. 2020. *Searching for Love: Courtney Love in Liverpool, 1982*. Manchester: Cōnfingō.

Hawkins, Stan. 2002. *Settling the Pop Score: Pop Texts and Identity Politics*. New York: Routledge.

Heap, Chad. 2009. *Slumming: Sexual and Racial Encounters in American Nightlife, 1885–1940*. Chicago: University of Chicago Press.

Heath, Chris. 1989. Review of Holly Johnson's *Blast*. *Q*, May, 80.

Heath, Chris. 1993. *Pet Shop Boys versus America*. Miami: Viking.

Hebdige, Dick. 1979. *Subculture: The Meaning of Style*. London: Methuen.

Hebdige, Dick. 1987. *Cut 'n' Mix: Culture, Identity and Caribbean Music*. London: Routledge.

Heise, Thomas. 2015. "Subterranean Worlds: Urban Redevelopment, Queer Spaces, and John Rechy's *City of Night*." In *The Textual Outlaw: Reading John Rechy in the 21st Century*, edited by Manuel M. Martín-Rodríguez and Beth Hernandez-Jason, 23–41. Madrid: Universidad de Alcalá.

Hepworth, David. 2016. "How Performing 'Starman' on *Top of the Pops* Sent Bowie into the Stratosphere." *Guardian*, January 15. https://www.theguardian.com/music/musicblog/2016/jan/15/david-bowie-starman-top-of-the-pops.

Hermann, Andy. 2018. "For Outsiders and Outliers, Danny Fuentes' Gallery Is a Place to Call Home." *Los Angeles Times*, August 28.

Hernandez, Gilbert. 1999. *Love and Rockets X*. Seattle: Fantagraphics.

Hernandez, Jaime. 1997. *Flies on the Ceiling: Love and Rockets*, vol. 9. Seattle: Fantagraphics.

Hibbert, Tom. 1985. "The Pet Shop Boys: An Ex-*Smash Hits* Writer and the Grandson of a Nitwit." *Smash Hits*, December 18, 13.

Hidalgo, Melissa Mora. 2016. *Mozlandia: Morrissey Fans in the Borderlands*. Truro, UK: Headpress.

Hidalgo, Melissa Mora. 2021. "Gente from La Puente: Underground Punk Icon Kid Congo Powers Still Rocks." *Artbound*, KCET, February 18. https://www.kcet.org/shows/artbound/gente-from-la-puente.

Hilderbrand, Lucas. 2013. "'Luring Disco Dollies to a Life of Vice': Queer Pop Music's Moment." *Journal of Popular Music Studies* 25 (4): 415–38.

Hizer, Bruno. 1984. *Give It Loads! The Story of Frankie Goes to Hollywood*. New York: Proteus.

Hoare, Philip, and Chris Heath. 2006. *Pet Shop Boys: Catalogue*. London: Thames and Hudson.

Hoggart, Richard. (1957) 2009. *The Uses of Literacy: Aspects of Working-Class Life*. London: Penguin.

Holden, Stephen. 2020. *Adolescent Alternatives: Road Trips with Japan, 1978–1980*. With Anthony Reynolds. Manchester: Diplomat Productions.

Homan, Shane, ed. 2006. *Access All Eras: Tribute Bands and Global Pop Culture*. Berkshire, UK: Open University Press.

Hunt, Leon. 1998. *British Low Culture: From Safari Suits to Sexploitation*. London: Routledge.

"If I Could, I'd Be a Recluse . . . I'm Trying Really Hard." 2013. *Daily Mail*, June 29.

Jackson, Danny. 1985. *Frankie Say: The Rise of Frankie Goes to Hollywood*. New York: Simon and Schuster.

Jacquemin, Jean-Pierre, Jadot Seirahigha, and Richard Trillo. 1999. "Rwanda and Burundi." In *World Music: Africa, Europe and the Middle East*, vol. 1, edited by Simon Broughton, Mark Ellingham, and Richard Trillo, 608–12. New York: Penguin.

Jaime-Becerra, Michael. 2019. "Todo se acaba: 11950 Garvey Avenue/7305 Melrose Avenue." *ZYZZYVA* 116 (fall): 103–21.

Jeffries, Georgia. 1979. "The Low Riders of Whittier Boulevard." *American Film*, February, 58–62.

Johnson, David. 1981. "I Thought I Was Geronimo." *New Sounds New Styles*, August 13, 12–14.

Johnson, Holly. 1994. *A Bone in My Flute*. London: Arrow.

Johnson, Holly. 2019. "Like a Pfuckking Taart!" In *A Love Letter to Europe*, edited by Melvyn Bragg, 62–65. London: Coronet.

Jones, Dylan. 2020. *Sweet Dreams: From Club Culture to Style Culture, the Story of the New Romantics*. London: Faber and Faber.

Jourgensen, Al. 2013. *Ministry: The Lost Gospels According to Al Jourgensen*. Cambridge, MA: Da Capo.

Katz, Robin. 1981. "Blue Rondo A La Turk." *Smash Hits*, November 26, 14.

Kemp, Gary. 2009. *I Know This Much*. London: Fourth Estate.

Kemp, Martin. 2000. *True: The Autobiography of Martin Kemp*. London: Orion.

"Kid Congo Powers Oral History." 2015. *New York Night Train*. October. http://www.newyorknighttrain.com/zine/issues/1/oralhist.html.

Kirk, Kris. 1999. *A Boy Called Mary: Kris Kirk's Greatest Hits*. East Sussex, UK: Millivres.

Klosterman, Chuck. 2002. "Viva Morrissey!" *Spin*, August, 88–92.

Kokinis, Troy Andreas Araiza. 2020. "El Monte's Wildweed: Biraciality and the Punk Ethos of the Gun Club's Jeffrey Lee Pierce." In *East of East: The Making of Greater El Monte*, edited by Romeo Guzmán, Carribean Fregoza, Alex Sayf Cummings, and Ryan Reft, 234–41. New Brunswick, NJ: Rutgers University Press.

Kun, Josh, ed. 2017. *The Tide Was Always High: The Music of Latin America in Los Angeles*. Berkeley: University of California Press.

Lawrence, Tim. 2016. *Life and Death on the New York Dance Floor, 1980–1983*. Durham, NC: Duke University Press.

Lees, Gene. 1979. "Tony Bill: Maverick Producer." *American Film*, February, 62–63.

Letts, Don. 2006. *Culture Clash: Dread Meets Punk Rockers*. With David Nobakht. Middlesex, UK: SAF.

Letts, Don. 2021. *There and Black Again*. With Mal Peachey. London: Omnibus.

Lime, Harry. 2020. *Marc Almond*. Morrisville, NC: Lulu.

Lipsitz, George. (1998) 2018. *The Possessive Investment in Whiteness: How White People Profit from Identity Politics*. Philadelphia: Temple University Press.

Long, Pat. 2012. *The History of the* NME*: High Times and Low Lives at the World's Most Famous Music Magazine*. London: Portico.

López, Marissa. 2012. "Soy Emo, y Qué? Sad Kids, Punkera Dykes, and the Latin@ Public Sphere." *Journal of American Studies* 46 (4): 895–918.

Lowe, Lisa. 2015. *The Intimacy of Four Continents*. Durham, NC: Duke University Press.

Lydon, John. 1994. *Rotten: No Irish, No Blacks, No Dogs*. New York: Picador.

Macias, Anthony. 2008. *Mexican American Mojo: Popular Music, Dance, and Urban Culture in Los Angeles, 1935–1968*. Durham, NC: Duke University Press.

Macilwee, Michael. 2015. *The Teddy Boy Wars: The Youth Cult That Shocked Britain*. London: Milo.

Majewski, Lori, and Jonathan Bernstein. 2014. *Mad World: An Oral History of New Wave Artists and Songs That Defined the 1980s*. New York: Abrams.

Mal-One and the Punk Collective. 2020. *Worlds End/Sex Pistols, McLaren and Westwood: A Chronology 1971–1978*. London: JR.

Marcus, Greil. (1980) 1993. "It's Fab, It's Passionate, It's Wild, It's Intelligent! It's the Hot New Sound of England Today!" In *In the Fascist Bathroom: Punk in Pop Music*, 109–34. Cambridge, MA: Harvard University Press.

Marks, Laura U. 2002. *Touch: Sensuous Theory and Multisensory Media*. Minneapolis: University of Minnesota Press.

Marshall, Bertie. 2006. *Berlin Bromley*. London: SAF.

Martin, Peter. 1984. "I've Changed the World!" *Smash Hits*, July 19–August 1, 48.

Martinez-Cruz, Paloma. 2020. "Chicano Dracula: The Passions and Predations of Bela Lugosi, Gomez Addams, and Kid Congo Powers." In *Decolonizing Latinx Masculinities*, edited by Arturo J. Aldama and Frederick Luis Aldama, 185–95. Tucson: University of Arizona Press.

Martins Junior, Angelo. 2020. *Moving Difference: Brazilians in London*. London: Routledge.

Masters, Marc. 2007. *No Wave*. London: Black Dog.

Mathur, Paul. 1988. "Born Again Savages." *Melody Maker*, July 9, 28–30.

Mattson, Kevin. 2020. *We're Not Here to Entertain: Punk Rock, Ronald Reagan, and the Real Culture War of 1980s America*. New York: Oxford University Press.

Maw, James. 1981. *The Official Adam Ant Story*. London: Futura.

McLeod, Jamie, and Jeremy Reed. 2001. *Marc Almond: Adored and Explored*. London: Creation.

McRobbie, Angela, ed. 1988. *Zoot Suits and Second-Hand Dresses: An Anthology of Fashion and Music*. Boston: Unwin Hyman.

McRobbie, Angela. 1991. *Feminism and Youth Culture: From* Jackie *to* Just Seventeen. Boston: Unwin Hyman.

Mehno, Scott. 1997. "Miami Thrice: Exposé Ride the New Miami Wave." *Spin*, May, 18.

Miles, Barry. 1981. *The 2-Tone Book for Rude Boys*. London: Omnibus.

Miller, D. A. 1988. *The Novel and the Police*. Berkeley: University of California Press.

Miller, Monica L. 2009. *Slaves to Fashion: Black Dandyism and the Styling of Black Diasporic Identity*. Durham, NC: Duke University Press.

Minian, Ana Raquel. 2018. *Undocumented Lives: The Untold Story of Mexican Migration*. Cambridge, MA: Harvard University Press.

Miranda, Carolina A. 2020. "Painter Shizu Saldamando Puts a Face to L.A.'s Latinx Art and Punk Scenes." *Los Angeles Times*, February 18. https://www.latimes.com/entertainment-arts/story/2020-02-18/painter-shizu-saldamando-latinx-art-punk-scenes.

Mooney, Jordan. 2019. *Defying Gravity: Jordan's Story*. With Cathi Unsworth. London: Omnibus.

Moore, Thurston, and Byron Coley. 2008. *No Wave. Post-Punk. Underground. New York. 1976–1980*. New York: Abrams Image.

Morales, Ed. 2003. *The Latin Beat: Latin Music from Bossa Nova*. Cambridge, MA: Da Capo.

Morrissey. 2019. "Blue Rondo a la Turk." Messages from Morrissey, Morrissey Central, July 8. https://www.morrisseycentral.com/messages frommorrissey/blue-rondo-a-la-turk.

Mort, Frank. 1996. *Cultures of Consumption: Masculinities and Social Space in Late Twentieth-Century Britain*. New York: Routledge.

mullets i have loved. 2014. "Star Hits Editors, David Keeps and Suzan Colón, Answer Your Questions." June. https://mulletsihaveloved.wordpress.com/2014/06/.

Muñoz, José Esteban. 1996. "Ephemera as Evidence: Introductory Notes to Queer Acts." *Women and Performance: A Journal of Feminist Theory* 8 (2): 5–16.

Muñoz, José Esteban. 1999. *Disidentifications: Queers of Color and the Politics of Performance*. Minneapolis: University of Minnesota Press.

Muñoz, José Esteban. 2013. "'Gimme Gimme This . . . Gimme Gimme That': Annihilation and Innovation in the Punk Rock Commons." *Social Text* 31 (3): 95–110.

Musto, Michael. 1984. *Downtown*. New York: Vintage.

Musto, Michael. 2016. "RIP LGBT Latin Dance Club Escuelita." *Paper*, March 2. https://www.papermag.com/rip-lgbt-dance-club-escuelita-1637308305.html.

Nama, Adilifu. 2020. *I Wonder U: How Prince Went Beyond Race and Back*. New Brunswick, NJ: Rutgers University Press.

Napier-Bell, Simon. 2002. *Black Vinyl, White Powder*. London: Ebury.

National Lesbian and Gay Survey. 1993. *Proust, Cole Porter, Michelangelo, Marc Almond and Me: Writings by Gay Men on Their Lives and Lifestyles*. New York: Routledge.

Neal, Charles. 1987. *Tape Delay*. Middlesex, UK: SAF.

Nericcio, William Anthony. 2007. *Tex[t]-Mex: Seductive Hallucinations of the "Mexican" in America*. Austin: University of Texas Press.

Newsroom. 2016. "Music Interview: Pet Shop Boys." *Yorkshire Evening Post*, April 8. https://www.yorkshireeveningpost.co.uk/whats-on/arts-and-entertainment/music-interview-pet-shop-boys-622437.

Noriega, Chon A., ed. 1992. *Chicanos and Film: Representation and Resistance*. Minneapolis: University of Minnesota Press.

Nowell, David. 2011. *The Story of Northern Soul: A Definitive History of the Dance Scene That Refuses to Die*. London: Portico.

O'Brien, Lucy. 1994. "A Kiss in the Dreamhouse." In *Love Is the Drug*, edited by John Aizlewood, 86–99. London: Penguin.

O'Brien, Lucy. (1995) 2020. *She Bop: The Definitive History of Women in Popular Music*. London: Jawbone.

Olalquiaga, Celeste. 1998. *The Artificial Kingdom: The Treasury of the Kitsch Experience*. New York: Pantheon.

O'Neill, Peter D., and David Lloyd, eds. 2009. *The Black and Green Atlantic: Cross-Currents of the African and Irish Diasporas*. New York: Palgrave Macmillan.

O'Shea, Mick. 2018. *Pocket Guide to Ska*. Cornwall, UK: Red Planet.

Pacini Hernandez, Deborah. 2010. *Oye Como Va! Hybridity and Identity in Latino Popular Music*. Philadelphia: Temple University Press.

Padilla, Felix M. 1985. *Latino Ethnic Consciousness: The Case of Mexican Americans and Puerto Ricans in Chicago*. Notre Dame, IN: University of Notre Dame Press.

Palmer, Robert. 1981. "The Pop Life; Latest British Invasion: 'The New Tribalism.'" *New York Times*, November 25, 13.

Palmer, Robert. 1982. "Britain's New Pop—Synthetic Bands." *New York Times*, March 7, D19.

Paphides, Pete. 2020. *Broken Greek: A Story of Chip Shops and Pop Songs*. London: Quercus.

Partridge, Christopher. 2010. *Dub in Babylon: Understanding the Evolution and Significance of Dub Reggae in Jamaica and Britain from King Tubby to Post-Punk*. London: Equinox.

Paytress, Mark. 2003. *Siouxsie and the Banshees: The Authorized Biography*. London: Sanctuary.

Paytress, Mark. 2015. *Marc Almond*. London: First Third.

Paytress, Mark. 2019. *To Show You I've Been There: Soft Cell*. London: Renegade Music.

Peellaert, Guy, and Nik Cohn. 1973. *Rock Dreams*. New York: Popular Library.

Peiss, Kathy. 2011. *Zoot Suit: The Enigmatic Career of an Extreme Style*. Philadelphia: University of Pennsylvania Press.

Perry, Leah. 2016. "Neoliberal Crimmigration: The 'Commonsense' Shaming of the Undocumented." In *American Shame: Stigma and the Body Politic*, edited by Myra Mendible, 57–83. Bloomington: Indiana University Press.

Petty, Kevin. 1995. "The Image of Siouxsie Sioux: Punk and the Politics of Gender." *disClosure: A Journal of Social Theory* 4, article 2. https://doi.org/10.13023/DISCLOSURE.04.02.

Pierce, Jeffrey Lee. (1998) 2017. *Go Tell the Mountain: The Stories and Lyrics of Jeffrey Lee Pierce*. Spokane, WA: Creeping Ritual Productions.

P-Orridge, Genesis. 2021. *Nonbinary: A Memoir*. With Tim Mohr. New York: Abrams.

Porter, Dick. 2007. *The Cramps: A Short History of Rock 'n' Roll Psychosis*. London: Plexus.

Porter, Dick. 2015. *Journey to the Centre of the Cramps*. London: Omnibus.

Prince, Bill. 1982. "Blue Rondo A La Turk." *Noise!*, October 12, 10–11.

Puterbaugh, Parke. 1983. "Anglomania: America Surrenders to the Brits—But Who Really Wins?" *Rolling Stone*, November 10, 31–32.

Quantick, David. 1989. "Master Blaster." *New Musical Express*, April 22, 31.

Rachel, Daniel. 2016. *Walls Come Tumbling Down: The Music and Politics of Rock against Racism, 2 Tone and Red Wedge 1976–1992*. London: Picador.

Raggett, Ned. 2019. "A Long Term Effect: Tim Pope on Four Decades of Work with the Cure." *Quietus*, July 8. https://thequietus.com/articles/26761-tim-pope-interview-the-cure.

Raheja, Michelle H. 2010. *Reservation Realism: Redfacing, Visual Sovereignty, and Representations of Native Americans in Film*. Lincoln: University of Nebraska Press.

Rambali, Paul. 1980. "The Promised Land Calling." *New Musical Express*, February 9, 30–33.

Ramírez, Catherine S. 2009. *The Woman in the Zoot Suit: Gender, Nationalism, and the Cultural Politics of Memory*. Durham, NC: Duke University Press.

Rechy, John. (1963) 2013. *City of Night*. New York: Grove.

Rechy, John. (1967) 1984. *Numbers*. New York: Grove.

Reed, Jeremy. 1994. *Pop Stars*. London: Enitharmon.

Reed, Jeremy. 1995. *Marc Almond: The Last Star*. London: Creation.

Reed, Jeremy. 1999. *Angels, Divas and Blacklisted Heroes*. London: Peter Owen.

Reed, Jeremy. 2010. *Piccadilly Bongo*. London: Enitharmon.

Reynolds, Simon. 2005. *Rip It Up and Start Again: Postpunk 1978–1984*. New York: Penguin.

Reynolds, Simon, and Joy Press. 1995. *The Sex Revolts: Gender, Rebellion and Rock 'n' Roll*. Cambridge, MA: Harvard University Press.

Rimmer, Dave. 1985. *Like Punk Never Happened: Culture Club and the New Pop*. London: Faber and Faber.

Rimmer, Dave. 2003. *New Romantics: The Look*. London: Omnibus.

Rivera, Raquel Z. 2003. *New York Ricans from the Hip Hop Zone*. New York: Palgrave Macmillan.

Rivera, Reynaldo. 2020. *Reynaldo Rivera: Provisional Notes for a Disappeared City*. Cambridge, MA: MIT Press.

Rivera-Servera, Ramón H. 2012. *Performing Queer Latinidad: Dance, Sexuality, Politics*. Ann Arbor: University of Michigan Press.

Roberts, John Storm. (1979) 1999. *The Latin Tinge: The Impact of Latin American Music on the United States*. New York: Oxford University Press.

Rockwell, John. 1981. "Rock: Bow Wow Wow." *New York Times*, September 17, C13.

Rodríguez, Juana María. 2003. *Queer Latinidad: Identity Practices, Discursive Spaces*. New York: New York University Press.

Rodríguez, Juana María. 2014. "Gesture in Mambo Time." In *Sexual Futures, Queer Gestures, and Other Latina Longings*, 99–138. New York: New York University Press.

Rodríguez, Richard T. 2009. *Next of Kin: The Family in Chicano/a Cultural Politics*. Durham, NC: Duke University Press.

Rodríguez, Richard T. 2017. "X Marks the Spot." *Cultural Dynamics* 29 (3): 202–13.

Rogers, Jude. 2013. "The Pet Shop Boys on Texting Cameron and Russian Homophobia." *New Statesman*, September 26. https://www.newstatesman.com/culture/2013/09/beyond-suburbs-utopia.

Román-Velázquez, Patria. 1999. *The Making of Latin London: Salsa Music, Place and Identity*. Brookfield, VT: Ashgate.

Roseberry, Craig. 2009. "Bauhaus/*Mask* (1981): Remake, Remodel, Reinvent." *Mask*, by Bauhaus. Beggar's Banquet. Liner notes.

Rothberg, Michael. 2009. *Multidirectional Memory: Remembering the Holocaust in the Age of Decolonization*. Stanford, CA: Stanford University Press.

Royster, Francesca T. 2013. *Sounding Like a No-No: Queer Sounds and Eccentric Acts in the Post-Soul Era*. Ann Arbor: University of Michigan Press.

Ruiz, Ariana. 2015. "In Transit: Travel and Mobility in Latina Literature and Art." PhD diss., University of Illinois, Urbana-Champaign.

Ruiz, Ariana. 2019. "*Ex-Voto #7*: Print Culture and the Creation of an Alternative Latinidad in the Work of Jim Mendiola." In *Latinx Ciné in the Twenty-First Century*, edited by Frederick Luis Aldama, 186–201. Tucson: University of Arizona Press.

Sabin, Roger. 1999. "'I Won't Let That Dago By': Rethinking Punk and Racism." In *Punk Rock: So What? The Cultural Legacy of Punk*, edited by Roger Sabin, 199–218. New York: Routledge.

Salas, Floyd. 1967. *Tattoo the Wicked Cross*. New York: Grove Press.

Salewicz, Chris. 1981a. "The Americanization of John Lydon: A Progress Report." *Face* 16 (August): 49. Salewicz, Chris. 1981b. "Funk and Roll: A Profile of Linx." *Face* 20 (December): 36–40.

Sanabria, Izzy. 1977. "'Spic Chic' Is Coming!" *Latin NY*, January, 6–7, 65.

Sánchez, Erika L. 2017. *I Am Not Your Perfect Mexican Daughter*. New York: Ember.

Sanchez, Thomas. 1978. *Zoot-Suit Murders*. New York: Dutton.

Sandbrook, Dominic. 2019. *Who Dares Wins: Britain, 1979–1982*. London: Penguin.

Santisi, Donna. (1978) 2010. *Ask the Angels: Photographs by Donna Santisi*. Los Angeles: Kill Your Idols.

Savage, Jon. 1990. "Tainted Love: The Influence of Male Homosexuality and Sexual Divergence on Pop Music and Culture since the War." In *Consumption, Identity, and Style: Marketing, Meanings, and the Packaging of Pleasure*, edited by Alan Tomlinson, 153–71. New York: Routledge.

Sedgwick, Eve Kosofsky. 1993. *Tendencies*. Durham, NC: Duke University Press.

Sedgwick, Eve Kosofsky. 1996. "Gosh, Boy George, You Must Be Awfully Secure in Your Masculinity!" In *Constructing Masculinity*, edited by Maurice Berger, Brian Wallis, and Simon Watson, 11–20. New York: Routledge.

Shankland, Guy. 2021. "Tension and Turmoil." *Vive le Rock!*, no. 83, 38–47.

Shapiro, Peter, ed. 2000. "Freestyle." In *Modulations: A History of Electronic Music: Throbbing Words on Sound*, edited by David Toop, 104–5. New York: Caipirinha.

Shatkin, Elina. 2007. "Chicano Portraiture Meets Siouxsie Sioux." *Los Angeles Times*, August 2, E12.

Shaw, William. 1988. "Holly Johnson: Frankie Say See You in Court!" *Blitz*, August.

Shimizu, Celine Parreñas. 2007. *The Hypersexuality of Race: Performing Asian/American Women on Screen and Scene*. Durham, NC: Duke University Press.

Shirley, Ian. 1994. *Dark Entries: Bauhaus and Beyond*. Middlesex: SAF.

Smith, Graham. 2011. *We Can Be Heroes: London Clubland, 1976–1984*. London: Unbound.

Smith, Liz. 1980. "Dandies in Hand-Me-Downs." *Evening Standard*, March 17, 20.

Smith, Richard. 1995. *Seduced and Abandoned: Essays on Gay Men and Popular Music*. London: Cassell.

Snicks. 2014. "The Essential Pet Shop Boys: Ranking Their Top Ten Songs." *Logo*, July 10. http://www.newnownext.com/the-essential-pet-shop-boys-ranking-their-top-ten-songs/07/2014/.

Spindel, Carol. 2002. *Dancing at Halftime: Sports and the Controversy over American Indian Mascots*. New York: New York University Press.

Spitz, Marc. 2012. "Pet Shop Boys' Neil Tennant Talks about American Homophobia." *Vanity Fair*, August 29. https://www.vanityfair.com/culture/2012/08/pet-shop-boys-neil-tennant-olympic-closing-ceremonies-performance.

Spooner, Catherine. 2004. *Fashioning Gothic Bodies*. Manchester: Manchester University Press.

Stanley, Bob. 2015. *Yeah! Yeah! Yeah! The Story of Pop Music from Bill Haley to Beyoncé*. New York: Norton.

Stanley, Carl. 2015. *Kiss and Make Up*. Croydon, UK: Ignite.

Steele-Perkins, Chris, and Richard Smith. 2002. *The Teds*. Stockport, UK: Dewi Lewis.

Stevenson, Ray. 1986. *Siouxsie and the Banshees: Photo Book*. London: Omnibus.

Stewart, Graham. 2013. *Bang! A History of Britain in the 1980s*. London: Atlantic.

Strange, Steve. 2002. *Blitzed! The Autobiography of Steve Strange*. London: Orion.

Stubbs, David. 2018. *Future Sounds: The Story of Electronic Music from Stockhausen to Skrillex*. London: Faber and Faber.

Suck, Jane. 1977. "avAntgarde." *Sounds*, September 24, 24.

Sullivan, Caroline. 2002. "'Anyone Over 30 Belongs to Me—Bisexual, Male, Female, Gay, Whatever.'" *Guardian*, January 10. https://www.theguardian.com/lifeandstyle/2002/jan/11/shopping.artsfeatures.

Sullivan, Chris. 1981. "The Zoot Suit: A Historical Perspective." *Face*, September, 50–51.

Sullivan, Chris. 2014a. *Chewing the Fat*, by Blue Rondo a la Turk. Cherry Red Records. Liner notes.

Sullivan, Chris. 2014b. "Zoot Suit." *Jocks and Nerds*, summer, 170–76.

Sullivan, Paul. 2014. *Remixology: Tracing the Dub Diaspora*. London: Reaktion.

Tashjian, Rachel. 2018. "In Praise of the Cramps, the Scariest Band of All Time." *Vice*, October 24. https://garage.vice.com/en_us/article/9k74m8/the-cramps-style.

Taylor, Leila. 2019. *Darkly: Black History and America's Gothic Soul*. London: Repeater.

Taylor, Steve. 1980. "Anti-Hero." *Smash Hits*, October 30, 40.

Tebbutt, Simon. 1982. "Animal Caracas." *Record Mirror*, August 21, 20.

Tebbutt, Simon. 1984. *Soft Cell: The Authorized Biography*. London: Sidgwick and Jackson.

Tennant, Neil. 1982. Review of Blue Rondo a la Turk's "The Heavens Are Crying." *Smash Hits*, August 19, 28.

Tennant, Neil. 2006. "Foreword." In *The Best of Smash Hits: The 80s*. London: Sphere.

Tennant, Neil. 2018. *One Hundred Lyrics and a Poem*. London: Faber and Faber.

Tennant, Neil. 2021. "A Year." In *Annually*, 13–57. London: Lithosphere.

Thompson, Dave. 2002. *The Dark Reign of Gothic Rock: In the Reptile House with the Sisters of Mercy, Bauhaus, and the Cure*. London: Helter Skelter.

Thompson, Dave. 2017. *Wheels Out of Gear: 2-Tone, the Specials, and a World in Flame*. Self-published.

Tobler, John. 1982a. *Adam and the Ants: Superstar*. Cheshire, UK: Stafford Pemberton.

Tobler, John. 1982b. "Soft Cell." In *Eclectic Rock: The Complete A-Z of Electronic Rock*, 17. East Sussex, UK: SB Publishing and Promotions.

Tongson, Karen. 2011. *Relocations: Queer Suburban Imaginaries*. New York: New York University Press.

Toothpaste, Lucy. 1978. "Wouldn't You Like to Rip Him to Shreds? Adam and the Ants." *Temporary Hoarding*, summer, n.p.

Tran, Phuc. 2020. *Sigh, Gone: A Misfit's Memoir of Great Books, Punk Rock, and the Fight to Fit In*. New York: Flatiron.

Turner, Luke. 2016. "Party Conference: Why the Pet Shop Boys Are Worthy of Academic Consideration." *Guardian*, March 18. https://www.theguardian.com/music/2016/mar/18/pet-shop-boys-academic-symposium.

Vague Rants. 2018. "*Vague* 7." http://www.vaguerants.org.uk/vague-7/.

Vargas, Deborah R. 2014. "Ruminations on *Lo Sucio* as a Latino Queer Analytic." *American Quarterly* 66 (3): 715–26.

Vasquez, Richard. 1970. *Chicano*. New York: Avon.

Vazquez, Alexandra T. 2010. "Can You Feel the Beat? Freestyle's Systems of Living, Loving, and Recording." *Social Text* 28 (1): 107–24.

Vazquez, Alexandra T. 2013. *Listening in Detail: Performances of Cuban Music*. Durham, NC: Duke University Press.

Veal, Michael E. 2007. *Dub: Soundscapes and Shattered Songs in Jamaican Reggae*. Middletown, CT: Wesleyan University Press.

Veloso, Caetano. 2002. *Tropical Truth: A Story of Music and Revolution in Brazil*. New York: Da Capo.

Vermorel, Frank, and Judy Vermorel. 1981. *Adam and the Ants*. London: Omnibus.

Villaseñor, Edmund (Victor). 1973. *Macho!* New York: Bantam.

Vozick-Levinson, Simon. 2019. "Los Angeles Proclaims 'The Specials Day.'" *Rolling Stone*, April 23. https://www.rollingstone.com/music/music-news/the-specials-day-los-angeles-826124/.

Warner, Michael. 2002. *Publics and Counterpublics*. New York: Zone.

Waters, Frank. 1977. *Book of the Hopi*. New York: Penguin.

Watkins, Tom. 2016. *Let's Make Lots of Money: Secrets of a Rich, Fat, Gay, Lucky Bastard*. With Matthew Lindsay. London: Penguin/Random House.

Webster, Sue. 2019. *I Was a Teenage Banshee*. New York: Rizzoli Electa.

Weiner, Joshua L., and Damon Young. 2011. "Queer Bonds." *GLQ: A Journal of Lesbian and Gay Studies* 17 (2–3): 223–41.

Westwood, Vivienne, and Ian Kelly. 2014. *Vivienne Westwood*. London: Picador.

Whitney, Karl. 2019. *Hit Factories: A Journey through the Industrial Cities of British Pop*. London: Weidenfeld and Nicolson.

Wilkinson, David. 2015. "Ever Fallen in Love (with Someone You Shouldn't Have?): Punk, Politics and Same-Sex Passion." *Key Words*, no. 13, 57–76.

Wilkinson, David. 2016. *Post-Punk, Politics and Pleasure in Britain*. New York: Palgrave Macmillan.

Williams, Raymond. (1958) 1983. *Culture and Society: 1780–1950*. New York: Columbia University Press.

Williams, Raymond. (1958) 1989. "Culture Is Ordinary." In *Resources of Hope: Culture, Democracy, Socialism*. London: Verso.

Woll, Allen L. 1980. "Bandits and Lovers: Hispanic Images in American Film." In *The Kaleidoscope Lens: How Hollywood Views Ethnic Groups*, edited by Randall M. Miller, 54–72. Englewood, NJ: Jerome S. Ozer.

Wombat, John. 2018. *The Cramps, Beast and Beyond: A Book about Bryan Gregory*. Self-published.

Worley, Matthew. 2017. *No Future: Punk, Politics and British Youth Culture, 1976–1984*. Cambridge: Cambridge University Press.

DISCOGRAPHY

Adam and the Ants. 1979. *Dirk Wears White Sox*. Do It Records.

Adam and the Ants. 1980. *Kings of the Wild Frontier*. CBS.

Adam and the Ants. 1981. *Prince Charming*. CBS.

Adam and the Ants. 2001. *Live at the BBC*. Strange Fruit.

Almond, Marc. 1984. *Vermin in Ermine*. Some Bizarre.

Almond, Marc. 1986. "A Woman's Story." Some Bizarre.

Almond, Marc. 1987. *Mother Fist and Her Five Daughters*. Some Bizarre/Virgin.

Almond, Marc. 1988. *The Stars We Are*. Some Bizarre/Capitol.

Almond, Marc. 1995. *Treasure Box*. EMI.

Almond, Marc. 1999. *Open All Night*. Blue Star Music.

Almond, Marc. 2016. *Trials of Eyeliner*. UMC.

Ant, Adam. 1982. *Friend or Foe*. CBS.

Ant, Adam. 1983. *Strip*. CBS.

Ant, Adam. 1985. *Vive le Rock*. CBS.

Ant, Adam. 1994. *B-Side Babies*. Epic.

Ash, Daniel. 1991. "Walk This Way." RCA/Beggars Banquet.

Aztec Camera. 1987. *Love*. Sire.

Bag, Alice. 2016. *Alice Bag*. Don Giovanni Records.

Ball, Dave. 1983. *In Strict Tempo*. Some Bizarre.

Bauhaus. 1979. "Bela Lugosi's Dead." Small Wonder.

Bauhaus. 1980. *In the Flat Field*. 4AD.

Bauhaus. 1981. *Mask*. Beggars Banquet.

Bauhaus. 1982. *The Sky's Gone Out*. Beggars Banquet.

Bauhaus. 1983. *Burning from the Inside*. Beggars Banquet.

Bauhaus. 2008. *Go Away White*. Cooking Vinyl.

Bell and James. 1979. "Livin' It Up (Friday Night)." A&M Records.

Blue Rondo a la Turk. 1982. *Chewing the Fat*. Virgin.

Blue Rondo a la Turk. 1984. *Bees Knees and Chickens Elbows*. Virgin.

Boone, Pat. 1962. "Speedy Gonzales." Dot Records.

Bowie, David. 1972. *The Rise and Fall of Ziggy Stardust and the Spiders from Mars*. RCA.

Bowie, David. 1974. *Diamond Dogs*. RCA.

Bronski Beat. 1984. *The Age of Consent.* London Records/MCA Records.
Cramps. 1982. *Psychedelic Jungle.* I.R.S. Records.
Cramps. 1984. *Smell of Female.* Enigma Records.
Creatures. 1989. *Boomerang.* Polydor.
Culture Club. 1982. *Kissing to Be Clever.* Virgin/Epic.
Culture Club. 1983. *Colour by Numbers.* Virgin/Epic.
Culture Club. 1984. *Waking Up with the House on Fire.* Virgin/Epic.
Cure. 1983. *Japanese Whispers.* Fiction Records/Sire.
Cure. 1985. *The Head on the Door.* Elektra.
Cure. 1987. *Kiss Me, Kiss Me, Kiss Me.* Elektra.
Depeche Mode. 1987. *Music for the Masses.* Mute/Sire.
Duran Duran. 1983. *Seven and the Ragged Tiger.* EMI.
Frankie Goes to Hollywood. 1984a. "Two Tribes." ZTT/Island.
Frankie Goes to Hollywood. 1984b. *Welcome to the Pleasuredome.* ZTT/Island.
Frankie Goes to Hollywood. 1986. *Liverpool.* ZTT/Island.
J, David. 2002. *Mess Up.* Heyday Records.
Japan. 1979. *Quiet Life.* Hansa.
Japan. 1980. *Gentlemen Take Polaroids.* Virgin.
Johnson, Holly. 1979. "Yankee Rose." Eric's.
Johnson, Holly. 1980. "Hobo Joe." Eric's.
Johnson, Holly. 1989. *Blast.* MCA.
Johnson, Holly. 2014. *Europa.* Pleasuredome.
Love and Rockets. 1987. *Earth, Sun, Moon.* Beggars Banquet/Big Time Records.
Marc and the Mambas. 1982. *Untitled.* Some Bizarre.
Marc and the Mambas. 1983. *Torment and Toreros.* Some Bizarre.
Matt Bianco. 1984. *Whose Side Are You On?* WEA.
McLaren, Malcom, and the World's Famous Supreme Team. 1982. "Buffalo Gals." Island Records.
Modern Rocketry. 1985. "Homosexuality." ZYX Records.
Modern Romance. 1981. *Adventures in Clubland.* WEA.
Morrissey. 1988. *Viva Hate.* Sire/Reprise.
New Order. 1983. "Confusion." Factory.
New Order. 1985. *Low-Life.* Factory/Qwest Records.
Pet Shop Boys. 1986a. *Please.* Parlophone.
Pet Shop Boys. 1986b. *Disco.* Parlophone.
Pet Shop Boys. 1987. *Actually.* Parlophone.
Pet Shop Boys. 1988. *Introspective.* Parlophone.
Pet Shop Boys. 1990. *Behaviour.* Parlophone.
Pet Shop Boys. 1993. *Very.* Parlophone.
Pet Shop Boys. 1996. *Bilingual.* Parlophone.
Pet Shop Boys. 1999. *Nightlife.* Parlophone.
Pet Shop Boys. 2013. *Electric.* x2.
Pet Shop Boys. 2016. *Super.* x2.

Prado, Pérez. 1954. "Cherry Pink (and Apple Blossom White)." RCA Victor.
Public Image Ltd. 1981. *The Flowers of Romance*. Virgin/Warner Bros.
Rutherford, Paul. 1989. *Oh World*. Island/4th and Broadway.
Sade. 1984. *Diamond Life*. Epic Records.
Scritti Politti. 1982. *Songs to Remember*. Rough Trade.
Scritti Politti. 1985. *Cupid and Psyche 85*. Virgin/Warner Bros.
Scritti Politti. 1999. *Anomie and Bonhomie*. Virgin.
Sex Pistols. 1977. *Never Mind the Bollocks, Here's the Sex Pistols*. Virgin/Warner Bros.
Siouxsie and the Banshees. 1978. *The Scream*. Polydor.
Siouxsie and the Banshees. 1979. *Join Hands*. Polydor.
Siouxsie and the Banshees. 1980. *Kaleidoscope*. Polydor.
Siouxsie and the Banshees. 1981. *Juju*. Polydor.
Siouxsie and the Banshees. 1982. *A Kiss in the Dreamhouse*. Polydor.
Siouxsie and the Banshees. 1984. *Hyaena*. Polydor/Wonderland.
Siouxsie and the Banshees. 1986. *Tinderbox*. Polydor/Wonderland.
Siouxsie and the Banshees. 1988. *Peepshow*. Polydor/Wonderland.
Slits. 1979. *Cut*. Island.
Smiths. 1986. *The Queen Is Dead*. Rough Trade/Sire.
Smiths. 1987. *The World Won't Listen*. Rough Trade.
Soft Cell. 1981. *Non-Stop Erotic Cabaret*. Some Bizarre.
Soft Cell. 1983. *The Art of Falling Apart*. Some Bizarre.
Soft Cell. 1984. *This Last Night in Sodom*. Some Bizarre.
Soft Cell. 2002. *Cruelty without Beauty*. Cooking Vinyl.
Soft Cell. 2022. **Happiness Not Included*. BMG.
Specials. 1979. *The Specials*. Two-Tone Records.
Specials. 1981. "Ghost Town." Two-Tone Records.
Time Zone. 1984. "World Destruction." Celluloid Records.
Various Artists. 1977. *Saturday Night Fever*. RSO.
Various Artists. 1983. *Now That's What I Call Music*. Virgin.
Various Artists. 2001. *Very Introspective, Actually: A Tribute to the Pet Shop Boys*. Dancing Ferret Discs.
Various Artists. 2018. *Revolutionary Spirit: The Sound of Liverpool 1976–1988*. Cherry Red Records.
Various Artists. 2021. *Shake the Foundations: Militant Funk and the Post-Punk Dancefloor 1978–1984*. Cherry Red Records.
Visage. 1982. "The Damned Don't Cry." Polydor.

FILMOGRAPHY/VIDEOGRAPHY

Anger, Kenneth, dir. 1963. *Scorpio Rising*.
Belfield, Richard, dir. 2006. *Stand and Deliver: The Documentary*.

Bond, Jack, dir. 1988. *It Couldn't Happen Here.*

Bond, Jack, dir. 2015. *Adam Ant: The Blueblack Hussar.*

Cavani, Liliana, dir. 1974. *The Night Porter.*

Chadha, Gurinder, dir. 2019. *Blinded by the Light.*

Chomsky, Marvin J., John Erman, David Greene, and Gilbert Moses, dirs. 1977. *Roots.*

Denyer, Ian, dir. 2016. *Boy George's 1970s: Save Me from Suburbia.*

De Palma, Brian, dir. 1984. *Body Double.*

Dobson, Zoë, dir. 2019. *Duran Duran: There's Something You Should Know.*

English, Keith, dir. 2018. *The More You Ignore Me.*

Filipiak, Gavin, dir. 2016. "Twenty-something."

Foster, Harve, and Wilfred Jackson, dirs. 1946. *Song of the South.*

Fowler, Gene, Jr., dir. 1957. *I Was a Teenage Werewolf.*

Godley, Kevin, and Lol Creme, dirs. 1985. "Two Tribes."

Griffith, D. W., dir. 1926. *The Sorrows of Satan.*

Hencken, George, dir. 2015. *Soul Boys of the Western World.*

Hickenlooper, George, dir. 2003. *Mayor of the Sunset Strip.*

Hill, Walter, dir. 1979. *The Warriors.*

Hitchcock, Alfred, dir. 1945. *Spellbound.*

Jarman, Derek, dir. 1978. *Jubilee.*

Klane, Robert, dir. 1978. *Thank God It's Friday.*

Lawrie, Claire, dir. 2018. *Beyond "There's Always a Black Issue Dear."*

Letts, Don, dir. 2000. *The Clash: Westway to the World.*

Mendiola, Jim, dir. 1996. *Pretty Vacant.*

Moulson, John, dir. 2003. *The Madness of Prince Charming.*

Mulcahy, Russell, dir. 1981a. "Bette Davis Eyes."

Mulcahy, Russell, dir. 1981b. "Planet Earth."

Nava, Gregory. 1995. *Mi Familia.*

Nelson, Ralph, dir. 1970. *Soldier Blue.*

Newton, Dione, dir. 2009. *The Queens of British Pop.*

O'Casey, Matt, dir. 2016. *Top of the Pops: The Story of 1982.*

Penn, Arthur, dir. 1970. *Little Big Man.*

Pennebaker, D.A., dir. 1989. *101.*

Pope, Tim, dir. 1982. *Non-Stop Exotic Video Show.*

Pope, Tim, dir. 1983. "Dear Prudence."

Pressman, Michael, dir. 1979. *Boulevard Nights.*

Rose, Bernard, dir. 1983. *Relax.*

Scott, Tony, dir. 1983. *The Hunger.*

Shah, Rubika, dir. 2020. *White Riot.*

Sinclair, Peter, dir. 1983. "Karma Chameleon."

Smith, Martyn, dir. 2001. *I Love 1984.*

Spheeris, Penelope, dir. 1984. *Suburbia.*

Stanford, Jennifer Juniper, dir. 2016. *Modern Day Virgin Sacrifice.*

Stone, Drew, dir. 2017. *Who the Fuck Is That Guy?*
Temple, Julien, dir. 2000. *The Filth and the Fury.*
Valdez, Luis, dir. 1981. *Zoot Suit.*
Waters, John, dir. 1988. *Hairspray.*
Watson, Eric, dir. 1986. "Suburbia."
Watson, Eric, dir. 1988. "Domino Dancing."
Watson, Eric, dir. 1989. "Americanos."
Wiene, Robert, dir. 1920. *The Cabinet of Dr. Caligari.*

PERIODICALS

BAM
Blitz
Classic Pop
Creem
Details
Electronic Sound
Face
Gay Times
Him Magazine
i-D
Jackie
Japan: Made in the USA (J:MUSA)
Jocks and Nerds
Journal
Latin NY
Louder Than War
Lowrider Magazine
Melody Maker
Mojo
New Musical Express (NME)
New Sounds
New Sounds New Styles
No. 1
Noise!
Q
Razorcake
Record Mirror
Rock Scene
Rolling Stone
Skin Two
Smash Hits

Sounds
Spin
Star Hits
Time Out
Trouser Press
Uncut
Vague
Video Rock Stars
Vive le Rock!
ZigZag

Index

Page numbers in italics refer to figures.